The Longest Week

Also by Nick Page

The Bible Book

What Happened to the Ark of the
Covenant and Other Bible Mysteries

The Collins Bible Atlas (Editor)

Phantastes (Editor)

Church Invisible

Lord Minimus

The Longest Week

Nick Page

HODDER &
STOUGHTON

ISBN 978 0 340 99526 6

Typeset in ITC Galliard and Gill Sans by Nick Page

Printed and bound in Great Britain by Clays Ltd, St Ives plc

The paper and board used in this paperback are natural recyclable
products made from wood grown in sustainable forests. The manufacturing
processes conform to the environmental regulations of the
country of origin

Hodder & Stoughton Ltd
338 Euston Road
London NW1 3BH

www.hodderfaith.com

CONTENTS

The past is never dead. It's not even past.

William Faulkner, *Requiem for a Nun*

Listen, I am casting out demons and performing cures today and to-morrow, and on the third day I finish my work. Yet today, tomorrow, and the next day I must be on my way, because it is impossible for a prophet to be killed away from Jerusalem.

Luke 13.31b–33, NRSV

On Friday 3 April AD 33, Joshua ben Joseph — commonly called Joshua of Nazareth — was executed.

He had come into the city just six days before, leading a crowd of supporters down the hillside from the Mount of Olives. Over the next few days the whispers, rumours and arguments about him swilled around the city: he had created a disturbance in the Temple; he had advocated non-payment of taxes; he had defied the Temple purity laws; he had attacked the authorities — both Jewish and Roman. In the end he was betrayed by one of his own followers, hurriedly tried by the local aristocracy, and extradited to the Roman occupying forces. After some political bargaining and negotiations with various powerful groups and individuals, the Romans agreed to execute him. Their soldiers — a group of auxiliaries from Samaria — beat him so badly that his death on the cross occurred with unusual speed. A rich well-wisher asked the Romans for permission to bury him and his corpse was hurriedly interred, in order to comply with local religious laws.

Another Galilean rabble-rouser. Another would-be Messiah. Another footnote in the history of Roman imperial politics. Just a routine killing at the edge of empire.

Nothing to write home about.

Introduction

This is a history of the last week of Jesus' life.

It's not a book of theology (although you can't easily divorce the one from the other). It's not a book of spirituality (although I think it has a spiritual impact). It's not a work of fiction (although there will be plenty of times when our imagination can be invited out to play). It's not a book of esoteric conspiracy theories (although it does involve a conspiracy). It's a book of history. A book of what we know about the life and times of Jesus and how that helps us to understand the stories. It is a book about the city and the people, the time and the place – a book about a week that changed the world entirely.

Some readers might be sceptical about seeing see the word 'history' applied to this story at all. These days, we're used to hearing that the whole thing is a myth or a metaphor, that the characters are inventions, that it is one enormous symbol. History? Not possible. Best leave it. Treat the whole thing as a story.

But the truth is that there are real, historical facts to be explored. The streets of this story are paved with reality. The people who tread these streets are real historical characters who lived and breathed and worked and sweated, who inhabited a society about which much is known. And, as we delve into the history, as we strip away the layers of pious iconography and theological interpretation, we discover a tale that, for all its spiritual significance, is characterised by some very real human passions. This is a story of fear and anger, of non-violent resistance and state brutality. It's a story of the outcasts and the powerful, of processions and perfume, of feasts and festivals, of death and darkness and, ultimately, of triumph. It's not exactly what we expect, this story. As a Christian, I went into this book prepared to give a guided tour of a city I knew well, only to find that there were alleys and side-streets that I had never explored, avenues and squares that I never even knew existed. It's a darker, more complex story than we realise, a tale of politics and double-dealing, of betrayal and compromise, of remarkable, earth-shattering events, of apparent failure and astonishing triumph.

It *matters*, this stuff, you see. Because, if you don't know the true history, you are at the mercy of other people's inventions. If we don't – both Christians and non-Christians alike – make an attempt to understand the culture of the times, to find out what really happened, then other people will make it up. And they'll use this story in a thousand different ways to claim a thousand different things. They'll get Jesus to say things he couldn't possibly have said, to obtain things he never would have wanted. They'll take the story and use it to screw money out of TV viewers, to justify positions of power, to peddle theories about the end of the world. They'll distort it to justify racism and bigotry. And they'll use this story – the greatest story of non-violent love in history – to justify acts of violence on a scale that has never been seen.

Yes, this stuff matters.

Hour by hour

Recreating the story is not, of course, just a matter of mere historical facts. No history – at least no history worth reading – is just about the facts. Even such apparently 'factual' sources of information as archaeology and numismatics need interpretation. We need not only to know the facts, but to reflect on them, play with them, stir them around in our minds, mix them into new possibilities, pile them up into new patterns. We need, in short, *imagination.*

One imaginative leap I have taken in this book, for which many scholars would beat me up behind the bicycle sheds, is that I have suggested the days – and even the times – at which these events could have taken place.

I accept that this is speculative, but I think it helps in showing the shape of the week, and how the pressure keeps growing and building until Friday morning when it all erupts in a sudden, savagely fast burst of activity.[1] This timetable is based on the mentions of days and times found in the Gospels. In the end it doesn't matter whether Jesus was taken to Pilate at 6 or 6.30. But putting some figures on it does help us as we consider the timescale of the events. It helps us to imagine it – and that brings the real meaning much closer.

But this is not the only imaginative leap that I think is helpful. In imagining the historical landscape, it helps to have other points of view, parallel experiences, even from different times and different people. I'm going to be drawing on data not just from Roman Palestine, but from mediaeval Saudi Arabia, Victorian Dublin, Nazi-occupied Greece and modern Africa. I realise that this runs the risk of confusing times and eras, of anachronistically applying feelings and attitudes from later centuries to people who, in their time, didn't feel that way. But there's also a risk involved in doing it the other way, and that is that we end up seeing the story of the Longest Week as something essentially irretrievable, which happened 'back then' and which has no relevance or meaning to us now.

The sources

Imagination, then. Modern parallels and other experiences, as well. But our main sources of information are resolutely historical, all from the time of the events, or thereabouts.

There are no official Roman or Jewish sources for the trial and execution of Jesus. Justin Martyr refers to official reports –

The Acts of Pilate – but these have been long lost.[2] The Roman historian Tacitus, writing around AD 100, describes how Christ (or Christus as he calls him) 'suffered the extreme penalty during the reign of Tiberius at the hands of one of our procurators, Pontius Pilate...' It may well be that he took this from official Roman sources of information.[3]

In the absence of official records, the primary – and most important sources – are the Gospels themselves.

The four gospels – Matthew, Mark, Luke and John – were written sometime between AD 65 and AD 80. Some scholars would put them earlier in this timeframe, others later. The first three gospels – Matthew, Mark and Luke – are known as the Synoptic Gospels, because they follow the same broad outline and contain a lot of the same material. Of these three, Mark is generally agreed to be the earliest source. John's is a very different type of gospel. It follows a different chronology, was probably written later than the first three and has a markedly different style.

Many scholars today are dismissive of the gospel writers; they view them as inventors more than historians. The attitude of modern critical scholarship to these works is, I think, rampantly colonial, treating the writers, and indeed the early church, as good-natured but essentially credulous and ignorant natives. *'It's not that they weren't intelligent, bless them. They were doing their best. It's just that we know better.'*

The Gospels themselves aren't objective – nor did they claim to be. Luke wrote his account so that his Roman patron, Theophilus, might 'know the truth concerning the things about which you have been instructed' (Luke 1.3–4). But when it comes to historical details, they have the advantage over us, in that both the authors and the audiences were alive at the time in question. They were part of a culture that had common features whether you were in Jerusalem or Rome. They knew more than we do about the world in which they lived. So, where there is doubt, the benefit of the doubt should go their way and not ours.

All of which is not to say that there are no conflicts in the writers' accounts. In the various Gospels, some events happen in a different order. Mark puts the 'cleansing' of the Temple on the day after Jesus arrived in Jerusalem; Matthew and Luke seem to imply that it was on the same day. There are events in one that are not reported in another. John has long speeches by Jesus that don't occur elsewhere. But, despite these differences, they do give a generally coherent and cogent account.

So the Gospels will be our primary witnesses, but there are some other sources which I will be using at length.

The letters of Paul have accounts of both the crucifixion and the resurrection which, in fact, date from earlier than the Gospels. Paul certainly mentions Jesus' trial before Pontius Pilate (1 Tim. 6.13), also the Last Supper and the fact that the 'rulers' crucified Jesus (1 Cor. 2.8). He passes on a tradition about the Last Supper and a list of people who saw the resurrected Jesus.

Outside the Scriptures, the main witness is the first-century Jewish historian Josephus.

Josephus was a Jew who, following the disastrous rebellion by the Jews in AD 67–70, moved to Rome and wrote a history of both the war and his Jewish people. He finished this around AD 93–4. He gives us masses of useful information about the atmosphere of Judaea at the time. Josephus lived in the region: he saw the Temple in action, and he was involved in the political activity of his day. He may be inconsistent at times, and he's certainly prone to exaggeration of numbers and to quite a bit of pro-Roman spin, but beneath that there is a real account of the times from someone who was actually there.[4]

Another Jewish source whom I will be quoting is a writer called Philo, a Jew who lived in Alexandria from c.20 BC to c. AD 50. Philo produced a great many works of literature, theology and philosophy, as well as writings that dealt with some of the major historical issues of his day.

There is also an enormous amount of Jewish rabbinic literature – works compiled by rabbis. The most important of these is probably the Mishnah, which represents the vast collection of

The Arch of Titus, Rome. Detail showing Roman soldiers bringing back the spoils from the destruction of Jerusalem in AD 70, including the golden candlestick.

oral law that had been accumulated by the rabbis in the period up to around AD 200.

A little bit of background might be helpful here. In AD 67 the Jews revolted against Roman rule. After initial successes, the Romans eventually besieged Jerusalem with 30,000 troops. The suffering and sickness and internal warfare within Jerusalem were awful. In the end, in AD 70, the city was recaptured and the Temple was completely destroyed. The Jews rebelled again in AD 130 under a leader called Bar Kokhba. Again, they were successful at first, but eventually the Roman military machine proved too powerful. After the second revolt, the Jews were expelled from Jerusalem completely. They took up residence elsewhere in Judaea and Galilee, notably in Tiberias, on the shores of Lake Galilee. It was there, or around there, that the Mishnah was compiled.

So the Mishnah is a book that is shot through with a sense of loss. The Mishnah accounts of Temple worship, sacrifice, taxes, council meetings and festivals reflect a world that has been irretrievably lost. There is, therefore, probably a degree of wistful idealisation in the accounts.

There may well be cases where the Mishnah reflects not Jerusalem and Judaea as it was, but how the later pharisaical editors thought it must – or even should – have been.[5]

Finally, we have the apocryphal Gospels, that is, Christian writings that are outside the New Testament and date, on the whole, from much later. Despite the claims of various academics, novelists and film-makers, there is very little in these works that is of historical value about the life of Jesus. They were not written near the time, or by eye-witnesses. They are useful in shedding light on the beliefs and practices of certain minority sects of Christianity in the late second century, but they tell us little new about Jesus. However, it may be that, hidden beneath the later additions, there are some fragments of Jesus' original teaching, and some stories and traditions that reflect real events.

Those, then, are our tools for the journey: archaeology and imagination; ancient literature and modern parallels. These are the guides to help us explore the sights, sounds and smells of the city of Jerusalem. Along the way we're going to meet soldiers and Sadducees, Pharisees and priests, prostitutes, brigands, traitors, heroes, villains, and all stops in between. We're going to encounter the heady smell of perfume from Nepal as well as the stench of sewage from the streets of Jerusalem; we're going to break fresh bread and drink bitter wine; we're going to see palm branches waved in acclamation and woven into savage crowns. We're going to explore the murky world of imperial politics and the explosive language of apocalyptic literature. We're going to see what happens when the kingdom of God crash-lands in the empire of Rome.

Above all, we're going to take a white-knuckle ride through the last days of the most amazing man who has ever lived.

Ready?

Tremors
Winter AD 32–Spring AD 33

'We are going up to Jerusalem'

By the winter of AD 32, Jesus seems to have come to a decision. He had spent some two years teaching and talking, telling stories and performing miracles – actions that gained him a significant following, as well as making him many enemies. The common people, the ordinary everyday folk, the poor, the outcasts, those starved of respect, loved him. Here was someone who fed them, lived like one of them, told them that God loved them. Wherever he went, crowds gathered. The leaders of the people were far less certain. Jesus was in constant conflict with the Pharisees, who had a significant influence in the towns and villages of Galilee. Scribes from Jerusalem came to monitor what he was doing (Mark 3.22). And even the ruler of that region – Herod Antipas, one of the sons of Herod the Great – wanted to kill him (Luke 13.31).

Such antagonism was manageable; for the most part, Jesus kept away from the political hotspots, restricting himself to the rural areas of Galilee or the Judaean wilderness. But sometime during AD 32 or early 33, he began to move. Accompanied by his followers he headed south, through Samaria and towards Judaea. And more and more, his thoughts and his words began to cluster around one place: Jerusalem.

He had been there before. In the Synoptic Gospels we have

details of only one trip to Jerusalem: the final journey to his trial and death.[1] In John's account, however, Jesus makes four more trips to the city.

In John chapter 2, Jesus goes to Passover and 'cleanses' the Temple and has a night-time meeting with Nicodemus, a member of the Pharisees (John 2.13–21). It is difficult to know whether this is a unique event, or whether it is a simple transposition of Mark 11.15–19. Mark's placing of the Temple incident in the last week makes more sense.

In John chapter 5, he is in Jerusalem at an unnamed 'festival of the Jews', which may be Passover, but, since it is unidentified, was probably one of the other festivals.

In John chapter 7 Jesus goes up for the festival of Booths or Tabernacles (Hebrew *Sukkoth*), a seven-day harvest festival in October. This was one of the three main pilgrimage festivals during the year, which drew thousands of pilgrims to Jerusalem. The festival included certain ceremonies such as the pouring-out of water and the lighting of the great lights in the Temple. Jesus uses these opportunities to describe himself as the light of the world (John 8.12). His presence at the festival causes arguments and disruption. An attempt is made to arrest Jesus, but the authorities are put off by the authority of his teaching. He is also defended by Nicodemus, who argues that Jesus should at least have a hearing.[2]

Whatever the timing of these trips – or whether John has simply, as in the case of the cleansing of the Temple, transposed an event from the last week of Jesus' life to much earlier – the end result is nearly always the same: Jesus is threatened with stoning, or arrest, or both.

Then there is the fourth visit, in the winter of AD 32/33.

'When Pontius Pilate was governor of Judaea...'

The dating of the Longest Week relies on a number of factors. The basic time frame is clear: we know that Jesus was crucified by Pontius Pilate, who was Prefect of Judaea between AD 26 and 36. Narrowing it down a bit more, John's Gospel, with

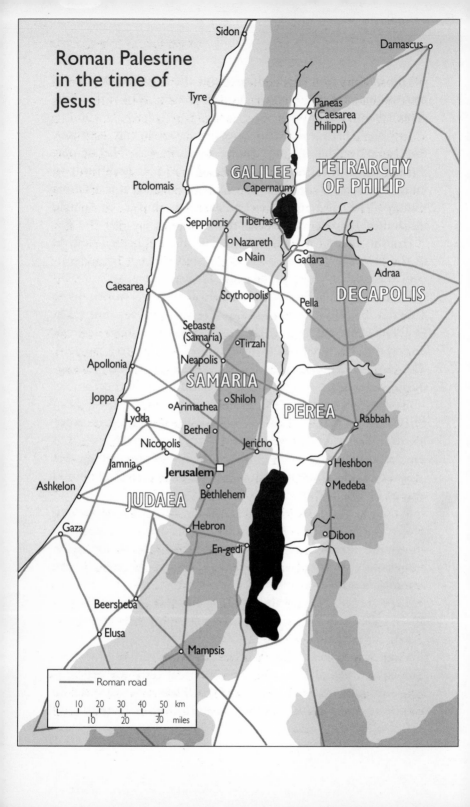

Roman Palestine in the time of Jesus

all those visits to Jerusalem for various annual festivals, implies that he had a public ministry lasting some two or three years. This, of course, culminated in his final trip to Jerusalem and his death – and it is this that helps us to ascertain the date more precisely, because all the Gospels agree that Jesus died on a Friday, just before the Sabbath began.[3] (In Jewish culture, the new day began at sunset, so the Sabbath began at sunset on the Friday.) They also agree that the events took place during the festival of Passover. However, the Synoptics say that the Last Supper was a Passover meal, whereas John says it was the night *before* Passover. Later on I will explain why I think John is right and the Synoptics are, if not right, then not exactly wrong. For now I will go with John's timing. Placing Jesus' execution on the morning before Passover began, rather than during Passover itself, makes more sense. So I'm going to assume that the Last Supper was on the night before Passover and that Jesus was executed on the 'day of Preparation', before Passover began at sunset.

Thus, for the date of the crucifixion, we need to find a year between AD 26 and 36 when the Passover festival fell on a Friday. Passover always takes place at a full moon. Philo tells us 'the feast begins at the middle of the month, on the fifteenth day, when the moon is full, a day purposely chosen because there is no darkness'.[4] So, from astronomical data, we can calculate in which years Passover fell on a Friday.[5] There are only two possible dates: AD 30 and AD 33.

There are supporters for both. My preference is for AD 33, largely because it makes more sense in view of the political situation. It explains, for example, why Pilate behaved in the way he did. As we shall see, in AD 30, Pilate had no need to even listen to the Jews, let alone compromise with them, but by AD 33 the situation had changed.

And remember that Passover full moon? Well, there's another detail which may be significant. When Jesus' followers came to speak about the events of those few days in Jerusalem, they found precedents and prophecies throughout the Jewish

Scriptures. In Acts chapter 2, we find Peter quoting the Old Testament prophet Joel, as part of a speech about 'Jesus of Nazareth, a man attested to you by God with deeds of power, wonders, and signs that God did through him among you…':

'And I will show portents in the heaven above and signs on the earth below, blood, and fire, and smoky mist. The sun shall be turned to darkness and the moon to blood, before the coming of the Lord's great and glorious day.' (Acts 2.19–20, quoting Joel 2.30–31)

It's the mention of the moon turned to blood which is intriguing. The Gospels claim that at Jesus' death there was an unnatural darkness, which fits in well with the prophecy. But what about that bloody moon? On the evening of Friday 3 April AD 33, there was a partial lunar eclipse, visible in Jerusalem. During a partial lunar eclipse, the moon turns orange or red. It may be that the quote from Joel was seen by the early church as a prophecy of two strange occurrences linked with the death of Jesus: an unusual darkness and a blood-red moon.[6] So that's what I'm going for here: AD 33. As we shall see, politically, culturally, perhaps even astronomically, this fits the bill.

The festival of Dedication

Where: Royal Portico, the Temple, Jerusalem

When: December AD 32

According to John, Jesus returned to Jerusalem in December AD 32 for the festival of Dedication, or Hanukkah (John 10.22–39). Like his previous trips, this visit is marked by confrontation and danger, but the tone is quieter, even surreptitious.

There is no mention of his disciples; it might even have been a lone visit. Perhaps his disciples did not know where he had gone – explaining why this episode is absent from the Synoptics, from Matthew, Mark and Luke. He was based at a place not far away. Mark 10.1 says that Jesus left Capernaum 'and went to the region of Judaea and beyond the Jordan'. It is not hard to imagine Jesus, in the late autumn and winter of AD 32, arriving in the Perea region from Galilee and setting up a base there. And from there he made a brief trip into

Jerusalem for the festival of Dedication, where he spent his time with followers in Jerusalem, not those he had brought with him from Galilee.

The festival commemorated the deliverance of the Jews from Antiochus IV Epiphanes, who had tried to eradicate their ancestral religion. The climax of his efforts was to put a pagan altar in the Temple itself – probably with his own likeness in the form of Zeus.[7] This act led to the Maccabaean revolt, in which the family of Judas Maccabaeus led Israel to independence and the Temple was cleansed and restored. Josephus called it *phota*, 'the festival of Lights'. According to Rabbi Hillel, one lamp was lit on the first day, with one extra on every succeeding day until all lamps were lit.

The popularity of this festival was not because of its scriptural authority: it wasn't mentioned in the Hebrew Scriptures. No, its popularity was due to the fact that it was a politically charged festival, a commemoration of the preservation of the Jewish state and the survival of their religious and cultural identity in the face of almost overwhelming pressure. This was the Jewish version of Independence Day. Only, sadly for them, it was not a celebration of independence, but the commemoration of a long-distant dream.[8]

'We have no king but the emperor'

The events of the Longest Week took place in a world controlled by one imperial power: Rome.

We think of the Roman Empire as a beacon of civilisation in the ancient world. Their culture and history – the roads, their military organisation, their literature and legal system, their architecture – continue to exercise a fascination on scholars and the general public alike. What we tend to forget is that Rome came to power not because of its impressive buildings, but because of its irresistible brutality. The Roman Empire was, above all, a military dictatorship. A speech attributed by Seneca to Nero sums up the emperor's power:

> I am the arbiter of life and death for the nations: it rests in my power what each man's lot and death shall be: by my lips Fortune proclaims what gift she would bestow on each human being: from my utterance peoples and cities gather reasons for rejoicing; without my favour and grace no part of the whole world can prosper; all those many thousands of swords which my peace restrains will be drawn at my nod...[9]

This is not idle posturing. This was fact. Just as the Romans built roads and bridges to last, when they conquered your country, you stayed conquered. It was this disciplined, organised approach to military conquest that made them so powerful.[10]

What was it like being occupied by such a force? Perhaps the response to another crushing military power – the Nazis – gives an impression of what it must have felt like when the Romans rolled into town.

> The men in helmets and carrying over their uniform light camouflage tunics, green, brown and black, armed to the teeth. Marching with a heavy but quick step, human 'robots' forming two rectangles of iron, they give an impression of invincible force.[11]

You were conquered and you knew it.

It was not that Rome hadn't provided some benefits. As with most occupying empires, the infrastructure had been improved and the defeat of piracy in the Mediterranean made travel a lot easier. There was peace – the famous *pax Romana* – but it was a peace gained through 'streams of blood and tears of unimaginable proportions'.[12] In the grim words of Tacitus, describing certain British tribes who refused to adopt Roman practices, there were tribes 'which feared our peace'; there were tribes and people who had learned to dread the arrival of the men in helmets.

Fear was the key. In a world where the Romans were in charge, life must have been lived according to a constant, low-level, background murmur of fear. As long as you paid your taxes and knew your place you were likely to be OK, but the minute you stepped out of line, the Romans would descend with crushing force. And there was no redress against such force. At a national level, the Romans 'always exacted from their conquered opponents the recognition that the war was entirely their fault'.[13] At a local level, civilians had little redress, not even in Rome itself, where the troops were effectively above the law:

> Let us consider first, then, the benefits common to all
> Military men. Not least is the fact that no civilian
> Would dare give you a thrashing – and if beaten up himself
> He'll keep quiet about it, he'd never dare show any magistrate
> His knocked-out teeth, the blackened lumps and bruises
> All over his face, that surviving eye which the doctor
> Offers no hope for.[14]

Such was the situation in Rome, among their own people. In the provinces, where the ultimate arbiter of judicial cases was the governor – himself a member of the military – civilians had even less chance of justice. Plutarch wrote with chilling honesty:

> You who hold office are a subject, ruling a state controlled by pro-
> consuls and by the procurators of the emperor… Do not have
> great pride or confidence in your crown, for you see soldiers' boots
> just above your head…[15]

The population of the empire was at least 31 million, maybe as high as 56 million.[16] It was split into provinces, each overseen by a Roman official. The size and economic importance of a province determined the kind of leadership it had. In the larger provinces, these officials were called governors; in the smaller provinces, such as Judaea, they were called prefects, or, later, procurators. Each province was administered from a city that housed the main Roman military and administrative services. The capital of the province of Syria was at Antioch-on-the-Orontes, a large cosmopolitan city. The smaller sub-province of Judaea was administered not from Jerusalem, but from Caesarea.

And the point of all this land, all these people, all this administration, was to make money. The Roman Empire was an economic exercise, designed to generate wealth for Rome. Soldiers were 'economic pioneers'.[17] Yes, they built bridges and roads and aqueducts, but they did so in order to exploit the land. Here's an instructive story from the Babylonian Talmud:

> For once Rabbi Judah and Rabbi Jose and Rabbi Simeon were sitting, and Judah son of proselytes was sitting with them. Rabbi Judah began and said: 'How excellent are the deeds of this nation. They have instituted market places, they have instituted bridges, they have instituted baths.' Rabbi Jose was silent. Rabbi Simeon ben Yohai answered and said: 'All that they have instituted they have instituted only for their own needs. They have instituted market places to place harlots in them; baths for their own pleasure; bridges, to collect toll.' Judah, son of proselytes went and reported their words and they were heard by the government. They said: 'Judah who exalted shall be exalted: Jose who remained silent shall be banished to Sepphoris; Simeon who reproached shall be put to death.'[18]

This event took place around AD 135, at a time when Rome was in no mood to tolerate criticism from Jews. But it shows how ordinary people felt about Roman development. Rabbi Gamaliel is reputed to have said, 'This empire gnaws at our substance through four things: its tolls, its bath buildings, its theatres and its taxes in kind.'[19] Roman imperialism gnawed at the very soul of the people it conquered.

The main way in which Rome raised money from the provinces was through tolls and taxes. Tolls had to be paid on goods brought into the country via various trade routes. Judaea and Galilee were important links in the trade route from South Arabia and trading centres such as Gerrha on the Persian Gulf. The overland route brought caravans through Nabatea and Galilee, to the ports on the Mediterranean coast.[20] Taxes were paid directly by the producer – the peasant farmer or city trader. According to Josephus, when the kingdom was ruled by Herod the Great, it provided the king with some 5.4 million denarii per annum, of which the bulk – 3.6 million denarii – came from Judaea.[21]

In many provinces, such as Judaea, the real business of government – the collecting of taxes and the keeping of order – was delegated to local elites. In Palestine, before AD 6, the government had been delegated to Herod the Great and then

The province of Judea and its subdivisions, c. AD 33

Judea and Samaria were under direct Roman rule, with the prefect residing at Caesarea. Galilee was ruled by Herod Antipas.

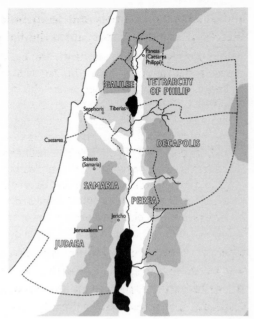

to his sons: Philip, Antipas and Archelaus. These ruled as client-kings, on behalf of the Romans. They had their own troops and their prestige meant – or the Romans hoped it meant – that Roman rule was accepted rather than fought against.[22]

When Archelaus was deposed, the Romans had to find a new local leader to run the province. They turned to the next layer down in the organisational chart: to the High Priest and the aristocratic families of Jerusalem. Thus, under Roman rule, the High Priest became a direct Roman appointment. He and his deputies were Roman retainers, reliant on the Prefect for their position. They were, in effect, collaborators with the occupying forces.

Rome believed that a rich, aristocratic leadership – combined with the religious power of the Temple – would command automatic respect, but they were wrong. To be a leader in Rome, it helped to come from the right kind of family and to have the right kind of background, but, above all, you had to be rich. The same, however, was not true of Jewish society. Jewish criteria for what constituted a 'leader' were different. Although they valued family history and breeding to some extent, money wasn't as important as wisdom; the real leaders in Jewish society were those with a passion for the purity of their religion, and those who were wise.

All of which explains why the official leaders of the Jewish people at the time of Jesus were almost universally hated.[23] To the people, the detestable Herodian dynasty had simply been replaced by its lackeys. And they made their distaste clear. The first of the high priests following direct Roman rule was so unpopular that he was removed from the post. The Roman leadership replaced him with a man plucked from obscurity – Ananus, son of Seth. Ananus – or Annas, as he is called in the Gospels – proved a much more canny operator, and his family was to dominate the post of high priest for the next sixty years. But although they proved to be shrewd political operators, the idea of a respected, powerful elite was a fiction; the Temple elite had the power, but never the respect.[24]

I doubt they were too upset. They might not have had respect but they had the consolation of considerable comfort and riches. Excavations in Jerusalem have uncovered a weight measure from a home in the Upper City with the name 'Bar Kathros' on it. Kathros was the name of one of the high-priestly families. There are the remains of other monumental houses nearby, indicating that this neighbourhood may have contained the residences of other elite aristocratic families of Jerusalem. One private mansion – the so-called 'Palatial Mansion' – covers 600 square metres. It had walls decorated with frescoes in contemporary Roman styles; it contained a piece of glassware by the famous glass-maker Ennion of Sidon. It also contained a number of baths for ritual bathing. One of the main tenets of Jewish religious law was the need for people to wash or bathe to achieve purification. Before entering the Temple or offering a sacrifice, you had to be clean. Jerusalem was full, therefore, of *miqvaot* – ritual baths – where orthodox Jews could be purified. These people had their own. This, then, was a house of wealth, but also of scrupulous attention to ritual purification: the kind of house, in fact, that might be owned by a high priest.[25]

Where did they get this wealth? Martin Goodman has suggested that one way they did it was by loaning money, and then when the debtor could not afford to pay them back, they took over his land. They were thus able to build up property portfolios. It is significant that in AD 66, when the revolution started and the rebels took over the Temple, the first thing they did was to burn the records of debts. This is clear evidence that the Temple functioned as a kind of bank – indeed, the only lending bank of any kind – and that its power was resented.[26] We shall explore the financial power of the temple in greater detail in later chapters.

So they had money. And they had power – power that could be wielded with violence. It is not only the New Testament that records the Temple aristocracy beating up its opponents. Both Josephus and other Jewish writers indicate that the various high-priestly factions were not above using violent or bullying tactics. The memory of the behaviour of these two families lasted a long time in Jewish society. In the Babylonian Talmud, Abba Saul ben Batnit says:

Woe is me because of the house of Boethus;
Woe is me because of their staves!
Woe is me because of the house of Hanin [i.e. Hanan or Ananus];
Woe is me because of their whisperings!
Woe is me because of the house of Kathros;
Woe is me because of their pens!
Woe is me because of the house of Ishmael the son of Phabi;
Woe is me because of their fists!
for they are High Priests and their sons are [Temple] treasurers and their sons-in-law
are trustees and their servants beat the people with staves.[27]

There you have it: all the main high-priestly families are represented in this lament – the houses of Boethus, Hanin (Hanan or Ananus), Kathros and Phabi. The memory of their behaviour – the nepotism, the physical force, the beatings with rods ('staves') and fists; the control they exercised over the finances, the whisperings and the pens, the secret, political machinations of the Temple authorities. These were people who had power and who knew how to hold on to it. The high priests did not merely rule Jerusalem through their position in the Temple hierarchy: they ruled with the rod and the fist.

This, then, is the group of people in charge of Judaea in Jesus' day. An aristocratic elite, appointed by the Romans and using the resources of the Temple to make themselves rich. Men who exhibited 'the illegitimate character, the compromised position and the exploitative behaviour of the Jewish ruling class'.[28] This is not to say that they did not care about the religion they espoused, or about the Temple. I think they cared passionately about both the Temple and the survival of the Jewish nation, but they were fatally compromised, as all collaborationist governments are, by their association with the occupying power. Power, once grasped, becomes hard to deny. The fact is that after the demise of the Temple in AD 70, not a single Jewish source expresses any kind of regret for the disappearance of the Temple aristocracy. They missed the Temple, of course, but never the people who ran it.[29]

'He has anointed me to bring good news to the poor'

As in Jerusalem, so in the wider Roman Empire. Throughout the Roman Empire, the wealth and power were in the hands of a small elite. The aristocracy – perhaps 2 to 5 per cent of the population – ruled huge areas of territory.[30] Ultimately, it was those lower down the scale who bore the costs of imperial occupation. Estimates of the tax burden on Jewish peasants and artisans vary greatly, but historians reckon that anything between 30 and 60 per cent of their production was claimed in taxes, not only taxes to the Romans, but also the tithes to the Temple, which Jews saw as an obligation to God.[31]

The impact of these financial pressures would have been enormous. One bad harvest and you've had it. Because if you have too little to survive, you have to borrow, and then you need a bumper harvest the next year to pay off the borrowing. And if that doesn't happen... the result for many families must have been a spiralling descent into poverty.

The Torah (the first five books of the Hebrew scriptures, i.e. Genesis, Exodus, Leviticus, Numbers, and Deuteronomy) had laws designed to protect people from falling into long-term debt. The Sabbath legislation meant that every seven years debts would be cancelled. Paradoxically, however, the effect of this was to make credit *harder* to obtain. After all, no one in their right mind was going to lend money near the Sabbath year.

Rabbi Hillel found a way round it, by inventing a loan secured by a *prozbul*, a declaration that the loan would not be remitted in the seventh year.[32] Hillel may have been trying to help an oppressed peasantry obtain much-needed credit, but the effect was to bypass the Sabbath legislation entirely, and so introduce permanent debt.[33]

And if you fell into debt, then where could you obtain money? In our society you would go to a bank: in Jesus' time, one source of finance was the Temple. The money that flowed into the Temple had to be used, it couldn't just sit there. The wealth of the Temple was invested in the land through high-interest loans to needy peasants, and if they defaulted on their loans, the land was passed over to the creditors.[34]

This, then, was the society into which Jesus was born, and within which he worked, taught and performed his miracles: a Roman province, governed at the local level by an illegitimate leadership under the rule of a pagan empire; a military dictatorship which saw its subjects as a means of producing wealth; a place where there was a huge gulf between rich and poor and where, for the bulk of people, a life of grinding poverty was made worse by the knowledge that there were 'soldiers' boots just above their head'.

No wonder so many people were looking for a rescuer, a hero, a Messiah.

'If you are the Messiah, tell us plainly'

Cut back to AD 32. In the chill December air, Jesus is walking in the Royal Portico, the long, covered colonnade at the south end of the Temple (John 10.22). Literally and figuratively he is under cover, but he is recognised and challenged. Jews gather round him – the verb actually means 'encircled' – to challenge him. 'If you're the Messiah,' they say, 'tell us plainly.' Their question draws on Jewish belief that God would one day send a liberator, the Messiah, the anointed one, who would usher in a new golden age of Jewish rule.

Jesus replies that he has already told them, but that they have not believed. Maybe some of those encircling him didn't *want* to believe in any of it. The Sadducees probably did not believe in the Messiah.[35] But just because they didn't believe in him it doesn't mean they didn't mind if one appeared. Not every Jewish group would have been awaiting the Messiah with keen anticipation. The Sadducees had power under the Romans. Admittedly, it was a limited kind of power, but it was power nonetheless. If the Messiah arrived, what power would they have? History shows that those who collaborate with occupying powers have, at best, an ambivalent attitude to liberation. They know that they will not be thanked for their role, but targeted as traitors. In the Second World War, Pierre Pucheu, former Minister of the Interior in the Nazi-authorised Vichy government, made his way to North Africa to join the Free French forces. He thought that his former army colleagues would welcome him, but instead he was the first member of the Vichy government to be tried for treason. He was eventually shot.[36] The same thing happened in Judaea. When the revolt eventually broke out, it was not the Roman prefect Felix who attracted the assassins' blades, but Jonathan, the former High Priest.[37] Such is the fate of those who work alongside 'the enemy'.

So their question to Jesus would not necessarily be a hopeful enquiry. Jesus' rejection was followed by a statement: 'The Father and I are one' (John 10.24–30), a statement that the assembled authorities viewed as blasphemous in the extreme.

He goes on to quote Psalm 82, a psalm that accuses Israel's leaders of judging unjustly and favouring the wicked, a psalm which calls for justice for the weak and the orphans, and rescue for the destitute and oppressed (Ps. 82.1–4).

So this brief visit to Jerusalem ends, as so many of Jesus' encounters did in the religiously charged atmosphere of this city, with threats against his life. The Jews took up stones again to stone him, says John. They tried to arrest him but he 'escaped from their hands' (John 10.31, 39), heading east from the city: down, down, down to the Jordan and across to where John the Baptist had previously been at work. There, we are told, many believed in him (John 10.42). Jerusalem, with its febrile atmosphere, its celebration of long-gone independence, its politically charged atmosphere, wants to stone Jesus; but in the wilderness, they believe.

What was the point, one wonders, of this trip? What was Jesus doing? Did he just go to confront the Temple elite? Did he slip into Jerusalem to enjoy the festival and wind up the powers-that-be?

Perhaps not. Perhaps it was a visit of preparation. Perhaps he was planning ahead. Perhaps he was meeting people: people with rooms, people with donkeys.

'Blessed is anyone who takes no offence at me'

What the visit shows is that Jesus had a breathtaking ability to offend people. He could hardly open his mouth, or sit down for a meal, without someone getting shirty. By January AD 33, Jesus of Nazareth had alienated, angered, irritated or simply bemused virtually all the powerful and influential people in Palestine.

Take the Pharisees, for instance. The Pharisees were a kind of grass-roots holiness movement, with a strong emphasis on religious observance. Their popularity in the villages and the poorer parts of the cities indicates that there must have been some dissatisfaction with the 'official' holiness party, the high priests. Popular 'holiness' movements generally arise in reaction to the official religion.

Unlike the aristocratic high priests in the Temple, the Pharisees had developed a body of oral teaching and traditions which explained, expounded and interpreted the law. This was a kind of vernacular Temple worship, a way of dealing with the complexities of Torah law in everyday life. Naturally this gave them a measure of popular sympathy; after all, the oral traditions had grown up from among the people. They reflected life in the villages and hamlets of Palestine, with all its myriad conflicts and difficulties.[38] The Pharisees were also an inclusive movement, drawing membership from all levels of Judaean society. Most importantly, they were not in charge. Although represented on the Sanhedrin, the Jewish ruling council, the Pharisees were an opposition group. So, like all opposition groups, they had the luxury of not having to be responsible for anything. To add to their popularity, the Pharisees were, in principle, opposed to the occupation of Judaea by the Romans.

You'd have thought that such a movement – a movement that was trying to help ordinary Jews interpret the law and live righteous lives – would have attracted Jesus' support. Indeed, several Pharisees were attracted to Jesus' teachings, although they had to be careful about openly supporting him. Like the Pharisees, Jesus called people to be holy. But his call was different. Whereas the Pharisees and the Temple authorities seem to have concentrated on the outward observance, Jesus pointed to an inner holiness.

In this he was following in the footsteps of his relative, John the Baptist. John was also the leader of a holiness movement and a reaction against the Temple. We have seen that the Jews placed a heavy emphasis on ritual bathing to purify a pilgrim or worshipper before they entered the Temple. John seems to have taken this idea and democratised it. No need for the Temple, no need for special *miqvaot* baths; John offered purification and forgiveness simply by immersing people in the river. Clearly, John – who came, we should remember, from a priestly family – was offering an alternative to the Temple.[39]

Jesus took this democratisation of holiness and expanded it.

He kept breaking the purity laws which formed such an important part of pharisaical belief. He didn't wash properly (Mark 7.15), he didn't see the need for fasting (Mark 2.19), he was somewhat flexible in his use of the Sabbath (Matt. 12.1–8) and he didn't even acknowledge the priority of Moses' instructions (Mark 10.2–9).

He spent his time in eating and drinking with those elements of society that no prophet should have touched: the prostitutes, tax-collectors and lepers. He spoke to women. Worse, he spoke to Samaritan women. *Loose* Samaritan women. As well as his stance on fasting, Sabbath observance and ritual bathing, he persistently associated with unclean people. To the law-abiding Jews of the time, it was outrageous to say that the unclean, infidel Samaritans could be closer to God's kingdom than they were. Never mind the Pharisees, any patriotic Jew would have found this deeply insulting.[40]

He even touched on one of the deepest of taboos: the burial of the dead. Taking responsibility for this was seen as an absolute priority. To say things such as, 'Follow me, and let the dead bury their own dead' (Matt. 8.22) was astonishing. For a Jew, it brought him into conflict with the Torah: the Ten Commandments told you to honour your father and mother.

Jesus' view of purity could be summed up in one statement, which seemed to undermine all the Jewish purity laws in one fell swoop:

> Then he called the crowd again and said to them, 'Listen to me, all of you, and understand: there is nothing outside a person that by going in can defile, but the things that come out are what defile.' (Mark 7.14–15)

Many scholars have challenged these statements, seeing in them a reflection of later Christian practice, rather than of Jesus' general practice. However, the sheer number of stories that mention Jesus' supposed infractions of Jewish purity laws must, at the very least, reflect something of an early tradition. Like his relative, John, he was to some extent defined by his opposition to a strict adherence to Jewish purity regulations. In the words of Martin Hengel, 'for Jesus the Torah formed no longer the ultimate standard… Jesus – unlike the whole body of his Jewish contemporaries – stood not under, but above the Torah received by Moses at Sinai'.[41]

And to cap it all off, he told stories with a clear bias against the Pharisees.[42] His insistence on teaching in his own name, and under his own authority, was not consistent with pharisaical practice, which would appeal to the Torah. He would use Scripture in a deeply subversive way.[43] We have seen that to be known as 'wise' was important, particularly for religious leaders.[44] Understanding the law gave you credibility with the public. Someone like Rabbi Gamaliel had huge influence among the people because he was known to be a wise Torah scholar (Acts 5.34).[45] It cannot have helped Jesus' popularity with the leading men, of either the Pharisees or the Sadducees, to have made them look like idiots. Jesus had powers that made everyone sit up and listen, and stories that made their listening worthwhile. He had an answer for everything – and a question, too.

And instead of showing the Pharisees respect for their teaching, he savaged them. He accused them of hypocrisy, satirising them, pointing out, time and again, the difference between their scrupulous observation of the law and their sometimes less than scrupulous observation of simple justice. Where the Pharisees believed that they were helping people to worship, Jesus charged them with burdening people with all their regulations. He was all about bringing people into the kingdom of God, making it possible for those on the outside to come into the feast. It was not that his creed was less demanding, but it was less exclusive.

So the Pharisees were 'hypocrites' and liars. But the list of opponents didn't stop there. To a wide range of orthodox Jews, Jesus' actions and statements would have been seen as provocative. Herod Antipas, the ruler of Galilee, was a 'fox' who wanted to kill Jesus (Luke 13.31–32); we've seen the Jews in the Temple so outraged at his claims that they'd tried to have him stoned (John 10.31–39). His own family did not support him (John 7.8). Only the Romans hadn't taken offence – and that was probably because they hadn't met him. Even John the Baptist had doubted. While imprisoned in Herod Antipas' jail, he had sent men to Jesus to ask him one key question: 'Are you the one who is to come, or are we to wait for another?' (Luke 7.19). Jesus' reply was simply to point to his actions: 'The blind receive their sight, the lame walk, the lepers are cleansed, the deaf hear, the dead are raised, the poor have good news brought to them. *And blessed is anyone who takes no offence at me* (Luke 7.22–23, my italics).

This, then, is the first thing to understand about the historical picture of Jesus in the Gospels. He was calling in those who were stuck outside, and in doing so he had the knack of the true radical: the ability to get under the skin of all those in power.

For if his attacks on the Pharisees, and his relaxed attitude to purity, alienated the Pharisees and other religious groups, his advocation of non-violence and his insistence on loving one's enemies alienated him from the political activists of his day. Historians have differed over the extent of armed resistance to Rome in Judaea during the time of Jesus. Jesus is recorded as having at least one disciple linked to a political group: Simon the Zealot. The Zealots were the left-wing radicals, the Provisional wing of the Pharisees, if you like. They advocated guerilla action against Rome and withholding all taxes and financial support. It was the Zealots (supported by the majority of the Pharisees) who gained control of Jerusalem during the great revolution of AD 66 – with disastrous consequences.

How active they were at Jesus' time is open to debate, but we know that there was some armed resistance going on, if only from the people who were crucified alongside Jesus. It seems likely that there was a continual undercurrent of insurgency against Roman rule and those who collaborated with it, which grew over the decades to a crescendo with the first Jewish revolt in AD 66. To people who advocated an armed struggle against Rome, 'loving your enemies' would have been impossible. Even for the church this has been a difficult, and at times unendurable, demand. Yet we can be sure that it formed the core of Jesus' teaching.[46] He challenged the idea that an armed struggle could change things; he even told a story which denied the idea that anyone could force the kingdom of God to come (Mark 4.26ff.).

We should remember that only a small minority of Jewish people were active supporters or adherents of these political–religious sects. Of the maybe 500,000 Jewish residents, Josephus estimates there were 6,000 Pharisees, over 4,000 Essenes and very few Sadducees.[47] But they were influential. And Jesus had annoyed them all.

There was, however, one group with whom Jesus was consistently popular: the poor and the marginalised. It was the poor who saw in Jesus one of their own. Jesus insisted on seeing things through the eyes of the poor. He understood the poor because he was poor. He understood that the poor needed more than food; he understood that the poor needed to worship God and to find a place in the kingdom of God. And he understood that there were so many hurdles in the way, that the things that should have been the highways to God were, in fact, the obstacles.

If Jesus lacked support among the powerful, he never lacked it among the ordinary people. They flocked to hear him teach and clamoured after him for healing. And, as we shall see, they never did turn against him, despite what their leaders said.

Thus, by the end of AD 32, Jesus' teaching, his miracles, his emphasis on the poor, the marginalised and the unclean and his almost total disrespect for religious leaders had resulted in distrust and even animosity. But although various groups had been moved to violence against him, there was no intentional coherent strategy to remove him. He was not seen as that much of a danger.

Then, in the early spring of AD 33, he did something that changed things entirely, something *really* annoying: he raised a man from the dead.

The raising of Lazarus

Where: Just outside Bethany

When: Spring AD 33

Jesus stayed across the Jordan for a while until, sometime in the early spring of AD 33, he received a cry for help. His friend Lazarus of Bethany was ill, and Lazarus' sisters, Mary and Martha, had sent an urgent message to Jesus to come to their aid. If Jesus was still 'across the Jordan', he was only around twenty miles from Bethany: perhaps a day's walk. Yet he delayed his trip, staying two days longer, during which time Lazarus died.

Why did he wait? John depicts it as being because he knew what was going to happen; he was preparing a sign (John 11.4–6). Perhaps, though, he really was anxious about returning so soon to a place where he had been threatened. Bethany is only a mile and half from Jerusalem, well within striking range of the Temple authorities. The disciples were aware of this tension. When Jesus eventually decided to answer the summons, the disciples reflected this concern: 'Rabbi, the Jews were just now trying to stone you, and are you going there again?' (John 11.8) When Jesus insists on going, Thomas, ever the pessimist, sums up the mood: 'Let us also go, that we may die with him' (John 11.16).

So Jesus and his followers crossed the Jordan and went up to Bethany, a little way from Jerusalem. There, in the graveyard just outside the village, he called Lazarus out of the tomb; he raised Lazarus to life. The issue of raising the dead to life is, obviously, something which gives the historian a few challenges! I shall be dealing with the idea of resurrection later, and looking more closely at the household of Mary, Martha and Lazarus. For the moment, whatever we might think about Jesus' miracles, it was clear that, from the start, he was associated with the miraculous. He was associated with acts of healing and deliverance and with supernatural acts of power.

For now, we should just note that the effect of this action was immense. It was not just that Jesus had performed a miracle, nor was it just that Mary and Martha had had their brother restored to them. It was an act that set alarm bells ringing in the Temple, for the action was reported to the Sanhedrin, the Jewish council:

> So the chief priests and the Pharisees called a meeting of the council, and said, 'What are we to do? This man is performing many signs. If we let him go on like this, everyone will believe in him, and the Romans will come and destroy both our holy place and our nation.' But one of them, Caiaphas, who was high priest that year, said to them, 'You know nothing at all! You do not understand that it is better for you to have one man die for the people than to have the whole nation destroyed.' (John 11.47–50)

This is the first mention of one of the chief players in the game which is about to commence: Caiaphas, the High Priest.

'It is better for you to have one man die for the people'

In 1990, in a cave in the northern Talpiot area of Jerusalem, archaeologists found twelve ossuaries – boxes containing the bones of the dead. Six of these were untouched, and in one of them was found a coin dating from the days of Agrippa (AD 42–3). Two of the ossuaries bore the name of Caiaphas and one contained the bones of a sixty-year-old man. We can't be sure that this is the same Caiaphas as the High Priest. But it was a wealthy tomb. And he was a wealthy man.[48]

By the time Lazarus stumbled out of the tomb, blinking in the sunlight, Caiaphas had been High Priest for around fifteen years, quite a remarkable feat given the volatile nature of the politics of his day.[49] And politics is what it was, for the office of high priest, though ostensibly a religious post, was, as we have seen, a political appointment, the gift of the Roman Prefect. There was supposed to be an annual review of the role, and the Romans had introduced the policy of rotating the appointment of the high priest among three or four families. These families were, in effect, the aristocratic families of Judaea, drawing their legitimacy from the Temple and from their priestly status. Members of the ruling class pointed proudly to their descent from one of the high-priestly families, and they guarded access to these families through marriage.[50] Extreme care was taken to find the right marriage partners for the sons of the most distinguished priestly families, and priests tried hard to avoid damaging their honour and position by mingling with the lower classes, whose women had to work for a living.[51] The result was a kind of religious aristocracy, in which power was transferred between members of the same family. Caiaphas, who had been appointed in AD 18, held the position till AD 36. His father-in-law, Annas, was High Priest from AD 6 to AD 15 and five of Annas' sons – Caiaphas' brothers-in-law – were to hold the same office.[52]

Caiaphas' longevity as High Priest may simply have been because he was in a position to keep paying Pilate for the privilege.[53] But there were always wealthy people around; it is much more likely that Caiaphas remained high priest because he did the job very well and because he and Pilate understood one another. It is noticeable that, when Pilate was recalled from Judaea, it was only a matter of months before Caiaphas was replaced. Whatever the case, if we can infer one thing about Caiaphas from history, it's that he was good at keeping his job.

And it really was a worthwhile job to keep. Caiaphas' position as High Priest was hugely influential, even allowing for the ultimate authority of the Romans. It was control of the Temple which gave the high priest his power. We tend to think of the Temple as a huge church. In fact it was a much, much greater and more powerful institution. The Temple was more than a place of worship: it was the economic powerhouse of Jerusalem. It was simply the biggest business in town, and certainly the leading employer. There was constant building work. There were animals to be slaughtered. There were workers needed to administrate the operations of the Temple, slaves and servants needed to keep the place clean and well run. The sacrifices required grain, wood, cattle, sheep, birds, olive oil, fruit and incense. All these had to be supplied. In turn, the Temple gained its enormous wealth through an annual donation from every Jew throughout the Græco-Roman world, as well as a tithe on the agricultural produce of the people in Judaea and beyond.[54]

Caiaphas must have already been a rich man when he ascended to the office, since the high priest had to provide certain key sacrifices – such as those on the Day of Atonement – out of his own pocket. The Gospels tell us that he lived in a house big enough to have a gatehouse and servants – most likely, as we have seen, in the wealthy Upper City. Although we don't have any data about the income of the high priest, it must have been significant and it was probably drawn from the Temple treasury. The fact that, as high priest, he appointed his own relatives to key posts such as Temple treasurer, would have given them access to a huge amount of capital.[55]

So the post had enormous benefits, but it also carried a high level of risk. There wasn't what you might call job security. It would take only one Roman decision for him to lose his position, and one decision by the Emperor for the Jews to lose their most holy possession. Managing relations with Rome was always difficult; things were always liable to be upset by religious zealotry. The conflicts which arose during the time of Pilate's rule were nearly always triggered by religious conflict. They arose over the use of images, or threats to the purity of the Temple, or the use of sacred money. Ironically, it was too much zeal for the Jewish religion that was the biggest danger to Caiaphas and his regime, the very religion that they were supposed to defend.

Hence Caiaphas' anxiety at this meeting of the council. Jesus' actions and growing popularity were seen as a threat to 'our holy place and our nation'. The two were intrinsically linked: in a way, the Temple *was* the nation. It was the symbol, the representation. In a world ruled by pagan forces, the Temple offered the Jews one shred of true independence. It was, apart from anything else, the one place where the Romans did not go. They observed it. They kept a careful watch from the fortress overlooking it. They controlled the worship, to a certain extent, through keeping the high priest's vestments under lock and key. But it was the one spot on the earth that belonged to the Jews. Some thirty years later, on the eve of the Jewish revolt, Agrippa is said to have used the same threat, foretelling that the Romans would burn down the holy place and wipe out the nation.[56]

It is to counter this threat – the nightmare scenario of the Jews losing everything they have – that Caiaphas is recorded as suggesting the 'sacrifice' of Jesus.[57]

It was a matter of compromise. And Caiaphas knew all about compromise, because he was a Sadducee.

'Some Sadducees came to him, saying there is no resurrection'

The received view of Sadducees is that they were politically aligned to the Romans but theologically conservative, that they were wealthy aristocrats, living secular, Hellenised lifestyles, and that they were the high-priestly class in charge of the Temple. The contradictions in this view are immediately apparent. A conservative, Torah-based theology does not sit well with a Græco-Roman lifestyle.

Their origins are difficult to fathom. The first reference to them is in the Hasmonaean period, in the third century BC, but that is more as a political grouping than as a religious affiliation. By the time of Jesus, the Sadducees had little in common with their ancestors except for the name.[58] The references to the Sadducees are not that extensive. In contemporary accounts, they appear in the Gospels and in Acts, and in the writings of Josephus. (Later mentions of them in the works of Christian writers are drawn mainly from the Gospels.) There are accounts in the Mishnah of conflicts between the Pharisees and the Sadducees, but by the time they were collected, the Sadducees had, apparently, completely disappeared.[59]

Josephus says that the doctrines of the Sadducees were 'received but by a few, yet by those still of the greatest dignity'.[60] A further clue comes from a passage in which Josephus writes:

> What I would now explain is this, that the Pharisees have delivered to the people a great many observances by succession from their

fathers, which are not written in the law of Moses; and for that reason it is that the Sadducees reject them and say that we are to esteem those observances to be obligatory which are in the written word, but are not to observe what are derived from the tradition of our forefathers; and concerning these things it is that great disputes and differences have arisen among them, while the Sadducees are able to persuade none but the rich, and have not the populace obsequious to them, but the Pharisees have the multitude of their side...[61]

These two accounts indicate that, although presumably anyone from any class could follow their teachings if they chose, the Sadducees had a particular following among the wealthy and politically powerful.

Although Josephus claims that the Sadducees refused to follow later Jewish religious traditions, it would have been practically impossible to obey the Torah without some kind of interpretation. But they do seem to have rejected the Pharisees' interpretations. This may have been a class issue. The Pharisees' oral law was drawn from life in the villages and communities of Judaea and Galilee. Perhaps the Sadducean interpretative structure came from the richer, upper echelons of Jerusalem.

They also, according to Josephus, rejected the idea of fate:

And for the Sadducees, they take away fate, and say there is no such thing, and that the events of human affairs are not at its disposal; but they suppose that all our actions are in our own power, so that we are ourselves the cause of what is good, and receive what is evil from our own folly.[62]

This is a hardline message and may well explain why the Sadducees were mainly the wealthy elite. If you are poor and oppressed, if the Romans have taxed you and the aristocrats have foreclosed on your land, it's not a popular message to hear that 'It's all your own fault'.

It is usually claimed that the Sadducees were the priestly party. Here we are on trickier ground, since neither Josephus nor the later rabbinic sources give any indication that the Sadducees were the priestly class.[63] The New Testament, too, distinguishes between the two: in Acts 4.1, Luke talks about 'the priests, the captain of the Temple, and the Sadducees'. Clearly, priests did not have to be Sadducees. As we shall see, there were pharisaical priests as well.

So, not all high priests were Sadducees, but some Sadducees were high priests. We know, in particular, of one High Priest who was a Sadducee: Ananus ben Ananus, the High Priest who, in AD 62, was responsible for the execution of James, brother of Jesus. Here's Josephus again:

> Now the report goes, that this elder Ananus proved a most fortunate man; for he had five sons, who had all performed the office of a High Priest to God, and he had himself enjoyed that dignity a long time formerly, which had never happened to any other of our High Priests: but this younger Ananus, who, as we have told you already, took the High Priesthood, was a bold man in his temper, and very insolent; he was also of the sect of the Sadducees, who are very rigid in judging offenders, above all the rest of the Jews, as we have already observed.[64]

This 'younger Ananus' was the son of Ananus, or Annas, whom we shall meet later. He was one of five of Ananus' sons who were to become High Priest. This is the House of Hanan, whom we have already encountered in the verses bemoaning their 'whisperings'. Significantly, Caiaphas, too, was part of this wider family: he was Ananus' son-in-law. So we're dealing with a dynasty here. It's highly likely that the younger Ananus was simply following in the family tradition: they were all Sadducees. That was their faith, their denomination, their political party. Their behaviour was certainly more akin to a modern political party. Josephus wrote that 'The behavior of the Sadducees one towards another is in some degrees wild; and their conversation with those that are of their own party is as barbarous as if they were strangers to them'.[65]

If Caiaphas was a Sadducee, it would explain why the resurrection of Lazarus provides the tipping point. For the one crucial issue that we know divided Pharisee from Sadducee was the resurrection of the dead. 'The doctrine of the Sadducees is this,' wrote Josephus, 'that souls die with the bodies.'[66] The argument between the Pharisees and the Sadducees over this matter was so intense that a fight could break out at any moment. Paul cunningly used the argument as a way of creating a disturbance during his hearing before the Sanhedrin. All he had to do was toss out an inflammatory remark and the place erupted (Acts 23.4–8). So, in raising Lazarus from the dead, Jesus was not only encouraging, as they believed, a nationalistic Messianic fervour, he was also undermining their theology. For what was the life of Lazarus, if not life after death?

The Sadducees, then, cannot be seen purely as the priestly class. They were not the liberal wing of Judaism against the fundamentalist Pharisees. If anything, it was the other way round. They were the *sola scriptura* party. Their practice was based on the Torah and the Torah alone. They were, in the words of Goodman, 'radical biblical fundamentalists'. And in Jesus' day, they were in power.

But wielding power can be less comfortable than we think. Because as soon as they come to power, all fundamentalists start to see that the world doesn't exactly operate along neatly doctrinal lines. Caiaphas, for example, is in charge of the Temple. But Josephus claims that ordinary Jews followed pharisaical practices 'with regard to prayer and sacrifices'. At a local level, in fact, the Sadducees may have been reluctant to take power, simply because it did mean so much compromise between them and the people:

> When they become magistrates, as they are unwillingly and by force sometimes obliged to be, they addict themselves to the notions of the Pharisees, because the multitude would not otherwise bear them.[67]

And the compromises were not restricted to the local level. In temples throughout the Græco-Roman world, the emperor was worshipped as a god. Sacrifices were made to him. In the Temple in Jerusalem, however, the sacrifice was different. There, in deference to the Jewish faith, sacrifices were made, not to the Emperor, but for his health, and for the well-being of the Roman people. In other words the Romans insisted that some form of sacrifice and obeisance to Rome had to be made, but it could be couched in language that was not offensive to Jewish ears.

That is, not *all* Jewish ears. Even within the Temple, there was disagreement about this compromise. In AD 66, on the eve of war with Rome, it was this daily sacrifice which was the target for the first act of revolutionary reform. Some of the priests, seized with revolutionary fervour, decided that no longer would they offer sacrifices for foreigners or on behalf of Caesar. The person who stopped the sacrifices was a man called Eleazar. He was the Temple Captain – a kind of second-in-command at the Temple – and a son of a former high priest (not part of the House of Hanan).[68] Eleazar's hotheaded action did not win total support – and the people opposing it included 'many of the High Priests and principal men'.[69] Clearly, not all of the major aristocratic families disagreed with this sacrifice.

So Caiaphas, High Priest and Sadducee, was a master of compromise. As a Sadducee he should have rejected any sacrifice that was not to be found in the Torah, but as a high priest he had to agree to this innovation. He understood, more than anyone, that the worship in the Temple survived only because of the goodwill of the Romans. And this sacrifice was not the only sign of their power: the vestments worn by the high priest at the times of festival were in the keeping of the Romans. They would be handed over to Caiaphas for the duration of that festival and then taken back into Roman 'safekeeping'. It was like owning the keys to the religion. The Jews were free to take the car for a drive, but only when the Romans let them have the keys.

In this light, therefore, Caiaphas' statement about Jesus, 'Better to have one man die…', shows a real understanding of the true nature of things in Judaea. Each day a bull and a lamb were sacrificed in the Temple with the sole purpose of keeping the Romans happy and keeping the Jewish religion alive. It was a very small step to sacrifice one man for the same purpose. At this point in time, Caiaphas knows that keeping the Temple alive is a political balancing act. And he knows that Jesus is a loose cannon, an uncontrollable factor in that very delicate equation.

And so, in the months leading up to the Longest Week, the decision has already been taken. We can feel the first tremors of what will happen. In effect, Jesus has already been sentenced. The Council leaders already know what is to be done with him. All they have to do is lay hands on him.[70]

And it is the Temple aristocracy who have decided this, a small cadre of family, friends and supporters who have one aim: to keep the Temple going and the Jewish nation alive. It would be wrong to see their actions as totally self-serving. They were trying to protect the one thing that the Jews still had left: the Temple. But they were also wealthy and powerful, and those are drugs from which it is difficult to free yourself.

So the order is sent out: Jesus is a marked man. After the resurrection of Lazarus, Jesus can no longer walk about openly, but instead heads to a town called Ephraim near the wilderness, possibly Aphairema, near Bethel. The text implies that it was near the Judaean wilderness to the north-east of Jerusalem. The exact place is uncertain. But Jesus was in hiding.

The authorities suspect that he will not be away for long.

> Now the Passover of the Jews was near, and many went up from the country to Jerusalem before the Passover to purify themselves. They were looking for Jesus and were asking one another as they stood in the Temple, 'What do you think? Surely he will not come to the festival, will he?' Now the chief priests and the Pharisees had given orders that anyone who knew where Jesus was should let them know, so that they might arrest him. (John 11.55–57)

Is he coming? That was the question on everyone's lips as Passover approached. In a city filled to bursting point with pilgrims, one pilgrim in particular was looked for. His followers looked for him to come and begin the revolution in full. His opponents were on the lookout to arrest him.

Both were to get their wish.

The Night Before
Saturday 28 March AD 33

Jesus in Bethany: Saturday evening

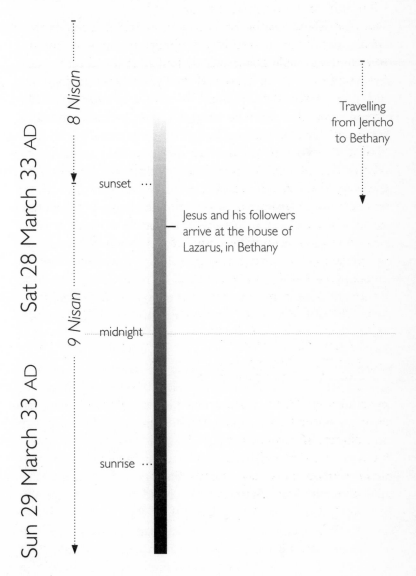

8 Nisan

Sat 28 March 33 AD

sunset ···

Jesus and his followers
arrive at the house of
Lazarus, in Bethany

Travelling
from Jericho
to Bethany

9 Nisan

midnight

Sun 29 March 33 AD

sunrise ···

Jesus in Bethany

Where: The house of Lazarus, Martha and Mary

When: Saturday evening

> Six days before the Passover Jesus came to Bethany, the home of
> Lazarus, whom he had raised from the dead. (John 12.1)

John places Jesus' arrival after sunset on the Saturday, six days
before Passover was to start on the Friday.[1] Jesus and his followers had arrived from Jericho where he had shared a meal – and
perhaps stayed – with a tax-collector called Zacchaeus (Luke
19.1–10). Would-be tax-collectors would bid for contracts,
promising to raise a certain sum each year for the authorities.
Anything over that amount was theirs to keep. It was in their
interest, therefore, to get as much money as they could.

Elsewhere in the Græco-Roman world tax-collectors were
generally respected, but in Judaea they were reviled, because
their success was gained not through knowledge of the Torah,
but through collaboration with the Roman authorities. In a
society in which the gulf between rich and poor was ever-widen-
ing, the tax-collectors, with their undeserved wealth, drew the
same kind of scorn as 'city investors' do today. They had done
nothing to deserve their wealth, except work for the occupying
powers.[2] But it was more than mere scorn or dislike: tax-collectors were considered ritually impure. The Mishnah records
that even 'if a tax-gatherer enter a house, [all that is within] the
house becomes unclean'.[3] They were contaminants, economic
lepers. Jesus' inclusion of such people among his disciples, his
invitations to them to be part of God's party and his habit
of eating with them do not so much contravene Jewish purity
taboos as smash them to pieces.

On his way out of Jericho, Jesus was accompanied by crowds,
eagerly anticipating, no doubt, his entry into Jerusalem. Matthew says that, as he left the city, two blind men called after him
and were given their sight (Matt. 20.29–34), while Mark also
records the healing of another blind man, Bartimaeus – son
of Timaeus. Significantly, the blind men had called him 'Son
of David' – a term which, by the time of Jesus, had become a

title for the Messiah, the deliverer who would rescue Israel and assume the throne.[4] No wonder the crowd was excited.

From Jericho the road took Jesus and his followers up along the hillside, some eleven miles to Bethany, where Lazarus lived with his sisters, Martha and Mary. This was to be Jesus' base for the climactic week of his life.

'So he appointed the twelve'

Jesus came to Bethany accompanied by a group of followers. The traditional view of Jesus and the twelve disciples is only partially correct; in fact the New Testament indicates he had many followers. The twelve, though, were his core group, although there are different accounts in the Gospels of the make-up of the group. Usually the discrepancies in the lists are explained by the fact that individuals might have different names or forms of identifiers. The list of the twelve disciples is as follows:

Matthew 10.2–4	Mark 3.16–19	Luke 6.13–16
Simon, also known as Peter	Simon	Simon
Andrew	Andrew	Andrew
James son of Zebedee	James	James
John son of Zebedee	John	John
Philip	Philip	Philip
Bartholomew	Bartholomew	Bartholomew
Thomas	Thomas	Thomas
Matthew	Matthew	Matthew
James son of Alphaeus	James son of Alphaeus	James son of Alphaeus
Thaddaeus	Thaddaeus	Judas son of James
Simon the Cananaean	Simon the Cananaean	Simon the Zealot
Judas Iscariot	Judas Iscariot	Judas Iscariot

John mentions the twelve in only three places (John 6.67, 70–71; 20.24), and nowhere gives a list of names. But, along with some of those mentioned above, Jesus' disciples include Nathanael (John 1.45) and Joseph of Arimathea (John 19.38). John's 'vagueness' reflects what, in fact, the Synoptics acknowledge, that there were many more disciples than the twelve. Luke has an account of 72 (or 70) followers being chosen. Indeed, Luke also lists women who supported Jesus financially, some of whom travelled with him as well:

> The twelve were with him, as well as some women who had been cured of evil spirits and infirmities: Mary, called Magdalene, from whom seven demons had gone out, and Joanna, the wife of Herod's steward Chuza, and Susanna, and many others, who provided for them out of their resources. (Luke 8.1–3)

The women who followed Jesus were, to all intents and purposes, disciples, but, in the Gospels at least, they are not referred to as such. In that culture, at that time, a disciple was male.[5] Even so, the role of women in supporting and travelling with Jesus was remarkable. Kenneth Bailey points out that, even today in the Middle East, if travelling with a group of men, women have to spend their nights with relatives.[6]

We can see, therefore, that the people who accompanied Jesus to Bethany came from a variety of backgrounds – often backgrounds that involved marginalisation or discrimination. Some had formerly been disciples of John the Baptist; at least four were fishermen; Matthew was a tax-collector; Simon is described as a Cananaean or a 'Zealot' in Luke's version. The word does not come from 'Canaan', as in the land, but from the Aramaic word meaning zealot or enthusiast. In other words, he had previously been associated with some kind of ultra-nationalistic political movement. It would be the equivalent of having a former Black Panther as one of the core supporters of Martin Luther King.

The presence of a Zealot among Jesus' disciples has led to speculation that Jesus himself was a political revolutionary of that sort.[7] Jesus, it has been pointed out, criticises every other section of Jewish political life, including the Sadducees, the Pharisees and the Herodians, but not the Zealots. However, Jesus' advocation of non-violence does not sit easily with this theory; nor do his evasive answers when challenged about tax. It is more likely that the Zealots escaped specific criticism because, in Jesus' time, they were a marginal and fragmented organisation, not the well-organised military force that they were later to become. And as for Jesus' lack of criticism – he didn't criticise the Romans, but that doesn't make him Italian.[8]

Attempts to portray Jesus as leading a class-based revolution can succeed only by ignoring all the references to members from other classes and groups. The presence of a tax-collector in the twelve, not to mention a female former demoniac, shows that Jesus was able to attract an unusually wide range of people.

'Jesus came to Bethany, the home of Lazarus'

John places dinner that night in the house of Lazarus, and has Mary anoint Jesus' feet with oil. Mark places this event in a different house – the house of Simon the Leper – and at a different time – the Wednesday night. Given that versions of the event happen in other places in the Gospels, it seems safe to assume that none of the evangelists is quite sure when it happened, or even who was involved. I prefer the Marcan tradition here, so will treat the event at happening at that time. However, Jesus' staying at the house of Lazarus is natural enough. They were his friends; he had been there only a few weeks before. Bethany was just a short walk from Jerusalem, yet far enough outside the city to escape the crowds and the attention on the eastern slopes of the Mount of Olives.

Lazarus, and his sisters, Mary and Martha, are some of the most familiar names of the New Testament. Yet the status of this household is intriguing. Lazarus, it seems, has no wife, Mary and Martha no husbands. Nobody else is mentioned in the household. So who were these people?

Individuals in the New Testament are identified in a number of ways. Since there was a relatively narrow choice of first names, there was normally some other form of identifier such as the place they came from (e.g. Joseph of Arimathea, Mary Magdalene) or even a family characteristic (e.g. Thomas Didymus – 'Thomas the Twin'). Probably the most common form of identifier was to define a person by their family relationships, most commonly by their father. So we have X, son of Y as a common designation. Simon son of Jonah, for example (Matt. 16.17), or James and John the sons of Zebedee (Matt. 10.2). Women were identified by their relationship to their husbands or sons, for example Mary the mother of James and Joseph (Matt. 27.56) or Mary the wife of Clopas (John 19.25). (This is one of the reasons why most scholars believe Jesus' father, Joseph, to have been dead by the time his son started preaching and healing; where Jesus is designated 'Jesus son of Mary', it is an indication that his mother is alive but his father is dead.) Daughters were normally identified by their father's name, as X the daughter of Y.[9] But Mary and Martha are only ever identified by their relationship to their brother. And Lazarus is not placed in any family context at all. He is identified only by his place of residence: Lazarus of Bethany (John 11.1). So we have a household here, of which Lazarus appears to be the head and in which he lives with his sisters.

Where are the parents? They are never mentioned. Nor is there any hint of a husband for either Martha or Mary. The marriageable age for Jewish girls was anything from twelve onwards, and rabbinic sources seem to indicate that both men and women were expected to marry earlier rather than later.[10] Certainly, it was normal for a Jewish girl to marry between fourteen and eighteen, and a Jewish man by the time he was twenty-one or so. So it seems unusual to have two older unmarried sisters in one home, not to mention an unmarried brother. This is a family of single people; it's the nearest we get to a first-century student house.

One possible reconstruction of this household, therefore, is that all three were young and that both parents were dead.[11] This would have forced Lazarus into the role of provider. They may not have been a poor household – evidently the house had enough room for Jesus and his followers – and the perfume incident, as we shall see, indicates a certain amount of resources. But they were a family in a perilous state. Because if Lazarus died, the girls could not legally inherit. What wealth they had would have passed to the next male relative. In such a scenario, the death of Lazarus would have had huge implications for the girls. This would not have been just the loss of a beloved brother, but the loss of house, money and, especially, status. What little self-determination they had as women would have been taken away from them. This adds a poignancy to Martha's response to Jesus: 'Lord, if you had been here…'

Lazarus' resurrection can be seen, therefore, as more than the return of a brother they had given up as lost: it meant the return of economic security and status. They had lost their parents, they had lost their older brother, now they turned to the only other man they trusted.

This absence of a father figure may also illuminate the story in Luke that depicts an earlier meeting between Jesus and the family, in which Mary sits at Jesus' feet. The presence of this story in Luke can be seen as tacit confirmation that Jesus made more than one visit to Jerusalem. Luke does not name the place; he merely talks of 'a certain village'. The village was Bethany.

It was at that visit that Mary chose to sit at Jesus' feet, rather than to help her sister (Luke 10:38–42). The story is often interpreted as showing the difference between the active and the contemplative life. In fact, it's about the difference between knowing your place and trying to break free. It's a story that illustrates Mary's relative disdain for social standards. In Luke's story, Mary sits at Jesus' feet to listen to his teaching. Rabbinic teaching seems to have excluded women from the study of the Torah. Rabbi Eliezer said that 'anyone who teaches his daughter Torah, it is as though he has taught her lechery'.[12] Women did attend various religious assemblies, but it was to listen, rather than to engage in debate. Eleazar ben Azariah interpreted the command, 'Assemble the people – men, women and children' (Deut. 31.12) to mean that the men should come to study, the women to listen and the little ones 'to receive the reward for those who bring them'.[13] It was likely that women knew some Torah, especially those laws which related to the kitchen and the household, and the Mishnah does include some instances where, on domestic matters, women seem to know more than the men. But women, on the whole, were not expected to learn anything beyond what they needed to. Martha's complaint against Mary, therefore, is that she is breaking the boundaries: by listening to Jesus' teaching she is stepping out of the kitchen. It's nothing to do with the active versus the contemplative life: it's everything to do with the way that women were supposed to be.

This, then, is one picture of the family with whom Jesus stayed while in Jerusalem: a young family, with two girls who saw in him rescue and protection and the hope that their life could be different. And a young man whose experiences can only be imagined. A family whom Jesus had rescued.

No wonder that Jesus' presence in Bethany soon attracted attention. A crowd began to gather to see, not only Jesus, but Lazarus as well:

> When the great crowd of the Jews learned that he was there, they came not only because of Jesus but also to see Lazarus, whom he had raised from the dead. So the chief priests planned to put Lazarus to death as well, since it was on account of him that many of the Jews were deserting and were believing in Jesus. (John 12.9–11)

The resurrection of Lazarus was the trigger which determined the Temple aristocracy to act. They planned to get rid of Jesus, whom they feared would bring the wrath of the Romans down on them. But why get rid of Lazarus as well? One might have thought that Lazarus had already suffered enough, without being put to death a second time.

As we have seen, one of the main planks of Sadducean theology was a disbelief in the resurrection of the dead. Here was living proof of the opposite. Part of the reason why they wanted to get rid of Jesus was that he had proved them wrong.

Part of the reason why they wanted to get rid of Lazarus was, surely, because they simply wanted to destroy the evidence.

But there's another factor as well. If there's one thing that the story of the Longest Week shows us, it is that resurrection is a political act. It is, in a way, the ultimate act of subversion. Lazarus was a danger to the state, because the story of his resurrection not only destroyed the theology of the political leadership, it destroyed the power of totalitarian leadership everywhere. If you don't fear death, if death is not the end, then what power does the state have over you? A later Christian wrote about all those whose lives 'were held in slavery by the fear of death' (Heb. 2.15), for throughout the Græco-Roman world the fear of death, and the idea that this life was all there was, was used to enslave and control millions of people. The problem, then, with the idea of Jesus as a nationalistic, Jewish revolutionary is that it's way too small a picture: his revolution was far greater than that, and the rebellion he began was aimed at a far, far greater power.

Day One: The Entry
Sunday 29 March

The triumphal entry: Jerusalem, Sunday morning
Jesus looks at the Temple: The Temple, Sunday morning
Greeks speak with Jesus: The Temple, Sunday morning

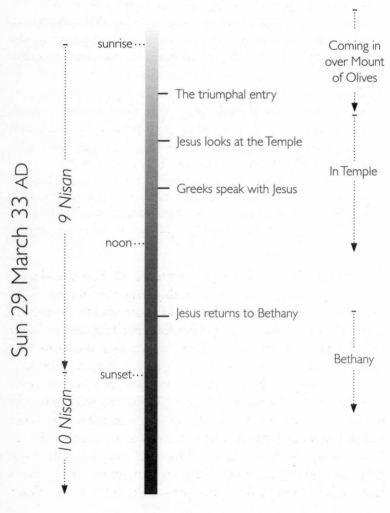

The triumphal entry

Where: Jerusalem

When: Morning

He came from the east, over the Mount of Olives.

Jerusalem sits on two ridges, with the valleys running around and between. To the south is the Hinnom Valley. Running north–south through the city itself is the Tyropoeon Valley. To the east of the city is the Kidron Valley, with the Mount of Olives rising above it. Bethany is just over the crest of the Mount.

So we can imagine Jesus that morning, rising with the dawn, preparing for the day ahead, setting out along the road to the west, knowing that just over the hill lay the greatest challenge of his life.

> When they were approaching Jerusalem, at Bethphage and Bethany, near the Mount of Olives, he sent two of his disciples and said to them, 'Go into the village ahead of you, and immediately as you enter it, you will find tied there a colt that has never been ridden; untie it and bring it. If anyone says to you, "Why are you doing this?" just say this, "The Lord needs it and will send it back here immediately."' They went away and found a colt tied near a door, outside in the street. As they were untying it, some of the bystanders said to them, 'What are you doing, untying the colt?' They told them what Jesus had said; and they allowed them to take it. (Mark 11.1–6)

Jesus orders his disciples to go and fetch a colt from the village. The colt is brought to him, probably near the crossroads on the main Jericho–Jerusalem road, where the road to Bethphage goes off to the south.[1] Many Christians see this, and the later coded arrangements for the Last Supper, as a prophetic act: Jesus miraculously 'knows' there is a colt waiting for him. But there's nothing in the text to indicate that the Gospel writers thought them miraculous. These were prearranged events, set in motion by coded signals. We should remember that Jesus had followers in Jerusalem and in the nearby villages, such as Emmaus and Bethany. He could have set things up either the previous evening or, more likely, in that quiet, surreptitious visit to Jerusalem in the winter of AD 32. What is significant is that Jesus needs to get the details right for this journey; he needs to enter on the right kind of animal. There is going to be more than one code at work this morning.

So Jesus embarks on a carefully staged entrance. He mounts the donkey and, sending disciples ahead of him to spread the news, he crests the hill and sees before him, spread out in the morning sunlight, the city of Jerusalem.

'See, we are going up to Jerusalem'

At the centre of Judaea, its pumping, pulsating heart was Jerusalem.

There are two main factors that determine the sites of cities: money and defence. Some cities – most cities, perhaps – start as trading places, expanding from points on trade routes, serving as a market place for local agriculture or mining, or standing in the perfect bay for a port. Other cities spring up because they are in places where defence is easy. They stand on the top of a hill, usually, in places where they cannot easily be attacked, or where they command views of the surrounding countryside.

Some cities start as one, and turn into the other. Jerusalem was founded as a Caananite city – the city of the Jebusite tribe – before David captured it some time around 1000 BC.[2] In those days, its strength lay in its strategic hillside position, which made it hard to attack. According to the Bible, David only managed to capture it by sending men up through the water shaft. Having taken Jerusalem, he set about transforming the city into the defensive capital of his empire.

However, by the time of Jesus, Jerusalem's defensive strength was a thing of the past. As armies grew larger, and siege warfare more sophisticated, its isolation and lack of a viable water supply made it vulnerable. After the Babylonians captured it in 586 BC, it never really managed to repel a determined siege again.

David had changed things by bringing in the Ark, and his son had built the Temple, but those glory days were long gone. The second Temple – the one built by Zerubbabel after the

Jews returned from exile in Babylon – was a small affair. It reflected Israel's situation. By the time the Romans arrived, in 63 BC, Jerusalem was a spent force. Jerusalem was a small capital in a backwater country. One man changed all that: Herod, the one they called 'the Great'.

Before Herod, rebuilding had concentrated mainly on defence and water supplies. The Hasmonaean dynasty, who ruled before him, built a large palace to the east of the Temple. Although its exact location has never been identified, it must have been on the eastern slope of the western hill, overlooking the location of the Temple. They also built new aqueduct systems in the lower part of the city and major reservoirs outside the walls. According to Josephus, the Hasmonaeans created a council chamber – sometimes identified with the Chamber of Hewn Stone – which stood in the Tyropoeon valley, west of the Temple.

Herod certainly improved Jerusalem's defences, but he also built a string of hill-top palaces and settlements around Judaea as alternatives. This was an implicit recognition that Jerusalem was no longer defensively strong. Herod recognised that Jerusalem had to change; it had, in short, to find something to sell. This was tricky. Jerusalem, as a city, had no great resources of agriculture or mineral wealth and no major river. But it did have one huge asset: the Temple, which had been built by Solomon and rebuilt by Zerubbabel. So that is what Herod decided Jerusalem could sell: it could sell religion.

When Herod captured Jerusalem, he determined to make the Temple into one of the wonders of the Græco-Roman world. Over the years, successive Judaean rulers added to the Temple, but it was Herod the Great who really raised the bar. He enlarged the platform around the building to form a huge raised enclosure. He built massive colonnaded walls all around, with a *stoa* – a long, colonnaded hall – at the south end. He added a large entrance porch to Zerubbabel's Temple, and a second storey, turning it into a kind of T-shape. The Temple was faced with white marble and inlaid with gold. It shone in the bright sunshine, a symbol of purity in an otherwise impure world.

And he didn't stop there. He rebuilt a fortress to the north of the Temple, naming it the Antonia, after Mark Antony. He built a magnificent new palace on the western edge of the city. He added some up-to-date cultural refinements from the Græco-Roman world, such as a hippodrome, an amphitheatre and, in all probability, bath complexes to cater for Gentiles or more westernised Jews. He also improved the aqueducts and the streets. The main thoroughfare ran north to south down the bottom of the valley. Shops lined each side and the street was colonnaded, as were almost all Middle-Eastern thorough-fares of the time. The street was lined with columns which sup-ported a roof linked to houses or shops behind.[3] This concept, although more developed, is still ubiquitous in the cities of the Middle East: the bazaar street (Arabic *suq*, Persian *bazar*) still forms the core of the town or city. In the heat and dust of the east, cities did not, on the whole, go in for wide open spaces like the Western-style market square. Instead, their streets were narrow and winding and shady.[4] Another main street – probably from the Hasmonaean period – led from what is now the Jaffa gate to the bridge across the Tyropoeon valley to the Temple. The outline of these roads persists today, the main entrance at the Damascus gate in the north of the old city splitting in two with the roads splitting at about a forty-degree angle heading south-east and south-west respectively.

It was the Temple, though, that really made Jerusalem dif-ferent. With the Temple, Herod turned Jerusalem into a must-see tourist destination – a pilgrimage city like no other. For Jews throughout the Roman Empire, it became the ultimate place of pilgrimage. Of course, pilgrims had always come to Jerusalem, but mainly from within Judaea. Herod saw the potential in attracting pilgrims from throughout the Græco-Roman Empire. This potential was further enhanced by the *pax Romana*, which made it possible for people to travel much more extensively than ever before.

Herod had other reasons as well. He developed the city for personal prestige, and to ingratiate himself with the people. (It didn't work. They appear to have hated him as much after he built the Temple as they did before. They might have admired – and used – the buildings, but they continued to despise the builder.)[5] He may even have had some pious reasons for improving the Temple, although, given that in Caesarea he also built a temple to Augustus, he was clearly not the world's most orthodox Jew.

No, the main reason he developed Jerusalem was so that it would bring in wealth. And it worked. By Jesus' day, Jerusalem was attracting hundreds of thousands of visitors every year. Descriptions of Jerusalem dating from earlier centuries make no mention of such a pilgrimage or such trade. Diaspora Jews had always sent money, but they did not feel the need to go there themselves. It was Herod who changed things. It was his expenditure on the Temple's infrastructure that turned it into one of the wonders of the age. His building programme and the magnificence of the Temple itself made them *want* to go. He encouraged, or allowed, Jews to donate to the Temple. The gates of the Temple were plated with gold by one Alexander the Alabarch, an Alexandrian Jew.[6] A man from Rhodes called Paris, son of Akestor, helped pay for the pavement.[7] And he established military bases to protect the pilgrim routes from the east.[8] Jerusalem did not see itself as a Greek or Hellenistic city. Many cities in the Græco-Roman world prided themselves on their Hellenistic heritage, claiming for themselves a sophistication as a modern city of culture. But Jerusalem, although it had certain features of a typical Græco-Roman city, was a place with its own, unique tradition and heritage.[9] A Roman visiting Jerusalem would be under no illusion that he was in a typical Græco-Roman city. It might have had bathhouses and even a theatre, but for many Jews these were symbolic of pagan depravity. The centre of Jerusalem did not consist of places of entertainment, but of the Temple.[10]

There were a lot of Jews in the Roman Empire; anything between four and eight million, that's between 6 and 12 per cent.[11] But unlike other nationalities they did not assimilate easily. Rome was no less tolerant of Judaism than it was of other religions. The problem was, perhaps, the other way round: that Judaism was intolerant of Rome. While the religions of Egypt and Greece and Rome could accommodate any number of gods, the Jews (and the Christians after them) had room for only one.[12] And the way that they followed their religion set them apart: they did not eat the same food, they did not worship the same gods, their calendar and their dress were different. And in particular, once a week, they just seemed to stop doing anything. To the pagan world, the Jewish Sabbath was a uniquely baffling institution.

The thing that made the Jews so different from the Roman world was also what gave them their strength. The steadfastness with which they had kept to their customs, their laws, was what had enabled them to survive the invasions, the exiles, the frequent changes of ruler, the oppression that had dogged them for the best part of a thousand years. It was the law, as found in their Scriptures, which gave them a sense of identity that few other ethnic groups in the Græco-Roman world (or, indeed, since) could match for intensity and perseverance. They knew who they were: they were the chosen race, the people of God. Such certainty, though, does not lead to popularity. Jews were seen as aloof. Pagans saw them as unwilling to share a table with them, or even to render basic human assistance. They were characterised as a 'hostile, prickly people, quick to take offence and unfriendly to aliens'.[13]

Jews had privileges under Roman law, ostensibly granted as a reward for the support of Herod during the civil war between Octavius (later Augustus) and Mark Antony. In cities of the diaspora, such as Alexandria, they had their own council of leaders. They were exempt from military service (as it would have forced them to fight on the Sabbath). They were allowed to follow their ancestral laws. In Alexandria, they were not subject to the poll tax.[14] Yes, the Romans might have tolerated the Jews, they might have granted them concessions, but they didn't respect them. The Jews' exemption from a military career

– the usual route to success for Romans – meant that they were never accepted into the upper strata of Roman society. Rich Jews from Judaea, unlike wealthy leaders from the other parts of the empire, rarely became citizens and no Jewish senator has ever been recorded. The Romans, accordingly, always looked down on their local collaborators.[15]

For Jews throughout the empire, labouring under suspicion, tolerated for the most part, but also frequently attacked, ridiculed and persecuted, Jerusalem and the Temple gave them something to be proud of. It was a symbol of their fortitude and heritage, in a city that was a match for anything in the Empire. All buildings are statements; all say something about their users or inhabitants. What the Temple said, among other things, was *we have kept the faith*. Thus, it became important to support the Temple and to visit the holy city itself. It was to do with your identity. And the high priests whom the Romans appointed took this one stage further. They turned support for Jerusalem into a duty. They instituted, or reinforced, the idea of an annual Temple tax, paid by all Jewish males over twenty, not to mention others who could pay it voluntarily.

All of which meant that money flowed into Jerusalem in vast amounts. It came via the Temple tax, via the visiting pilgrims, via the tithes that all Jews in Palestine had to provide. Jerusalem was rich. And like all rich cities, it attracted the elite from throughout the nation. If we look at the names, we can see that the members of respected families holding important positions included people from Sepphoris, Gamla in the Golan Heights, Galilee, and rural settlements. Jerusalem, in that sense, worked like any modern metropolis. It was a magnet, drawing people from throughout Palestine, a place where people could make their name – and, perhaps, their fortune. This centrality was resented by the regions, which saw it as aloof and arrogant, and even rejoiced in its downfall.[16]

Later Rabbis wrote, 'He who has not seen Jerusalem has not seen a beautiful city.'[17] But, by then, the Rabbis were no longer allowed in Jerusalem, and, if we look closer, we shall see that not all the city was as glamorous as the Temple. Cities attract wealth and they attract talent. But they also attract people who have neither. The Roman Senator Flavius Magnus Aurelius Cassiodorus said, 'Let the wild beasts live in fields and woods; men ought to draw together into cities.'[18] And so they did, only to find that the jungle of the city had beasts of its own.

'No city or house divided against itself will stand'

The city itself was small in modern terms – about one square kilometre. There were, however, suburbs in the north-west, which may have been densely populated. How extensive these were in Jesus' time, we don't know.[19] It consisted of three main areas: the Temple to the east, the Lower City in the south-central valley, and the Upper City to the west.

The Upper City, as the name implies, stood on higher ground. This was a wealthy, elite neighbourhood. The biggest building in this part was the old palace of Herod the Great. As we have seen, the remains of palatial dwellings have been found in that area. Throughout the Roman world the rich tended to site their

Traditional site of the Upper Room   Site of palace of Herod the Great   Golgotha and the site of the Tomb

houses on the hills. They were sunny and well-ventilated and, most importantly, the drains all ran downhill.[20] (In that sense, at least, Græco-Roman cities are similar to those today. The richer live higher up, the poorer lower down in the valleys. The richer get the better views and the cooling breeze; the poor get the crowded airless streets and the winter flooding.) The 'Upper' City, then, in every sense of the word. A place for the upper classes, for the aristocracy of Jerusalem and Judaea, the home of the Roman Prefect when he chose to visit; it was a place that smelt of power and prestige.

Unlike the Lower City, which smelt of something altogether less pleasant. We mistake the nature of ancient cities. We are fooled by their ruinous emptiness, tricked by their marble pillars and pale pavements and statuesque columns bleached white by time. Because what has survived from them is substantial and permanent and, often, beautiful, we think that the real, live city was all like that. Jerusalem was dominated by the beautiful, clean, white Temple, so we think that the whole place was as glorious.

That's the problem with big buildings: they obscure the view.

Roman steps to Lower City   Hinnom Valley   Dung Gate   Site of Antonia Fortress

The truth is that, to modern eyes, ancient cities would have been places of almost unimaginable squalor. Most people in ancient cities lived in conditions more akin to slums than to anything else. In Rome, the majority of people were crammed into dangerous, unsanitary apartment blocks, sometimes as high as five or six storeys. In Jerusalem, most housing would have been one- or two-storey dwellings, closer to the type of housing in Alexandria or that found at Pompeii. And most of the people would have found somewhere to live in the Lower City.

The Lower City was, in every way, a place of shadows. Josephus records only one major residence in this area – the Palace of Helena of Adabiene; apart from that, and a few public buildings around the south entrance of the Temple, we should imagine narrow confined alleys, and simple, even slum housing. In the shaded streets and narrow alleys, there would have been relatively little direct sunlight. To enter Jerusalem's Lower City was to enter a world of dappled darkness and shadows, the alleys and lanes filled with shuttered shopfronts, curtained with cloth from the tradesmen or the dyeing workshops, fruit and

Temple Mount   Steps to Temple Mount   Kidron Valley

produce crowding the thoroughfare, vines and washing spanning the space in between. To go from the Lower City onto the steps of the Temple or the courtyards of the Upper City was to surface from a sea of shade.

The better-off among the working classes of Jerusalem might have had enough room in their townhouses to allocate different wings or storeys for men and women. Some would have had rooms on the ground floor that served as shops.[21] But poorer people would have had to resort to multiple occupancy, or rented rooms in cheap boarding houses. And the very poor made do with what they could: shelters and hovels pieced together from the stuff the rich people threw away.[22] The alleyways of the ancient city were not for the faint-hearted. Unsanitary and unhealthy to live in, they would also have been difficult to police. In Rome, the soldiers, despite their fearsome reputation, refused to patrol these illegal neighbourhoods, where losing your way might easily mean losing your life.[23] In Jerusalem there must, too, have been areas where anyone wearing a Roman uniform would have been advised not to go.

Gethsemane

Mount of
Olives

Squatters have always been part of urban development, and it was no different in the ancient world.[24] In Rome, people built *tuguria*: lean-to sheds sometimes on the edge of the city, but often above workshops or up against public buildings, or even between the columns of porticos.[25] These coagulated to create a kind of shanty-town. The authorities regarded them as a fire risk and might occasionally engage in some slum clearance and tear them down, but providing they were not obstructive, they could remain, and enterprising landlords would even charge rent.

If you couldn't find a hut, then it was whatever shelter you could find: the spaces under the staircases, underground cellars or vaults or simply in the open air. Those too poor even to live inside the city would find what shelter they could outside. For the real outcasts – the lepers and the possessed – there was always the necropolis, with its house-like tombs. Certainly in Rome these provided housing space, not to mention serving as makeshift brothels and lavatories.[26] Living there would have offended against Jewish purity laws about contact with the dead, but some were not in a position to care. In Galilee, Jesus met a demon-possessed man living among the tombs (Mark 5:1–17). The tombs, whether built to resemble houses or as caves carved out of the hillside, offered respite to people too disturbed or desperate to worry about the consequences of ritual impurity through coming into contact with dead people. Today, people still live among the tombs: in Cairo's City of the Dead, some one million people use the Mameluke necropolis as ready-made housing. The original use has been, if not forgotten, then adapted, with grave markers used as tables and shelves and washing lines strung between the gravestones.[27]

Slums, like death, like taxes, like the poor, are always with us.

'The poor, the crippled, the lame, and the blind'

And what was life like in these places? Away from the cool fountains and the calm courtyards of the Upper City, what was life like for the labourer, the tradesman, the street vendor, the beggar of the Lower City?

There was no privacy. With people living so close together there was always someone there. For Jesus, as we shall see, finding private space in Jerusalem meant either planning ahead for the use of a room, or leaving the city altogether for a more secluded olive grove. Within the city, there was no privacy for the masses. Perhaps, as in the slums of latter-day Dublin, rooms were divided for bathing and dressing purposes by sheets hung on a clothes line. Or the husband and sons might be sent out into the hallway to give the females some private time.[28]

Along with the struggle simply to get enough to eat, there would have been the constant difficulty of obtaining enough water. People need a basic amount of water to stay alive: anything from two to five litres a day. In addition they need water for cooking, washing and cleaning their clothes, houses and public spaces. It has been estimated that, in Rome, only about one-third of the water brought into the city was available to ordinary people. Most of it went to the emperor and wealthy individuals. And Rome's rainfall was higher. For Jerusalem water must have been scarcer still.[29]

Generally, people had to rely on water from publicly available spaces. There would have been public fountains, cisterns and springs where the water could be collected. The function of a roof in ancient Jerusalem was to collect water. Water was harvested with great care. Although there might have been a drainage system in place at the times of abundance, it would have followed the terrain, down the hill, filling the Tyropoeon valley and out through the Dung Gate. This, indeed, would be why the Dung Gate was at the bottom of the city and why the Hinnom Valley was the place of refuse.[30] When the rain fell, that's where all the water went anyway.

There were two areas in the city that were marked, however, by their abundance of water – that is the Upper City and the Temple. The Upper City had two aqueducts supplying it, the Lower City just a channel from the Struthion Pool. The other aqueducts ended either in the Temple, or in pools just to the north.[31] The Temple, certainly, required an abundance of water for purification and for cleansing and there were many cisterns for water storage beneath the Temple mount. In the work of Aristeas, which probably dates from 100–200 BC, a visitor to the Temple describes the 'endless supply of water, as if indeed, a strongly flowing natural spring were issuing forth from within... and in addition there exist marvellous and indescribable reservoirs underground – as they showed me – for five *stades* around the foundation of the Temple'.[32] The spring may have issued from the Gihon.

Then, of course, there was the smell.

As far as we know, Jerusalem, like Rome, had no official waste removal service. So whatever you produced had to be dumped somewhere. If you were reasonably well off you might have a toilet in your house, built over a cesspit. The accumulated waste would just pile up until there was a need to call a local manure merchant. He would come, empty the pit and take its contents away through the Dung Gate to be resold as fertiliser. Human dung, being particularly rich in ammonia, is good for trees, so some of it would have been piled up around the base of the olive groves on the Mount of Olives. In more Roman, wealthier houses, the toilet might be connected to a cesspit in the gardens by means of terracotta pipes. You would flush the toilet by pouring a bucket of water down it. But the demand for water in Jerusalem would have made this a luxury in the extreme.

For the poor, the waste was simply tipped outside. For others it would have been a case of going to an open ditch or a nearby dung-heap, or of simply emptying a pot onto the street itself at night.[33] There, it would have been left to the dogs and the carrion birds – the vultures and the kites. Sometimes this led to unpleasant surprises. Suetonius records that, while the Emperor Vespasian was having lunch, a dog brought in a human hand from the street and deposited it under the table. Vespasian saw it as an omen.[34]

It is possible that Jerusalem took the waste disposal problem more seriously than other Eastern cities, since there was such an emphasis on purity. Practically speaking, however, keeping the city clean would have been impossible. Even Rome, with the famous Cloaca Maxima, relied on open sewers running down the middle of the streets. One of the Emperor Nero's favourite tricks was to push unwary inhabitants into the sewer when he went out at night incognito.[35] Pliny reported that in the elegant and beautiful city of Amastris, in Bithynia, there was an open sewer running down the middle of the main street.[36] This picture – of cramped streets with sewers in the middle – may be the background of an otherwise obscure verse in the Mishnah, which says that normally anyone who walks in the middle of the street would be deemed unclean, except at festival time.[37] During festival times it must have been virtually impossible to avoid the foulest parts of the streets, so crowded was Jerusalem.

In the south-east of the city, down towards the Dung Gate, there would have been large terracotta jars out on the street, which served as urinals. The Dung Gate was the most impure part of the city, in every sense. It was there that the weavers were, and probably the fullers nearby. Fullers used urine for dyeing cloth. However, the jars, being terracotta, were porous, so were not the best way of collecting the waste.[38]

But Jerusalem, as we've seen, was a pilgrimage city, a city of animal sacrifice on a huge scale. The endless parade of sheep, goats and cattle on their way to be sold or slaughtered, never mind those used as food, must have left the streets near the Temple in a filthy state. And after the sacrifice, the waste from the Temple had to go somewhere. Carcasses had to be dumped; blood had to be washed away.

Some of it ended in the city's dump, the Hinnom Valley – which by Jesus' day had become *gehenna* – a synonym for hell (e.g. Matt. 13.42; Mark 9.43–47). If we want to imagine the rubbish tips at Hinnom, then perhaps we get a glimpse from the seventy-five large pits excavated in the Esquiline graveyard at Rome, each pit filled with 'a nauseating mixture of the corpses of the poor, animal carcasses, sewage and other garbage'.[39] Dogs would have been a feature of the valley, gnawing at the bones of the corpses. Martial, in a poem about a beggar, shows the man listening to the dogs as they howl in anticipation of feeding on his corpse, and flapping his clothing at birds of prey to keep them away from him. Without anyone to care for them, the poor and destitute must have died in the streets, to be taken away by slaves anxious to keep the city 'pure'.[40]

The mass of people in the ancient city lived in the kind of conditions which would have been familiar to inhabitants of large European cities until the middle of the nineteenth century.[41] The slums of nineteenth-century Dublin or Naples – slums not produced by industrialisation – are perhaps a better guide to living conditions in Jerusalem than the archaeological guidebooks. In the early years of the twentieth century, nearly a third of all Dubliners lived in single, small tenement rooms. There, families of between six and twelve children would conduct all the activities of family life. 'The whole cycle of life from births to weddings to wakes was played out in the same tiny room the poor called "home".'[42] Here are some contemporary descriptions of tenement life:

> Most landlords kept their houses just one jump ahead of the law. They were very old houses and falling apart at the seams and they just did the minimum of what they had to do. And then, if they did any repairs, the rent went up! So people didn't complain.[43]

> The stagnant gutters in the middle of the lanes, the accumulated piles of garbage, the pools accumulated in the hollows, the disjointed pavement, the filth choking up the dark passages which open like rat-holes upon the highway – all these with their indescribable sights and smells leave scarce so dispiriting an impression on the passenger as the condition of the houses…[44]

Such experiences have been common to slum-dwellers throughout the centuries. The bulk of the city's residents would probably have been the low-income tenants, people who bought what little comfort they could from landlords who no doubt cared little about the conditions. The slums of ancient cities were like the modern 'rent plantations' of modern cities; owned by rich urban landlords, administered by slaves or managers. In Nairobi today, such landlords are called *wabenzi* – that is, someone who is rich enough to drive a Mercedes-Benz.[45] In Jesus' Jerusalem they were probably the chief priests, and the elders.

How would the residents of such places have viewed the Temple? Jews were proud of their Temple, but it is hard to believe that a poor family, living in a squalid hut in the dim Lower City, didn't once or twice wonder whether all that money couldn't have been better spent elsewhere. Herod's building programmes, magnificent though they were, must have led to widespread urban displacement. You cannot build the largest Temple complex in the Roman Empire without moving a few people on. As Scobie writes of Rome's public spaces: 'If an unskilled worker was by the very nature of his housing denied privacy for the most fundamental life functions, if he could never be sure of adequate food and clothing, and if he lacked resources to gain access to formal education and the protection of the law, what compensation would he be likely to derive from costly public buildings… or from a few public parks?'[46]

The same must surely have been true for Jerusalem. When you are trying to survive on a handful of bread every day, when there is no work for you, when your small plot of land has been foreclosed and taken into the possession of the rich, when you have little more than the clothes on your back, what joy can you take in the marble-clad Temple on the hill? As the dawn trumpet rings across the city, announcing the morning sacrifice, does your heart leap with joy? Or do you dread the struggle of the day ahead? What is the point of queuing to enter the ritual baths? How can you ever be clean again?

This then was Jerusalem. A magnificent Temple on one ridge, rich housing and a sumptuous palace on the others. And, in between, alleys and gunnels, cramped streets and crowded houses; shops and shanty-towns, and the sound of animals nervously awaiting slaughter. A city of ritual purity and unimaginable filth. A city where they burned incense in the Temple and corpses in

Gehenna. A city of sunlight and shadows, upper and lower. And into this city, a new king was about to enter.

'Then he entered Jerusalem'

> Then they brought the colt to Jesus and threw their cloaks on it; and he sat on it. Many people spread their cloaks on the road, and others spread leafy branches that they had cut in the fields. Then those who went ahead and those who followed were shouting, 'Hosanna! Blessed is the one who comes in the name of the Lord! Blessed is the coming kingdom of our ancestor David! Hosanna in the highest heaven!' (Mark 11.7–10)

Jesus' route would have taken him down into the Kidron Valley and into Jerusalem, either by the gate to the north of the Temple, or by the Dung Gate in the south. He could also have gone straight into the Temple by the gate from the valley itself, where the Golden Gate stands today. However, it seems to me more likely that he would have gone into the city from the south and then up the main steps.

But the time is crucial. As we know, this is the beginning of Passover week, one of the most important weeks, if not *the* most important week, of the Jewish calendar. Which means that, whichever route he took, Jesus would have been engulfed in a sea of pilgrims. As he rode over the crest of the Mount of Olives on that spring morning there would have been a sea of tents and makeshift shelters spreading out in the valley below, and to the north. Josephus refers to Passover pilgrims staying in 'tents outside the Temple'.[47] Those pilgrims who could afford to, or who had relatives, stayed in the city; but many thousands would have had to camp outside. So Jesus' route takes him not only down the hill, but into a mass of people: devout Jews and poorer pilgrims. No wonder the word spread. It would be like leading a carnival procession through a pop festival: the king coming to Glastonbury or Woodstock.

We will consider the full impact of Passover on the city later on: for now, all we need to know is that the city was packed to bursting. And here is Jesus, descending through the crowds, surrounded by his followers, by those he had preached to, healed, released; those whose lives had been transformed. And gathering new followers as well, scooping up those who were desperate for change and hope; they wave their branches and join in the chanting, they wrap themselves around the procession like seaweed, as Jesus wades through the sea of people.

It has been suggested that the waving of palm branches and shouting of 'Hosanna' fits better with the festival of Tabernacles, at which, according to the Mishnah, it was usual to cry 'Hosanna' and wave branches.[48] But there is no reason to believe that this was the only time when such a celebration could have happened.

This is a deliberate, prophetic statement. It's a staged event, an act of religious theatre that makes reference to a number of Old Testament prophecies, notably Zechariah 9. It's the ancient equivalent of one of those orchestrated demonstrations that are usually seen at global summits. It has been carefully arranged to send out the exact message that Jesus wants to send. Jesus is using the symbolism of Zechariah:

> Rejoice greatly, O daughter Zion! Shout aloud, O daughter Jerusalem!
> Lo, your king comes to you; triumphant and victorious is he, humble
> and riding on a donkey, on a colt, the foal of a donkey. (Zech. 9.9)

This is the vocabulary of the Messiah, the anointed one, the king of Israel. On the road out of Jericho, Jesus had been acclaimed as the Son of David, now he was riding in, clothed in the same pictorial language. 'I'm the king' is the message, at least for those who know their Old Testament prophets. Whether they have spotted the reference or not, the people greet him with a custom usually associated with royalty; they throw their cloaks on the ground.[49]

David Catchpole has identified some twelve other examples of 'triumphal' entries into Jerusalem, by people such as Alexander the Great and Judas Maccabaeus. All of these operate on a kind of fixed pattern: the victory is already achieved; there is a formal, ceremonial entry; there are greetings and acclamation from the crowd; and the entry is climaxed by entry to the Temple.[50]

So, as well as operating in a religious context, Jesus is also making claim to a kind of kingly triumph. This, however, is a curious kingdom and a strangely wild king. One gets the sense of a wild, joyous, uncontrolled element here. The colt, for example, is a young animal – one that has never been ridden. He's riding a donkey a few sizes too small for him, like a grown man riding a kid's bike. And the element of fun, of satire and mockery, is underlined when we further realise that it was not the only procession entering Jerusalem that day.

Someone else had to come into the city that day. And he came from the opposite direction, in every sense.

'And many went up from the country to Jerusalem before the Passover to purify themselves'

The sheer weight of numbers, combined with the religious fervour of the festival, made for a combustible atmosphere. Josephus records several major disturbances and wrote that the feasts were 'the usual occasion for sedition to flare up'.[51] It takes just one spark to start a fire. On one notorious occasion a soldier on guard duty in the Antonia fortress – overlooking the Temple – chose to bare his backside to the Jews below and make 'a noise as indecent as his attitude'. In the riot that followed, Josephus claims that 30,000 people were crushed to death.[52]

Which is why, for each of the major pilgrimage festivals, Pontius Pilate entered town.[53] There were only a handful of Roman soldiers in Jerusalem – one cohort, maybe 500 men, in the Antonia Fortress overlooking the Temple. These were, at best, a token force, for most of the time, security in the city was delegated to the high priest and his Temple police. This force was several thousand strong – during the first Jewish revolt, 8,500 Temple guards were killed defending Ananus, a former High Priest.[54] Their responsibility would have continued during the festivals, but, given the intense atmosphere – the city filled to bursting with Jews with a strong sense of history and a zeal for the purity of their religion – the Roman authorities would have made sure that there was a Roman military presence there as well.

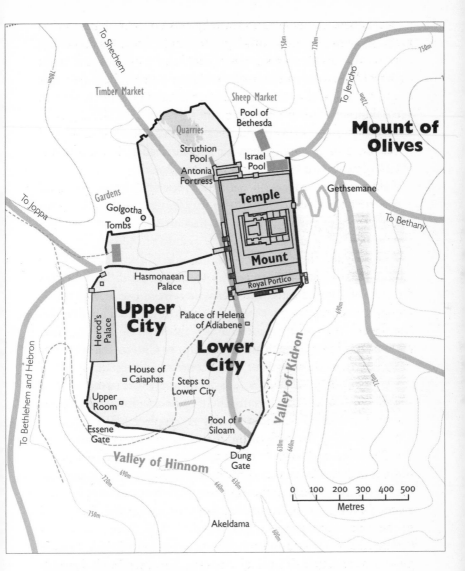

Jerusalem c.33 AD

During the triumphal entry on Sunday, Jesus entered from the Mount of Olives to the east. Around the same time, Pilate was entering from the road to Joppa from the west.

The other reason that the Prefect had to enter was, of course, to hand over the ceremonial vestments, to give Caiaphas the keys to the car. Just for a bit. There was an important truth embodied in the symbolism of handing over the vestments; it was a picture of the political reality. The soldiers marching into Jerusalem were just the tip of the spear; Caiaphas and his people should not forget the Roman boot always poised above them.

So, imagine gleaming armour and burnished leather. Imagine cavalrymen on horseback and the imperial eagle on a standard leading the procession. Imagine foot soldiers beating and pushing the populace out of the way. A display of power. An entrance to let the city know he had arrived. The Emperor's representative, marching in to take charge of the city.

And he's entering on the opposite side of the city. The road from Caesarea probably took him via Joppa on the coast, then up through the hills and into Jerusalem from the west. Pilate's headquarters would have been in the former palace of Herod the Great – the most impressive private building in Jerusalem and, as we've seen, a feature of the Upper City to the west.[55]

In this context, therefore, Jesus' entry to Jerusalem is much more than an act of prophetic symbolism, more, even, than a statement of Messianic intention. It's a deliberate parody of the procession which had either already taken place – or was still to take place – on the other side of the city. On the west side of Jerusalem there was power and prestige, there was Pilate with the economic, political and military authority; but on the east there was an entirely different, radical form of power. To the west the kingdom of the world; from the east comes Jesus and the kingdom of God.

The 'political' aspect of this event is also picked up in Jesus' conscious embodiment of Zechariah. His choice of an animal was a Messianic reference. But the passage goes on:

> He will cut off the chariot from Ephraim and the warhorse from Jerusalem; and the battle-bow shall be cut off, and he shall command peace to the nations; his dominion shall be from sea to sea, and from the River to the ends of the earth. (Zech. 9.10)

Not a warlike Messiah, then. Not like the military procession on the other side of the city. No, on the other side of the city there was the Roman war machine, making its home in the wealth and privilege of the Upper City; but from the east came the tumbledown, ragamuffin regime of the Prince of Peace. This was the choice that Jesus presented to the people that day: to the leaders of the Temple, to the scribes and the lawmakers and the Temple police, to the pilgrims in their tents and the poor in their tenements – and to everyone who has sought to follow him ever since: which king are you going to choose? The rule of Rome or the kingdom of God? Whose side are you on?

Jesus looks at the Temple

Where: The Temple

When: Afternoon

Jesus' entry into Jerusalem is a carefully staged triumph. His Messianic symbolism is a challenge to the priestly aristocracy; his version of a Roman triumphal march is a challenge to the military and political power on the other side of the city. Yet what is curious about Mark's account is the ending: the event just seems to dissolve into nothingness.

> Then he entered Jerusalem and went into the temple; and when he had looked around at everything, as it was already late, he went out to Bethany with the twelve. (Mark 11.11)

Jesus enters the city in triumph, has a look round and goes away again, because 'it was getting a bit late'. In one sense there is no need for him to do any more: the procession, with its clear symbolism, has made his point. Indeed, the other Synoptic accounts go straight into the incident in the Temple. But Mark has Jesus making his way into the Temple, with that curious detail about looking around. What, one wonders, was he looking at? And why?

There is, in fact, one other reference to Jesus looking at things in the Temple. It comes, not from the New Testament, but from a scrap of parchment found in an Egyptian rubbish dump. And it may hold a clue as to what Jesus was looking at, and how his triumphal entry concluded.

'Blessed are the pure in heart, for they will see God'

As we saw in our brief overview of Jesus' career, purity laws in Judaism covered a wide range of areas. A person was impure or unclean if they had not done the proper ritual bathing or washing. A woman who was menstruating was unclean, as was a leper. You were unclean if you ate with Gentiles, if you entered the home of a tax-collector, or if you engaged in certain professions. You were unclean if you touched a corpse. There were complex and demanding food purity laws. One extreme view was that certain food, if touched by a Gentile, could become impure. Gentile oil, bread and wine could be impure. In the midst of such uncertainty, it was better not to eat with Gentiles at all.[56] Yet, throughout the Gospels, we find Jesus flouting these impurity laws. And he keeps telling stories in which the impure people are the heroes.

The story of the good Samaritan is a story about ritual purity. Consider the cast: a Jew attacked by robbers, a priest and a Levite – both staff of the Temple; and a hated Samaritan who could never, under any circumstances, be admitted by Jews to be 'pure'. Two clerics from the Temple ignore the man lying by the side of the road, not only because of a lack of mercy, but because they think he is dead: by helping him they would make themselves ritually unclean through coming into contact with a corpse. Jesus' story is an attack on religious hypocrisy, as it is framed in the purity laws. These people considered keeping clean more important than helping their fellow man.[57]

There has been major debate among experts about how Jews of the time viewed these rituals, and whether the many minute observances in the Mishnah were really widely followed by the inhabitants of first-century Palestine. What not many experts appear to have focused on is that purity is a luxury. As we have seen, if you are a poor, agricultural peasant, or if you're living a hand-to-mouth existence in the slums of the Lower City, then the idea of storing up enough food so that you do not have to scavenge on the Sabbath is impossible. If you are crammed into a squalid tenement where disease is rife, you don't have much of a hope of avoiding corpse defilement.

In practice, the strict legal observance of the Pharisees and Sadducees was only possible for the middle or upper classes. Take, for example, the prohibitions on contact with menstruating women. According to the Mishnah, any woman who was menstruating had to be secluded during that time so that she would not come into contact with either the utensils of the house or the other residents. In some of the better-off houses there may have been separate women's quarters, possibly on the second storey of the house; or where there was a clan dwelling, one room might have been available to serve a number of families.

But for the poorer working class, the idea of having an extra room at all would have been a luxury, let alone a room set aside for only one use. Rich people could afford stoneware vessels, which were reckoned to be immune from impurity, but the poorer had to make do with normal pottery, which demanded cleaning. If you were wealthy you could afford to have your own *miqvaot* for ritual bathing: if you were poor, you would have to use one of the public pools like everyone else.

It is this that motivates Jesus to attack the Pharisees:

> They tie up heavy burdens, hard to bear, and lay them on the shoulders of others; but they themselves are unwilling to lift a finger to move them. (Matt. 23.1–4)

The laws are laws which, in effect, make it impossible for poor people to achieve righteousness. It was not the emphasis on righteousness that was wrong, nor even, perhaps, the attempt to interpret the law. It was the fact that interpretation according to their standards was the preserve of the middle and upper classes. It was the way in which the interpretation made life harder for people to survive.

Jesus could see, in the poor and in the impure, the possibility of righteousness. Indeed, he could see that poverty was almost a precondition of true righteousness. For the wealthy to gain admittance to the kingdom was as impossible as threading a camel through the eye of a needle. This is why his disciples were surprised at the statement: in their understanding, the way to righteousness was through purity, and purity was a function of wealth. It was not that Jesus ignored Jewish law or did not obey it. On the contrary, his very presence in Jerusalem was testimony to his adherence to the main tenets of the law. But what he recognised was that there were many people in that city who had been locked out of righteousness.

The wealthy had the resources to observe the law in all its minutiae. The poor did not. But, in Jesus' teaching, it was the poor who gained heaven; it was the beggar who joined the feast.

'Why do your disciples break the tradition of the elders?'

Purity is also a control. The Temple authorities could bar people they considered unclean from entering the Temple, or from engaging in Temple worship. Just as mediaeval Popes used the threat of excommunication, the sanction of exclusion from the Temple must have been a powerful weapon. Indeed, the end of the second Temple period seems to have seen an increase in the practice and interpretation of purity practices and one wonders if that went hand in hand with the feeling that the authorities were actually losing influence and control. When the political leaders feel that no one is obeying them, they don't relax the rules: they issue new ones and make harsher penalties for non-observance.

This is one reason why pilgrims for Passover went to Jerusalem early: they had to make sure that they would be allowed to take part in Passover. Some rituals required elements that could only have been available in Jerusalem. Purification from corpse defilement, for example, required the impure person to sprinkle themselves with the ashes of a red heifer mixed with water. How widely available such ashes were outside Jerusalem is debatable. Philo indicates that elsewhere in the world people underwent a sprinkling with 'unheifered' water, which made them clean, but not clean enough to enter the Temple.[58]

Washing, as we have seen, was a widespread purification practice. The Mishnah says, 'None may enter the Temple court for [an act of the Temple] service even though he is clean, until he has immersed himself.'[59] The Palestinian Talmud went further, interpreting this as meaning anyone who even entered the Temple, even though they might not be making a sacrifice.

But Mark's account of the triumphal entry makes no mention of washing; indeed, nowhere in the Gospels is there any mention of Jesus ritually bathing. This doesn't mean that he didn't do it, of course; but equally it doesn't mean that he did. And we do know that he and his disciples were criticised for not washing before meals. Not washing before eating is one thing, however; not washing before worshipping is another thing entirely. And there is a story from outside the New Testament which shows Jesus doing just that.

'When he had looked around at everything'

In the Bodleian Library in Oxford there is a fragment of a miniature codex – a book – from the fourth century AD. Although it is called Papyrus Oxyrhynchus it is actually a piece of parchment, not papyrus.[60] The forty-five line fragment appears to come from a kind of gospel and contains two stories, which have no equivalents in the Gospel traditions. The first deals with a discourse apparently spoken by Jesus on the way to the Temple, in which he warns of the fate awaiting evil-doers. The second tells of an encounter with a Jewish chief priest called Levi, who accuses Jesus of entering the Temple without having undergone the purification ritual:

> And having taken them he brought them into the place of purification and was walking in the Temple. And having approached, a certain Pharisee, chief priest, whose name was Levi, joined them and said to the Saviour: Who gave you permission to enter this place of purification and to see these holy vessels, when you have not washed yourself, nor have your disciples surely bathed their feet? But you, in a defiled state, have entered this Temple, which is a pure place that no one enters nor dares to view these holy vessels without having first washed themselves and changed their clothes.

> And immediately the Saviour stopped, and standing with his disciples answered: Are you then pure in your present state here in the Temple?
>
> And he replied to him: I am pure, for I have washed myself in the pool of David, and having descended by one staircase I came up by another; and I have put on white and I pure clothes, and only then did I come and lay eyes on these holy vessels.
>
> The Saviour answered him saying: Woe unto you, O blind ones, who do not see! You have washed yourself in these running waters where dogs and pigs have wallowed night and day, and you have cleansed and wiped the outside skin which the prostitutes and flute-girls anoint, which they wash, and wipe, and make beautiful for human desire; but inwardly these women are full of scorpions and every wickedness. But I and my disciples, who you say have not bathed, we have bathed in waters of eternal life, which come down from the God of Heaven. But woe unto those…[61]

And that's where it ends. When this was first published, it was dismissed as a fabrication, largely on the grounds that the editors thought that none of the historical details were accurate. Now we have to acknowledge that the reference to Jesus as 'Saviour' reflects a later theology. But even allowing for some later terminology, the claim that this fragment shows ignorance of the Jewish customs and the topography of the Temple is simply not true.

This, along with Mark 11.11, is the only instance of Jesus 'looking' at objects in the Temple. He is shown to have entered a place of purification – presumably one of the inner courts of the Temple – and 'viewed the holy vessels'. Some of the vessels of the Temple were stored in side rooms, but the 'holy vessels' in the story may just refer to the sacred tools used every day in the Court of Priests.[62] Or it may be that Jesus and his followers went far enough to see right into the heart of the Temple sanctuary itself. Josephus implies that at festivals the veil across the entrance to the sanctuary was drawn back to allow the many pilgrims to see inside. This is backed up by statements in the Talmud that talk about pilgrims being allowed to see the table where the showbread was kept, and the gold plates. This is entirely understandable: not only would pilgrims want to see the treasures, but that the priests would want to show them to add to the awe and the majesty of the institutions.[63]

The identification of the priest is uncertain. He is identified as a Pharisee called Levi, but the word *archiereus* does not have to mean 'high priest'. Indeed, the Greek lacks the definite article ('*the* High Priest'), which probably means that we are talking about one of the chief priests. It could mean that it was a presiding priest, or an overseer, or simply one of the leading religious figures among the Pharisees.[64]

The pool of David has never been identified, but this is hardly a problem given the amount of *miqvaot* in Jerusalem. We should expect hardly any of them to appear in the rabbinical literature. Indeed, one of the most famous – the pool of Bethesda – is mentioned only in John 5.2. Frankly, in a city obsessed with David, it seems highly likely that one of the many ritual baths would be named after him. It would be more surprising if one wasn't. Indeed, archaeologists have identified at least three miqvaot on the Temple Mount itself.[65] And the detail about the two stairs is accurate: numerous archaeological findings in Jerusalem have revealed pools with two staircases, presumably

Miqvaot on the Temple Mount

Archaeologists have identified three possible *miqvaot* on the Mount itself. These would have been filled with rainwater from cisterns.

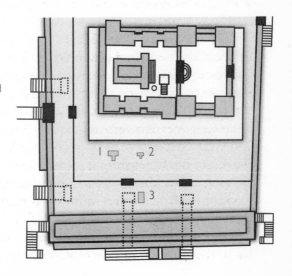

to ensure that the person was not contaminated by going out the way he came in.[66] As to the running water, that reflects a particular aspect of pharisaical practice. Pharisees believed that a *miqveh* was valid only if it had running water. This is why many excavated *miqvaot* had another pool beside them which served as a kind of cistern.[67]

As for the clothing, it was required that any visitors, if they wanted to enter the inner courts, had to divest themselves of staff, shoes and bag or purse, and ensure that their feet were not dusty. The Court of Israel could be entered only by those in a state of 'complete levitical purity'.[68] It is quite conceivable that to achieve this level of advanced purity a change of clothing was required. The Essenes, in their version of the Temple ceremonies, required their members to fully immerse and then change into white garments.[69] The fact that the priest has changed his clothing completely doesn't mean that this would be required of lay visitors. The point of this fragment is that Jesus and his followers have not washed their feet.

That such an event was possible can also be shown from the rabbinic literature. There's a story about a man called Shimon the Virtuous, who claimed that he had managed to get into the Temple – between the Temple sanctuary and the altar of burnt sacrifice – without washing his hands and his feet and without being challenged by 'the overseer'.[70] The details, then, are consistent with the archaeology – which is not bad if the fragment was, as the first editors claimed, a second-century invention. Someone has been doing their research.

But what about the pigs and the dogs? If the water was fed by an aqueduct from without, then the phrase could be used to imply that the purity of the water is somewhat suspect.[71] Certainly the rest of the attack from Jesus is hyperbolic and dripping with sarcasm, so there is no need to take this literally. Jesus' point is that even the prostitutes scrub up; washing, apparently, is no sign of cleanliness.

Papyrus Oxyrhynchus 840 records a strong tradition that Jesus entered one of the holiest places in Judaism without paying any attention to the ritual that was required. He entered in an unclean, impure condition. And it doesn't seem to have bothered him much. So, is this a true story? Is it a missing episode from the Gospels? Well, undoubtedly it has passed through the hands of a later editor. But there is nothing in the tale itself that is inherently unbelievable; it fits into the wider picture of Jesus' attitude to purity and the outrage that this caused among some of his more orthodox opponents. The real issue for Jesus was inward purity, not outward observance. Even the prostitutes and dancing girls bathe. Even pigs can wash.

If purity rituals are about control, then someone who no longer worries very much about them is, by definition, uncontrollable. The Oxyrhynchus fragment offers a compelling portrait of Jesus in the Temple (albeit one that may well have undergone later editing). Whether it is an authentic story will probably never be resolved. But it demonstrates, at the very least, the tradition – prevalent throughout the Gospels – that Jesus was repeatedly at odds with the purity legislation of his day.

Jesus is, literally, out of control. And who knows what he will do next?

Greeks speak with Jesus

Where: Jerusalem

When: Afternoon

Jesus' triumphal entry was, indeed, a triumph. Surrounded by his supporters and by the joyous pilgrims who sensed that perhaps change was in the air, the Pharisees took one look at Jesus and exclaimed, 'You see, you can do nothing. Look, the world has gone after him!' (John 12.19):

> Now among those who went up to worship at the festival were some Greeks. They came to Philip, who was from Bethsaida in Galilee, and said to him, 'Sir, we wish to see Jesus.' (John 12.;20–22)

The world has gone after Jesus. There are Greeks in Jerusalem, and they wish to see Jesus. But they are uncertain of their reception; would this holy man have contact with Gentiles? So they contact Jesus through an intermediary. Perhaps they were expecting the response they might have got from the Pharisees and the Sadducees. Indeed, even the disciples seem uncertain: Philip consults his brother before going to Jesus.

Jesus' reply is enigmatic and includes a typically Johannine speech from Jesus, full of dense imagery and concluding with the sound of thunder:

> Then a voice came from heaven, 'I have glorified it, and I will glorify it again.' The crowd standing there heard it and said that it was thunder. Others said, 'An angel has spoken to him.' Jesus answered, 'This voice has come for your sake, not for mine' (John 12.28–30)

Was it a voice? An angel? A clap of thunder? It's an echo, certainly: the voice from heaven echoes the one that spoke at the baptism of Jesus, while Jesus' concern about enduring this hour points ahead to his desire in Matthew 26.38–39 that the cup should pass from him. Whatever the reality, John's message is clear: the world has gone after Jesus. The triumphal entry was a proclamation of a kingdom that would not be limited to Jerusalem, but which would spread to Greeks, throughout the world and to all people.

Day Two: The Temple
Monday 30th March 33 AD

The fig tree is cursed: Mount of Olives, Monday morning
The temple protest: Temple Mount, Monday morning

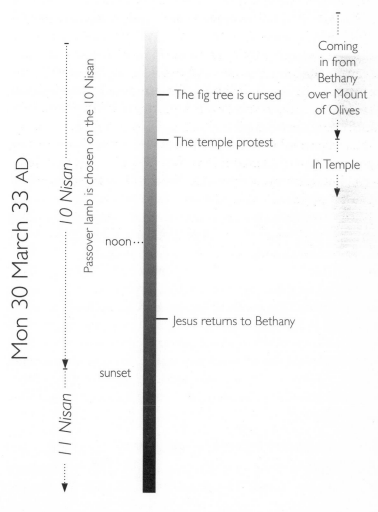

Mon 30 March 33 AD

11 Nisan

10 Nisan

Passover lamb is chosen on the 10 Nisan

noon···

sunset

The fig tree is cursed

The temple protest

Jesus returns to Bethany

Coming in from Bethany over Mount of Olives

In Temple

The fig tree is cursed

Where: Mount of Olives

When: Morning

> On the following day, when they came from Bethany, he [Jesus] was hungry. Seeing in the distance a fig tree in leaf, he went to see whether perhaps he would find anything on it. When he came to it, he found nothing but leaves, for it was not the season for figs. He said to it, 'May no one ever eat fruit from you again.' And his disciples heard it. (Mark 11.12–14)

On the face of it, this is a strange tale. Jesus curses a fig tree for not having any fruit on it, which is hardly the tree's fault since the fig tree produces only two crops: the earlier ripens from late May into June, and the later and larger harvest ripens from the end of August into October. It's like wandering up to an apple tree in May and moaning because of the lack of Golden Delicious. What did he expect?

Nothing. That's the point. The point is not about finding food, it's about *not* finding food.

This is what scholars call a Marcan Sandwich. Mark has a habit of taking stories or events, splitting them in two, and sandwiching between them another event, on which the first event is a comment. So, Mark 11.12–14 is 'The Fig Tree Part One'. But we don't see the conclusion of the story until Mark 11.20, which, according to Mark's timetable, takes place the next morning.

Jesus is using this tree as a symbol, a metaphor. His hunger, his futile search for fruit and his curse are all symbols of something that is about to happen. And the fate of the fig tree will be bound up with what is going to happen this day; something that will happen on the other side of the valley. Mark is specific about the location: Jesus is on the Mount of Olives, he's looking across the Kidron Valley. And on the other side of the valley is the Temple.

'Something greater than the temple is here'

The Temple in Jerusalem was one of the greatest buildings in the ancient world. The wonder was not just the Temple building – the sanctuary itself – it was the entire complex, a massive, raised plaza covering an area of around fourteen hectares: some 12 per cent of the city's area.[1]

As we have seen, Herod the Great was the man responsible for this. He doubled the size of the Temple area, cutting away a large portion of the bedrock to the north and building a monumental retaining wall to the west, on the eastern side of the Tyropoeon Valley. The enormous size of the building blocks can still be seen today in the Western or 'Wailing' Wall.

Raising the Temple to this height resulted in some complicated architectural and engineering problems. For one thing, the mound could not be solid; had it been filled, the pressure of the earth inside pushing outwards would have been too great. So behind this wall the mound was filled with arches and vaults – spaces that have been a lure to archaeologists, adventurers and conspiracy theorists ever since. Second, because of its height, access to the Temple plaza was difficult. Entry from the south was therefore via a large flight of steps leading to sloping tunnels which eventually emerged onto the Temple platform. To the west there was a bridge spanning the Tyropoeon Valley and more stairs from the streets below.

There was also, unlike in other temples in the Græco-Roman world, no major processional way, no route which led pilgrims and worshippers directly to the sanctuary. Instead, one had to negotiate the narrow streets or find one's way to the major entrances on the south or across the bridge from the west.

'Two men went up to the temple to pray'

A pilgrim arrives in Jerusalem. It's been a long journey from his home, wearisome boat journeys bringing him along the coast, an arduous journey on the road from Ptolomais, the fulfilment of a lifetime's ambition to see the Holy City and to worship in the Temple. Now, he stands at the southern entrance of the city. Ahead of him, he can see, rising above the buildings and the houses, the huge slab that is the Temple Mount. He can even glimpse the glittering golden light from the spikes on the roof of the Temple building itself. He joins the tide of pilgrims, drawn up along the stepped street with its limestone paving worn smooth by the feet of countless worshippers. To his left, the streets are steeper; narrow shafts disappearing into the darkness of the Lower City. All around him, stallholders and street vendors are plying their trade: everything from fruit to fancy glassware, jars of cheap wine, mounds of bread, cloth and animals to slaughter or to sacrifice.

Eventually he reaches the staircase to the Temple. A wide flight of steps, monumental, leads to a triple gate with darkness beyond. He ventures in, joining the crush of people. They are climbing now through the Mount itself, up a sloping set of stairs through a tunnel that runs under the Royal Portico on the south side. The darkness is a shock after the bright light of the city; the crush more oppressive with every step. And then suddenly he emerges from the gloom to find himself in the heart of the Temple Plaza. And suddenly everything is light and space and noise…

It was known as the Court of the Gentiles, for the simple reason that this was as far as Gentiles were allowed to go. The outer court was open to all, foreigners included (only menstruating women were refused admission).[2] And it was the place where people came to meet, to discuss, to talk, even to do business. In a city with cramped, crowded streets, the Temple Mount was one of the few places where there was space to meet in any significant numbers. This is why Jesus habitually taught there when in Jerusalem, and why the early church continued to meet there in the early days.

It was also the place where the moneychangers had their tables, and the traders sold doves, lambs and other animals for the sacrifices. It was a blend of a churchyard, a marketplace and a livestock market.

The first thing that would strike the visitor would be the cleanliness. Unlike the filth of the Lower City, the Temple plaza was kept, according to Philo, in a state of exceptional purity and cleanliness.[3]

Then there was the noise. On the south side of the Temple, the Royal Portico was alive with the sounds of animals and birds. This was where pilgrims and worshippers would purchase the animals they required for sacrifice.[4] From within the sanctuary itself came the sound of the Levites' voices, a low blur of chanting and singing. There would be periodic blasts on the trumpet from the high walls and, from within the inner compound, the pained bleating and cries of animals on their way to the slaughter. And all around the buzz of people, especially at festival time – the noise of people shouting, debating, selling, exclaiming, the splashing of water as people use the ritual baths, the low murmuring of prayers.

And the smells! The smell of blood, splashed against the steps of the altar. From the inner courtyard the smell of roasting meat as the animals were burnt on the altar; if you were close enough, perhaps, the exotic scent of incense burning on its embers inside the sanctuary. And everywhere, at festival time, the smell of perspiration as pilgrims crammed together.

Looking north, you could see the Temple itself, rising above the surrounding wall, white and gold and glittering in the sun. And beyond the Temple, at the far end of the plaza, the looming presence of the Antonia fortress.

The Hasmonaean kings had built a citadel called the Baris, where they kept the high priest's special robes which he put on for the major festivals. Herod developed this building into a major fortress which he called the Antonia – after Mark Antony. He covered the rock on which it stood with slippery flagstones – the first-century equivalent of anti-climb paint. Josephus describes the interior: 'from its possession of all conveniences it seemed a town, from its magnificence a palace.' It had four towers, one at each corner, three of which were fifty cubits high and one (the south-east) seventy cubits high. Its position and size shows that, from the first, the Temple was seen as a potential source of trouble – even for Herod. The only point of the Antonia was to overlook the Temple; there were stairs from the fortress leading straight into the Temple courtyard. In fact, it was rare to have a garrison in a major city. But Jerusalem was a special case, and the positioning of the garrison overlooking the Temple gives a clear enough indication of why it was necessary. When trouble kicked off, it usually kicked off in the Temple.

By the time of Jesus, the Roman army had taken over the fortress. The Antonia served as the home for the single cohort of troops that garrisoned Jerusalem, led by a 'Tribune of the Cohort' who seems to have served as the Roman commander-in-chief in Jerusalem. They served more as a snatch squad than anything else. When Paul caused an uproar in the Temple precincts, the soldiers descended and grabbed him (Acts 21.31–40).[5] Josephus describes how a Roman cohort was permanently stationed there, and sentries were posted during the festivals along the walls, 'to watch the people and repress any insurrectionary movement'. The soldiers were in their little city within a city: Samaritan and Greek auxiliaries looking down on the Jews, in every possible sense of the word.

For anyone wanting to go further, from now on, a filtering system takes effect, each gate narrowing further the number of people who are allowed to go through it. Into the big plaza anyone could go, but at the first wall around the Temple, only Jews could enter. Josephus again:

> All the Jews went into the second court, as well as their wives, when they were free from all uncleanness; into the third went the Jewish men when they were clean and purified; into the fourth went the priests, having on their sacerdotal garments; but for the most sacred place, none went in but the High Priests, clothed in their peculiar garments.[6]

This concern for levels of purity was expressed in the very geography of the Temple layout itself. Unlike many other cities with major temples in the ancient world, Jerusalem had no sacred way, no major avenue leading to the entrance. At Ephesus, for example, there was a major sacred way leading out of the city to the Temple of Artemis itself. At Jerash there was an elaborate sacred way which began at the eastern entrance of the city. In Babylon there was a major processional way leading from the Ishtar Gate to the Temple complexes.[7]

So why not in Jerusalem? It was not that Judaism didn't have processions; there are plenty of processional psalms. Nor would the topography of Jerusalem have made building such a route impossible; it would have been difficult, but no more difficult than constructing the Temple Mound itself. The answer must be that they didn't want a direct route to the heart of the Temple: you weren't supposed to go straight to God. Indeed, even within the Temple it wasn't straightforward. There was no entrance onto the Temple Mount that left you facing directly into the inner courtyards. Instead, you had to go to the east side of the plaza and then turn west. It was a kind of spiritual filtration system, a gradual ascent through different levels of holiness.[8]

Let us assume that you are Jewish. You head north-east to the East Gate of the Temple Courtyard itself. On the wall around the courtyard, you will notice the signs of warning to all Gentiles – written in Greek – not to enter on pain of death.

The main entrance to the Temple itself opens into the Court of Women. Here there are four chambers, in each corner of the courtyard, two storing wood and oil for the sacrifices, the others serving two groups of men who needed particular ritual purification: Nazirites and (recovering) lepers.

Ahead of you now is a small flight of steps rising to the Nicanor Gate, a magnificent gate of Corinthian bronze, donated by a man called Nicanor.[9] This is the entrance to the Court of Israelites. If you are a woman, this is as far as you can go. Only a few women around the Nicanor Gate would have been able to see into the inner court, where the activity of the Temple took place. From now on, it is for Jewish men only.

During crowded times – such as the major festivals – witnessing the ritual must have been rather a remote experience. In the small Court of the Priests, the devotee would have had a distant view of what was happening to his animal. For women it would have been all but impossible to see, since they were barred from the inner courtyards completely.[10]

So, upwards once more, and through the Nicanor Gate, to the Court of the Israelites, a place open only to Jewish men

The walls of the Temple

Top: The huge Herodian stones of the Western Wall originally formed the retaining wall of Herod's Temple Mount

Bottom left: The Golden Gate. Beneath this structure (which probably dates from Byzantine times), there are remains of the Herodian gate, originally the Shushan Gate, leading from the Kidron Valley.

Bottom right: The outline of the Herodian Triple Gate and the restored steps leading to it. Through this gate was an underground passage which led up to the Temple Mount.

Temple Mount

Herod the Great doubled the size of Temple Mount and built the magnificent Temple building. It was dedicated around 10 BC, but work on the Temple complex continued for decades. The Temple stood until AD 70 when it was destroyed by the Romans as they crushed the Jewish revolt.

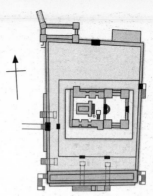

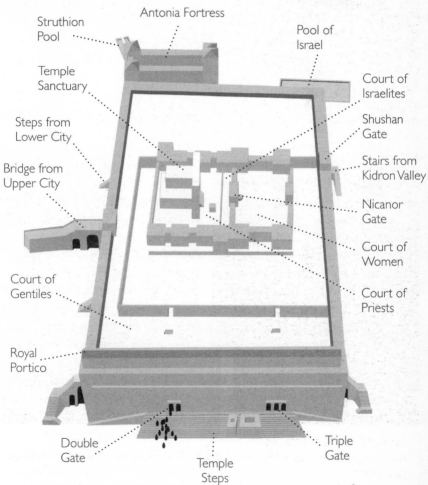

Struthion Pool

Antonia Fortress

Pool of Israel

Temple Sanctuary

Court of Israelites

Steps from Lower City

Shushan Gate

Bridge from Upper City

Stairs from Kidron Valley

Nicanor Gate

Court of Women

Court of Gentiles

Court of Priests

Royal Portico

Double Gate

Temple Steps

Triple Gate

who have completed all the necessary purification rituals. There are priests on duty at the gate to check you as you go in. If you pass inspection, you can progress into the forecourt of the Temple itself, a space that, compared to the rest of the complex, is shallow.

Ahead of you is another barrier, this time a low wall, separating the Court of Israelites from the Court of Priests. This is where only the priests can go and, beyond this wall, you can see the priests performing their duties: animals are being sacrificed, their blood collected and splashed against the steps of the altar, their bodies roasted on the burning embers of the altar. There is the huge basin containing water for ritual washing. And there is the Temple sanctuary itself.

'What large stones and what large buildings!'

Herod's Temple was more than an extension to the small Temple of Zerubbabel; it was a complete resetting. He raised the height of the building to 100 cubits, by adding a second storey. He also added new wings on each flank of the entrance hall, turning the overall building into a kind of T-shape. One of the wings, according to the Mishnah, served as a storehouse for knives used during the slaughtering of sacrifices. The other probably held the staircase to the upper storey.[11]

The width at the rear of the Temple matched that of Zerubbabel's Temple. The lower storey was sixty cubits high and the upper storey, which was narrower than the ground floor, was forty cubits high. The upper storey was surrounded by a roof porch fifteen cubits wide with a parapet that may have been up to five cubits high. The interior measurements remained the same as Zerubbabel's Temple as well: sixty cubits long, twenty cubits wide and fifty-five cubits high.

The entrance to the porch is open. There is a heavy curtain, but it is pulled back allowing visitors to catch a glimpse of the interior of the building, most notably the huge golden vine which hangs from vertical posts or columns. Individuals can donate a leaf, or a berry to this vine, and can bring it and hang it there.[12] This, then, is as far as you can go. You know that beyond the Court of the Priests, beyond the porch, through the golden doors lies the Holy Place, with the golden tables and the candlesticks and the incense smouldering in the dappled darkness. You know that beyond this porch, in the sanctuary itself, there is the Holy of Holies: the still, silent eye of the storm, the cube-shaped space, where only the High Priest himself can go and only once a year. But these things are not for you.

And so, having made your sacrifice, you make your way back through the courts, down through the steps, through the gates, through the opulence and the symbolism and the history, back south towards the traders and the moneychangers and the southern gates.

Where there seems to be some sort of disturbance going on…

The Temple protest

Where: Temple Mount

When: Morning

> Then they came to Jerusalem. And he entered the temple and began to drive out those who were selling and those who were buying in the temple, and he overturned the tables of the money-changers and the seats of those who sold doves; and he would not allow anyone to carry anything through the temple. He was teaching and saying, 'Is it not written, "My house shall be called a house of prayer for all the nations"? But you have made it a den of robbers.' (Mark 11.15–18)

All four Gospels record this incident, although John puts it earlier in Jesus' ministry. Mark's version has three actions: Jesus overturns the tables of the moneychangers and the seats of those who sold doves, and stops people carrying stuff through the Temple; Luke's is the simplest version, just two verses, which tell of Jesus driving out 'those who were selling things there' and the verse about making the house a den of robbers; Matthew mentions the moneychangers and the doves, but nothing about people carrying stuff through the Temple. John's account is the most developed and dramatic, with Jesus driving out 'people selling cattle, sheep, and doves, and the money-changers seated at their tables' with a whip he has made from ropes. 'Take these things out of here! Stop making my Father's house a marketplace!' (John 2.14–16).

This incident is often seen as the spark, the tipping point, the single thing which triggered Jesus' arrest. Certainly it would have been used by his opponents; anything that could be construed as violence against the Temple would be useful in cobbling together a case. But it wasn't the action, so much as the *meaning*, which really determined things.

It was not, for example, a serious attempt to start a riot. There's no indication that Jesus hoped that his actions would spread, that he hoped that more people would start chucking the furniture about. Jesus was not intending to provoke a riot here.[13] In fact, it wasn't even a major incident. None of the guards intervened, either the Temple police who routinely patrolled the area, or the Roman soldiers looking down on things from the Antonia fortress.

Nor was it an attempt to stop the Temple functioning. If the aim was to stop sacrifices, then the incident would have happened in an entirely different place – in the inner courtyards, for example. Turning over the tables of a few moneychangers is not going to stop them sacrificing on the altar. Even when Jerusalem was under siege, even when war was raging all around, the priests carried on doing their thing. Jesus' throwing a couple of tables around wouldn't register on their Richter scale.

Finally, it was not a 'cleansing' of the Temple. That comes from a later Protestant interpretation of the event. Changing money and selling doves was perfectly legitimate business. It gave people the chance to offer a sacrifice and to pay their tax to the Temple.[14]

So what was it? It was a message, a sign, a statement. It was the equivalent of lobbing a brick through the window of the clergy. It was theological graffiti. A clue to understanding the incident comes from the Old Testament line that Jesus quotes: 'My house shall be called a house of prayer for all the nations' (Mark 11.17). He is quoting a line in Isaiah:

> These I will bring to my holy mountain and give them joy in my house of prayer; their burnt-offerings and sacrifices will be accepted on my altar; for my house shall be called a house of prayer for all peoples. (Isa. 56.7).

In Isaiah, this is a prediction of the future, where Gentiles who worship God will be allowed to worship in the Temple. So we could see this as talking about Gentiles – especially as Jesus is standing at this time in the Court of Gentiles, the largest space in the Temple. But another look at the Isaiah passage reveals a bit more detail. It's not just about Gentiles; Isaiah also talks about eunuchs (Isa. 56.3–5). Eunuchs, by virtue of their mutilation, could not worship in the Temple (Lev. 21.20), but here they are symbolic of all those who are excluded from the worshipping community.[15]

But, according to Jesus, this place of prayer has become a den of thieves. The word he uses is *lestes*, which means not just robbers, but bandits. Banditry was not just petty theft; it was a systemised robbery against the state. Crucifixion was the penalty for banditry, since it was seen as a crime against Roman government. Jesus is accusing the Temple authorities of being as bad as the bandits whom they and their Roman masters so hated.

'My house shall be called a house of prayer'

It has been suggested that what Jesus was really doing was not attacking the processes in the Temple as such, but signifying its future destruction. In this interpretation, the quote from Isaiah is a later addition by the Gospel writers: what Jesus was actually doing was performing a piece of prophetic symbolism. Judgement has been pronounced on the Temple and it will be destroyed. Such a message was inherently dangerous – any perceived threat against the Temple was seen as a threat against the state itself.

It may well be so. Jesus does, after all predict the Temple's destruction in other places. (Remember the fig tree? Judgement is coming on the Temple and it's not going to be good.)

And the charge that Jesus threatened to destroy the Temple formed a main plank in the accusations against him during his trial. But when you examine those charges as recounted in the trial scenes, they don't actually relate to this incident. They relate, instead, to Jesus' statement that he will rebuild the Temple in three days and that not a stone would be left standing. They relate, in fact, to Jesus' words, not his actions.

If judgement is coming against the Temple, one has to ask, 'Why?' What was going on there that made such judgement inevitable? More to the point, one has to ask why the symbolic action wasn't, well, a bit more symbolic. Overturning the tables of the moneychangers and letting the doves go free doesn't, to me at any rate, seem that good a symbol of destruction. The fig tree is good. The fig tree, as we shall see, is completely destroyed. But the tables aren't even smashed. They're just turned over. At least when Jeremiah prophesied destruction, he smashed a pot.

And there is still Jesus' quotation to deal with: *'My house shall be called a house of prayer for all the nations... But you have made it a den of robbers.'* It will not do, as some scholars do, to simply dismiss this as a later invention.[16] If we're looking for meaning, we have to look at the specific elements. And the specific elements here are the tables of the moneychangers, the sacrificial animals and the charges that the house of prayer has become a nest of bandits. Take any of those away and the action no longer makes sense. It seems to me rather more sensible to begin with the simpler theories: that Jesus really did have an objection to the moneychangers and to the dove-sellers and that he thought a house of prayer actually *had* become a robbers' den. That, after all, would be entirely the kind of thing that would bring judgement on the Temple.

So why might Jesus have thought that?

The Jerusalem Temple was one of the richest organisations in the Græco-Roman world. In addition to the money charged every year in Temple tax to Jews living throughout the empire, there were tithes of agricultural produce as well as the money it

made through the sale of sacrificial animals and the daily offerings from thousands of pilgrims. It also served as the storehouse for the liquid assets of rich people, who would give the
money to the Temple for safekeeping. So the Temple was not
just a place for religious worship, but it was also the heart of the
Jerusalem economy and the central bank for Judaea.[17]There
were other ways in which it gained money. The Temple may,
for example, have owned farm estates in the balsam-growing
region around Jericho.[18] But the bulk of its income came from
two sources: local tithes and the international Temple tax.

The tithes produced a huge amount of money and goods. In
the third and sixth years of the seven-year cycle, farmers were
obliged to set aside a percentage of their harvest and take it
and consume it in Jerusalem (in a state of purity, of course). If,
however, their farm was located more than a day's walk from
Jerusalem, they could sell the produce and bring the money
instead. How many Jews observed this, or could afford to
observe it, we don't know. The tithe could be presented to any
priest, so perhaps a lot of it stayed in the locality. But a significant amount – certainly nearer to Jerusalem – would have made
its way to the city.[19]

The second major source of income was the Temple tax, the
annual half-shekel paid by every Jewish man over twenty years
old towards the upkeep of the Temple. The Temple authorities
may have claimed a precedent from Exodus 30.13ff., where a
half-shekel is demanded on occasions when a census takes place,
but otherwise there is no precedent in the Old Testament. It has
been suggested that the half-shekel tax arose only during the
Hasmonaean period, perhaps in the reign of Salome Alexander,
or even later. In fact, in AD 33, it was probably still a fairly recent
innovation, which may have added to the controversy.[20]

In particular there seems to have been an argument over
whether it should be an annual tax or a one-off payment. The
Pharisees also advocated the annual tax but it was clear that
many others were strongly opposed. Another source of controversy was that priests were exempt from paying the tax. A saying

attributed to one Rabban Johanan ben Zakkai blames priestly non-payment of the tax for the destruction by the Romans:

> You would not serve God, now you are made to serve the lowest of the Gentiles, the Arabs: you would not pay to God the beka a head, now you pay fifteen shekels under your enemies' rule: you would not repair the roads and open places for the pilgrims, now you repair the posts and stations for those who go to the kings' cities.[21]

That there were widespread attempts to avoid paying the tax may be imagined, because throughout history there have always been widespread attempts to avoid paying tax, no matter how noble the cause. But this was clearly the source of some controversy.

Jesus' attitude to the Temple tax was ambivalent to say the least. When challenged he paid it only through a miracle!

> When they reached Capernaum, the collectors of the temple tax came to Peter and said, 'Does your teacher not pay the temple tax?' He said, 'Yes, he does.' And when he came home, Jesus spoke of it first, asking, 'What do you think, Simon? From whom do kings of the earth take toll or tribute? From their children or from others?' When Peter said, 'From others', Jesus said to him, 'Then the children are free. However, so that we do not give offence to them, go to the lake and cast a hook; take the first fish that comes up; and when you open its mouth, you will find a coin; take that and give it to them for you and me.' (Matt. 17.24–27)

As Jesus points out, earthly kings exempt their sons from paying the tax. The inference is clear: if the worldly kings exempt their own family from paying, how much more should the priestly aristocracy do so?[22] Jesus pays, in order to stop others from stumbling, but he pays by means of a miracle, rather than out of his own pocket. He pays in a way that conforms to the rules but which implicitly criticises the rules.

The Temple tax had to be paid at certain times of year. The Mishnah states that the moneychangers' tables were set up in the provinces from the 15th Adar, and in the Temple from 25th Adar and that the dues had to be paid by Nisan 1, two weeks before Passover.[23] So some scholars argue that this event happened earlier, not a few days before Passover but a couple of weeks. I think this is extremely unlikely to be the case. First, even the Mishnah shows that payment was more flexible than we think. There was a mechanism for late payments.[24] Second, a two week period to collect the money and bring it to Jerusalem is far too short. The Temple dues may have had to be paid over a ten-day period in Judaea and Galilee, but it is less clear when it had to be paid for the rest of the world.[25] Much more likely is that, as Jews arrived from throughout the Græco-Roman world for Passover, they brought their local Temple tax with them. Finally, we should recall that the only evidence we have for these dates comes from 130 years after the Temple stopped functioning.

It's much simpler to imagine that the Temple tax was paid throughout the year, whenever pilgrims visited. And, let's face it, has there ever been a religious institution of any kind that has ever turned down money when it was offered? Jerusalem was an economy built on the Temple and the Temple required feeding. It is perfectly possible, indeed probable, that many of the pilgrims arriving in Jerusalem for the festivals took the opportunity to pay their Temple tax then. Passover, immediately after the tax was supposed to be collected, would have been a boom time for tax revenue. All those visitors piling in from Alexandria, Antioch, Rome... and all bringing their local offerings.

And all this money had to be processed by the moneychangers. According to the Torah, the shekel had to be paid in the 'shekel of the sanctuary' (Exod. 30.13). Later interpretation led to the conclusion that it had to be paid in silver. The Mishnah records that it had previously been paid in a variety of coinage, including Persian darics, and even Roman denarii.[26] By Jesus' day, however, you could pay in only one, official, currency: the Tyrian shekel.

In one sense the choice of currency was painful, because it reminded the Jews that they were not permitted by the Romans to mint their own silver coins. Imperial mints produced silver coins, local Jewish mints only bronze and copper coins. This was a sensitive issue because coins carried images of emperors, or symbols of victory. To the Jews, any such image was offen-sive. (When they revolted in AD 67, one of the first things they did was to set up their own mints and produce silver coins with images of the Temple on them.) So whichever coin they chose was going to entail some compromise. In the end, the coin that the Temple authorities decreed had to be used – the only 'official' coin with which you could pay your Temple tax – was the Tyrian shekel. The Talmud records that all 'the money of which the law speaks is Tyrian money'.[27]

Why choose that particular currency? Certainly the choice was not made out of friendship or allegiance. Josephus records that the Tyrians always hated the Jews.[28] Some scholars claim that the Tyrian shekel was chosen because, unlike other coins from the Roman Empire, it did not have on it a picture of the emperor, and was therefore less offensive to the strict prohibi-tion on 'graven images'. However, Tyrian shekels had the god Melkart (Heracles) on the obverse and a Tyrian eagle on the reverse, with the inscription 'Tyre the Holy and Inviolable'.[29] This, it seems to me, is not exactly a holier alternative to a picture of Tiberius or Augustus; a pagan god is no better than the emperors. Another suggestion is that the Tyrian currency was chosen because it was widely available in the region. This might be true in Judaea, but can hardly be true elsewhere in the empire. Given that the Temple tax came from far and wide, it would be much easier, surely, if it were in Roman currency. And it's not as if Roman coins were not available in Judaea – as we shall see.

No, the real reason the Tyrian shekel was chosen was far more mundane. Of all the silver coins in circulation, the Tyrian shekel had the most silver in it. Silver coins from Antioch contained only 80 per cent silver on average: Tyrian shekels averaged 90 per cent and their silver content was tightly regulated.[30] The Roman Empire was not on a gold standard: gold was a com-modity, whose price expressed in normal currency, the denarius, might vary like that of wheat.[31] So silver was actually safer. In other words this was a commercial decision wrapped up as a religious choice. *All* the images on the shekels were pagan; so the Temple authorities went for the Tyrian shekel, the most valuable coin, the one with the highest proportion of silver.

Tyrian coinage came in two denominations – a didrachma or half-shekel, and a tetradrachma or one shekel. The one-shekel coin was perceived as a more valuable coin – presumably because it had the most silver in it. Yet the set rate of Temple tax for one man was half a shekel. The Temple authorities, naturally, would want the more valuable coin. So what they did was place a surcharge of 8 per cent on every individual half-shekel payment. In other words, if you went to the Temple and paid what you were supposed to pay, you were charged extra.[32] You were actually penalised for paying the correct amount. The idea was to offer people a discount for clubbing together and paying with the tetradrachma – the most valuable coin.[33]

So if we go for the simplest explanation of Jesus' action – that there was something wrong with the moneychangers – we can actually find three possible charges against the system: they chose the most valuable currency as the only way of paying tax; they insisted on its being an annual and not a one-off payment; and they charged a surcharge if you paid the correct amount of money.

The moneychangers themselves, of course, were sanctioned by the high priest and the Temple authorities. The moneychangers didn't decide which coins you had to use. It was not them, but the system of economic exploitation, that Jesus was attacking.

Which brings us to the doves.

'A pair of turtledoves or two young pigeons'

The Temple tax was one way in which the Temple made money. Another way was through the sale of animals for sacrifice.

The Græco-Roman world smelt of blood. Animal sacrifice was an integral part of virtually all the religions in the Græco-Roman world. Temples were like religious abattoirs, with priests well versed in performing sometimes quite complicated surgical operations on the animals that were sacrificed. It was, in fact, a lousy time to be a vegetarian. (Or an animal, for that matter.) However, Jewish sacrifice was different from the often drunken celebrations of the pagans. Josephus wrote that:

> When we offer sacrifices to him we do it not in order to surfeit ourselves, or to be drunken; for such excesses are against the will of God, and would be an occasion of injuries and of luxury: but by keeping ourselves sober, orderly, and ready for our other occupations, and being more temperate than others.[34]

The daily ritual of the Temple began and ended with sacrifice. A lamb was sacrificed at dawn and towards the end of the evening. These were thanksgiving sacrifices, one for the benefits of the day, the other for blessing at night.[35] Festivals were marked by extra sacrifices. Through sacrifice, people gave thanks to God and shared in his peace. With sacrifice they celebrated major festivals and asked for forgiveness. It was through sacrifice that people were able to be cleansed from impurity. In the case of forgiveness and purification there were other actions as well, but the ritual always culminated in an act of sacrifice.[36]

Clearly it was reasonable, therefore, to have animals available. A pilgrim from Alexandria, arriving in Jerusalem for Passover, could not be expected to bring an animal with him. He would expect to buy one there, and therefore to be able to participate in the feast, which was the point of the journey. Without sacrifice, how could you be forgiven? Without sacrifice, how could you be purified? To engage in the worship of the community you needed to sacrifice. And that meant you had to buy an animal.

Let's assume that our pilgrim has decided to buy an animal to sacrifice from the stalls in the south portico of the Temple. How much would that cost in today's money? Comparing prices and costs across decades is difficult enough; across millennia and cultures it is nigh on impossible. Commodities change their availability; different tools affect the costs of different types of work. But if we take the everyday world of Jesus' stories as evidence (Matt. 20.2), as well as references elsewhere, it seems that a labourer's daily wage was one denarius.[37]

Here are some other costs, with their equivalent:

▷ Porters' fee to carry stone from lower Galilee to Jerusalem
  = 20d for five men.
▷ Wages for working a field of ten kor of wheat = 200d.
▷ Wages for weaving a tallit (prayer shawl) = 8d.
▷ Daily wages of a good scribe = 2d.
▷ Rabbi Hillel's daily wage = ½ d.[38]

The scribal wages come from a century later than Jesus' time, but probably reflect little, if any, inflation, while Hillel, as a famous rabbi, may have made a point of living below the poverty line. So one denarius a day is probably accurate as the wages of an unskilled working man; the basic minimum wage of the time.

Wheat cost one denarius for between eight and twelve litres.[39] A daily ration of bread – enough to provide two meals – cost around one-twelfth of a denarius.[40] Crops were more expensive in the city than in the countryside and fruit cost between three and six times as much as it did in the country. Figs are recorded as being sold in Jerusalem at three to four for an isaar, and there were twenty-four isaars to the denarius.[41] So your basic food for the day – some bread and fruit – would cost between one-twelfth and one-tenth of your daily wage.

For the sake of comparison, let's try that out on today's wages. The UK minimum wage today is, at the time of writing, £5.73 per hour. This is what many fruit-pickers and farm labourers have to survive on. A basic day's pay, then, is around £40. That works well enough for our comparison; it would cost at least a tenth of your daily wage to have enough food to survive on. So how do sacrifices compare?

The cost of animals for sacrifice varied, of course, with the size of the animal. An ox cost between 100 and 220 denarii; a calf twenty denarii; a ram, eight denarii and a lamb four denarii.[42] The pigeons – the offering for the poor – cost one denarius. The Temple tax – the Tyrian shekel, actually equates to two denarii, or two days' wages. So, if we were just to convert it on this rough and deeply unscientific comparison, the Temple tax would be £80, a pair of pigeons £40, a Passover lamb £80.[43] We can see that, whatever the comparative costs, for those many thousands in the city who were existing at poverty level, participation in the Temple worship at a very basic level must have been hugely expensive. And at festival time, when the laws of supply and demand kicked in, it must have been almost impossible.

'They went up as usual for the festival'

Back to our imaginary pilgrim. Having arrived in Jerusalem, he had to find somewhere to stay. Perhaps he had relatives here, or perhaps he would stay in a hostel attached to a synagogue. An inscription discovered in Jerusalem in 1914 reads:

> Theodotus, son of Vettenus, priest and synagogue chief, son of a synagogue chief, grandson of a synagogue chief, had the synagogue built for the reading of the law and for the teaching of the commandments, as well as the hospice and the accommodations and the water-works as lodging to those who need it from abroad, [the synagogue] whose foundations had been put down by the fathers and the elders and Simonides.[44]

This synagogue, which was a place for teaching and discussion, was also for Jews from the Græco-Roman world who came to visit the city. As this inscription shows, there were synagogues in Jerusalem at the time of Jesus and they seem to have catered for specific groups or nationalities; Paul went to debate in the Hellenistic Synagogues and Acts also mentions the synagogues of the Freedmen (Acts 6.1–10).

But what if you hadn't got accommodation lined up? Where would you stay? We can learn something, perhaps, from a festival that has survived, almost from the time of the Temple. Every year, huge numbers of Muslim pilgrims make their way to Mecca to take part in the Hajj, the largest annual pilgrimage in the world. For centuries, the inhabitants of Mecca have made a major part of their livelihood by providing for these millions of pilgrims, giving them somewhere to stay and food to eat,

A group of Russian pilgrims arriving in Jerusalem in the early years of the 20th century. Pilgrimage groups such as this had made their way to the city for centuries.

and helping them find their way around. They also served as brokers, finding the pilgrims accommodation, perhaps, like all tour guides before and after, using favoured connections and gaining commission. As the wonderfully named Snouck Hurgronje noted in 1888, nearly all the inhabitants of Mecca were engaged in the 'business' of Hajj:

> Mecca has no hotels, but, on the other hand, in the last months of every [lunar] year, every Meccan becomes an hotel keeper whether he has a whole house, or only one storey or half a storey… all Meccans therefore are interested in getting on good terms with several sheikhs *[i.e. mutawwifin – local guides]* as on the other hand the latter set great store on extensive connections among the public.[45]

This relationship between host and pilgrim in the Hajj could be easily exploited, and, indeed, complaints about such behaviour go back many centuries. The Islamic jurists of the thirteenth century considered that the obligation to make the Hajj should no longer apply 'given the incredible vexations to which the pilgrims were submitted at the hands of the inhabitants of the Hijaz'.[46]

Mecca is not Jerusalem and the Hajj is not Passover. But there are similarities. Like Passover, the Hajj is surrounded by many complicated rites, including ritual bathing – the *ghusl* – before the pilgrim can approach the holy shrine.[47] Indeed, the basic rituals of the Hajj – ritual purifications, feast, sacrifice and vigil – date back way before the advent of Islam and probably have their origin in ancient Semitic practice.[48] The Hajj is a survivor from the days of the great festivals. Despite the dangers in projecting back from one to the other, we can guess that what was common at the Hajj was common in Jerusalem: that people made money from the pilgrims – indeed, that people *had* to make money from the pilgrims. The great festivals, and the tithes and taxes, were the only harvest that Jerusalem could reap. Indeed, there is evidence that pilgrims were offered a range of products to commemorate their visit: archaeology has revealed that Jerusalem glass was as good as the high-quality ware from Sidon and the city had a thriving and expert stone-carving community.[49] And, according to certain rabbinic writings, pilgrims bringing money earned in exchange for second tithe were required to spend the money inside the city.[50] Saudi merchants view the Hajj much as those in the UK and the US view the Christmas season. It is where they make most of their money. Passover must have had a similar economic importance to Jerusalem's economy: it was their busiest time of the year.

Significantly, pilgrims to the Hajj are expected to make a sacrifice and supply and demand means that the cost of an animal can skyrocket. In 1967, for example, the price of sheep jumped from around $9 to $22.[51] And this is exactly what seems to have happened in Jerusalem. A passage in the Mishnah runs:

> Once in Jerusalem a pair of doves cost a golden denar. Rabban Simeon b.Gamaliel said: By this Temple! I will not suffer the night to pass by before they cost but a [silver] denar.[52]

There were twenty-five silver denarii to one golden denarius, so the price was clearly extortionate. The Rabbi began to teach that women could offer a pair of pigeons for as many as five live births or miscarriages and that, having done so, 'she may then eat of the animal-offerings', which means she could take part in the festivals, since that was the time when those sacrificing could eat their offerings (normally they were eaten by the priests). There are three points of interest here: first, the Rabbi considered one denarius to be an acceptable price for a pair of doves; second, it's clear that cases of extortionate overcharging could arise; and third, this case was clearly connected with festivals. Naturally, festivals would have been the time of highest demand. Someone who had travelled many hundreds of miles to Jerusalem to take part in the feast would be desperate to do things properly. They simply had to have the sacrifices, otherwise they would not be able to take part and an expensive and arduous journey would be wasted.

So the Temple, through the tithes, the taxes and the sale of animals, was a huge money-making machine. It needed to be: the Temple economy had to generate large amounts of cash in order to function; it kept thousands of people in work, and its operation was vital to the economic well-being of Jerusalem. But it was a monopoly. It was the only real economic power in town. And that meant that its financial muscle could be abused.

In their trading with the local economy, for example, the Temple always came out on top. If a supplier agreed to supply the Temple with flour at twelve litres per denarius, but the price rose to nine litres per denarius, he still had to provide it at the twelve-litre rate, as agreed. But if he had undertaken to provide it at nine litres per denarius, and subsequently found he was getting twelve litres per denarius, then he had to give the Temple twelve litres instead of the nine promised, since, according to the Mishnah, 'the Temple has the upper hand'. Precisely.[53]

Then there was the lavish luxury of the setting and the clothing. The high priest's vestments are said to have cost 10,000 denarii, an almost unbelievable amount. We're talking about clothing that on our scale would cost £400,000.[54]

We can see now that those who argue that moneychangers and traders were simply providing a service so that people could pay their Temple tax or make sacrifices are rather missing the point.[55] The argument is not whether animals were necessary, but how much they cost and who was profiting. And it's not about the moneychangers themselves, but the need to change money in the first place. There was nothing in the Torah even to say that it had to be paid annually, let alone that it had to be paid in silver, and then only in the purest Tyrian silver. The Temple itself used its economic muscle to pay the minimum price possible, and those in charge chose always to interpret the law in a way that effectively penalised the poorest people.

The evidence from the Mishnah – not exactly what you'd call anti-Temple propaganda – shows that abuses did occur. But these abuses were not down to the traders; this was part of the system. The surcharge wasn't the work of the traders but the work of the Temple authorities. These were the people who set the prices. The Temple had the upper hand.

'But you have made it a den of robbers'

We must return to those scattered tables and flapping doves, to the chimes of the coins on the pavements, the outrage of the stallholders and the delight, perhaps, of the people around.

A Temple economy is not a market economy. For the Jews in the Græco-Roman world, there was an emotional and spiritual attachment to their Temple, which made any alternative unthinkable. There was, in fact, another Jewish Temple during this period, in Egypt, at Leontopolis. It operated for over two hundred years until the Romans closed it in AD 72, but it barely registers on the radar of most first-century Jews. Philo, who lived in Alexandria, some 140 miles from this Temple, never mentions it, concentrating on the one 350 miles away.[56] It's the same kind of emotional appeal – albeit on a greater scale – that a football team has for its supporters. The owners of the clubs can put the season-ticket prices up in the knowledge that the true fan cannot just simply switch to another club if it's cheaper. This is his club, part of his identity. He might complain about the overcharging, but in the end he'll pay to worship at the shrine.

If you earn enough money to buy some bread and some figs and rent a place to sleep, what hope do you have of buying a pair of doves? The people who were most dispossessed by the Temple aristocracy were the Jews themselves – the ordinary Jews, living in their squalid tenements, struggling to make a living, as millions in the cities have done in the past and will continue to do in the future. The poor will be with us always, and always there will be churches and chapels to rip them off in the name of religion.

Jesus, then, was not attacking the moneychangers or the animal sellers as such. He was attacking the people behind the system; he was accusing the authorities of turning the Temple into a house of robbers, a den of thieves selling season tickets to God at prices that the poor could not afford.

Was this a deliberate policy on the part of the Temple leadership? Or was it simply the way that the system operated? We can't tell precisely. An economic entity the size of the Temple must have been hard to control. But there is one final twist in this tale.

It is possible that the trade in animals was a profit-making enterprise not of the Temple, but of the high priest. The animals were bought and sold in the Temple precincts (and probably in some markets elsewhere in the city), probably on the south side near the Royal Portico. Significantly, near to the Temple there were the shops of Hanaun or Hanan.[57]

We must be careful here, because the name is not an uncommon one, but Hanan is a version of the name of the high-priestly family, Ananus. So there is the possibility that the stalls selling animals in the Court of Gentiles were not just some anonymous individual traders, but, in the words of Jeremias, 'supported by the powerful high-priestly family of Annas [Ananus]'[58] Suddenly this puts an extra spin on the Temple protest. What if Jesus was protesting against the disproportionate prices of the animals – animals that were actually being sold by a business owned by the high-priestly dynasty currently in power in the Temple?

A line in some later rabbinic writings might also imply that the House of Hanan played the tithe system quite well:

> The Sages said: The [produce] stores for the children of Hanin *[Hanan]* were destroyed three years before the rest of the Land of Israel, because they failed to set aside tithes from their produce, for they interpreted *Thou shalt surely tithe…* and *thou shalt surely eat* as excluding the seller, and *The increase of thy seed* as excluding the buyer.[59]

In other words, they weren't paying their taxes. They were operating like those big corporations today, who manage their accounts so that they pay nothing in corporation tax, as, on paper, they make no profit.

Jesus' Temple protest, therefore, was never a real physical threat to the Temple, nor was it intended that way. By turning over the tables, Jesus was attacking the economic exploitation that had become part of the way the Temple worked. In doing so, he may well have offended the very family who were ruling the Temple at the time. The family of Ananus would not take kindly to such criticism: they would remember it. This would be another reason why Caiaphas was so determined that Jesus should be punished. And it would also explain why the family of Ananus, as we shall see, continued to bear a grudge against the family and followers of Christ, even many years later. It was personal.

That Jesus' actions were an attack on the Temple aristocracy can be seen from the reaction:

> And when the chief priests and the scribes heard it, they kept looking for a way to kill him; for they were afraid of him, because the whole crowd was spellbound by his teaching. (Mark 11.18)

This is the first revelation in Mark's account of the Temple authorities' active hostility to Jesus. He had openly opposed their management of the Temple, he had accused them of banditry, like some common rebel-thief on the road to Jericho, and, worst of all, the crowd was on his side.

So Jesus left the city – over the Mount of Olives to Bethany, where he spent his nights (Luke 21.37). The attacks on the Temple would continue tomorrow, although the weapons would be very different.

Day Three: The End Times
Tuesday 31 March AD 33

Fig tree part two: Mount of Olives, early Tuesday morning
The four questions: The Temple, Tuesday morning
The prophecy about the Temple: Outside the Temple, Tuesday afternoon
The prophecy about the future: Mount of Olives, Tuesday evening

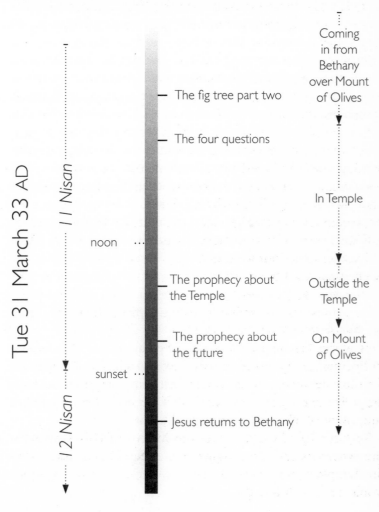

Tue 31 March 33 AD

11 Nisan

noon

12 Nisan

sunset

The fig tree part two

The four questions

The prophecy about
the Temple

The prophecy about
the future

Jesus returns to Bethany

Coming
in from
Bethany
over Mount
of Olives

In Temple

Outside the
Temple

On Mount
of Olives

Fig tree part two

Where: Mount of Olives

When: Early morning

Early the next morning, Jesus and his followers returned to Jerusalem.

Mark reports that, as they descended the hill, they noticed that the fig tree from the day before had 'withered away to its roots' (Mark 11.20). Mark uses the story to record Jesus' sayings about faith. If the disciples truly believe, they will be able to move mountains, Jesus says. But the context of the story, its position as the second slice of bread in this Marcan sandwich, reveals the other meaning. Before visiting the Temple, Jesus curses the fig tree; after cleansing the Temple the fig tree is withered 'to its roots'. The Temple was a barren tree. It would wither and die.

Given the disturbance he had caused the day before, it is odd that Jesus heads straight back into the Temple and starts walking around. Clearly the Temple protest cannot have been a widespread disruption, otherwise, despite their reservations about Jesus' popular support, there is no way that the authorities would have allowed Jesus to re-enter the Temple precinct. But the Temple afforded Jesus the space to sit and teach. Open space was at a premium in Jerusalem. Used to the hillsides and open spaces of Galilee, it would be natural for Jesus to seek similar venues in Jerusalem, and the Temple, with its wide-open plaza or the wide steps leading up from the south, fitted the bill perfectly.

It was easier for Jesus to hide in plain sight. While he was in the open, among the crowds, it was virtually impossible for the Temple authorities to act against him. At this point Jesus was commanding considerable public support. They could not arrest him in the open because of the fear of rioting.

Faced, therefore, with the impossibility of arrest – at least in the short term – the authorities try a different tack: they try to discredit him.

The four questions

Where: The Temple

When: Morning

Mark's account of Day Three contains a series of verbal attacks on Jesus in the form of trick questions. The Temple authorities have sent out their crack troops not to arrest Jesus, but to destroy his credibility. Mark records four direct challenges to Jesus:

▷ 'By what authority are you doing these things?'
   Challengers: 'the chief priests, the scribes, and the elders' (Mark 11.27–33);
▷ 'Is it lawful to pay taxes to the emperor, or not?'
   Challengers: 'some Pharisees and some Herodians' (Mark 12.13–17);
▷ 'In the resurrection whose wife will she be?'
   Challengers: 'some Sadducees' (Mark 12.18–27);
▷ 'Which commandment is the first of all?'
   Challenger: a scribe (Mark 12.28–34).

One of these is a genuine enquiry. The others are deliberate traps, each as delicate as a bomb and as tricky to defuse.

'By what authority are you doing these things?'

One of the things that worried the authorities the most was that Jesus, too, had authority – just of a different sort. Jesus, from the start, was perceived to have a different sort of authority. People realised that there was something different about Jesus' teaching: 'for he taught them as one having authority, and not as the scribes.' (Mark 1.22). When challenged by a demon-possessed man, he casts the demon out. 'A new teaching – with authority!' is the people's response (Mark 1.27). Jesus was not one of the trained legal scholars – the scribes. He did not back up his argument with precedent: he just *said* things. And they seemed to be true. And the more he did things, the more it backed up the things he said.

The authority of Jesus is one of those things which most

scholars would not dispute: whoever he was, people took notice of him. Jesus' wisdom springs from his own convictions and insight, his independence. What he says stands on its own merits. His sayings come with 'their own self-evidencing power'.[1] From the point of view of those in power, Jesus had the most threatening form of authority: credibility.

But such authority has potentially fragile foundations. For, without precedents and scriptural authority to back it up, it stands only on its own truth and the life of the speaker. So Jesus' personal integrity, his manner and his actions were of the utmost importance in his teaching. In that sense, the whole of the Longest Week is an argument for the authority of Jesus. The events of this week show a man who will go to the ultimate extreme to demonstrate the proof of what he is saying.

The first challenge, then: 'By whose authority do you do this?' – 'Who gave you permission to say all this stuff?' (Mark 11.27–33) – is easily rebuffed. In typical rabbinical fashion, Jesus bargains with his opponents: he's going to answer their question only if they can beat him at this game of 'who's got more wisdom?' Jesus quite astutely uses one of his key weapons here: the crowd. When he asks, 'Did the baptism of John come from heaven, or was it of human origin?' (Mark 11.30) his questioners are trapped. Because of the crowd's reverence for John the Baptist they can't actually say what they believe: that John the Baptist was deluded. This would turn the crowd against them even more. But if they say that John the Baptist had heavenly authority then the next question is – why didn't you follow him, then? In the end, it is not Jesus' credibility that is destroyed, but that of the questioners.

'He began to speak to them in parables'

Jesus does, however, go on to answer their question, albeit in an oblique way.

All three of the Synoptics follow this challenge with a selection of stories. Mark, Luke and Matthew have the parable of the wicked tenants in the vineyard (Matt. 21.33–46; Mark

12.1–12; Luke 20.9–18). Matthew adds two more parables: the parable of the two sons (Matt. 21.28–32) and the parable of the wedding feast (Matt. 22.1–14).

Matthew's first parable, the parable of the two sons, is a direct rebuttal of their implied criticism of John's ministry and a swipe at the emphasis on purity. Those who do the will of the father are those who change their minds when confronted by John, who believed in him: and those are the tax-collectors and the prostitutes (Matt. 21.32).

The second story in Matthew – and the one shared between the Synoptics – is the story of the wicked tenants in the vineyard. The meaning is unmistakable for the Sadducees: the vineyard was a recognised symbol for the land of Israel and the king could only be God, who created the country and gave it to his people. The wicked tenants kill first the slaves – the prophets – sent from the father and finally kill the son of the vineyard owner himself. It's a peculiar parable in some respects, because, although it sounds triumphant, it culminates with the death of the son. But it is pointing ahead to what Jesus will address later that day: the day of the Lord, the time when God will come and transform everything. 'Everything you have will be taken away from you,' Jesus is saying to them. 'You have killed the previous messengers from God and you're going to kill me. But justice will come.' The story also reinforces Jesus' credibility as an outsider. Jesus uses the image of a cornerstone, rejected by the builders. He is the king of the outcasts, the regent of the rejects. Jesus makes the point that his authority comes not only from his origins, but also from his independence. He is the ultimate outsider.

The third story, in Matthew, is similar to the parable of the wicked tenants. The kingdom of heaven is a wedding banquet for a prince. The king sends out slaves with invitations, but the invited guests refuse to come. Some issue an excuse, some actually murder the slaves. The king responds by sending troops to execute the murderers and destroy their city. Then he sends his slaves out to invite those they find on the road – 'the good and the bad' (Matt. 22.10). So far the story has a familiar arc. In Luke's version (Luke 14.16–24) this is where the story ends, with a wedding feast filled with the uninvited and unimportant, the 'poor, the crippled, the blind and the lame' (Luke 14.22). But Matthew adds an unexpected coda. Someone creeps into the wedding banquet who is not wearing a wedding robe. When challenged by the king about his dress, he has no excuse and so he is thrown into the outer darkness, 'where there will be weeping and gnashing of teeth'. Jesus goes on to say that many are called, but few are chosen (Matt. 22.13–14).

The first part of the tale is fairly straightforward, historically. Once again the wedding feast is a biblical image, conjuring images of the heavenly banquet in Psalm 107.1–9 and Isaiah 25.6–8. The slaves are most likely the prophets again, and their fate echoes the parable of the tenants. Verse 7 can be read as a foretelling of the destruction of Jerusalem by the Romans in AD 70. Again, this is a story of judgement on the official rulers, on the official invitees. These people who would not answer the summons will be replaced by less 'honourable' guests, and their refusal to answer the summons will result in death and destruction.

But what of the coda? First, it looks very likely that this is another parable, which Matthew has added to the end. Otherwise it seems a bit harsh that someone who has just been dragged off the street should be criticised for not wearing his poshest clothes! Luke's version probably records the original 'shape' of the story. Second, the phrase about weeping and gnashing of teeth occurs elsewhere in Matthew's Gospel, for example in 8.12, where the 'heirs to the kingdom' will be cast out in favour of the Gentiles. The episode is probably emphasising that it is not just the call that makes someone a member of the kingdom, but the response. Everyone is invited, but not everyone will choose the right way.

We think of parables as a 'tale with a meaning', a way of sugaring the pill. Jesus' parables weren't sugared pills so much as chocolate-covered chili peppers. Without the chocolate. Viewed in their social and political context, we can see

Jesus' parables for what they are: explosive, unsettling, even enraging. Told in the Temple courts, amidst the surging, explosive atmosphere of Passover, we can see these stories as taunts to which the Temple authorities respond with anger and resentment and a desire for revenge. These are not children's stories. These are incendiary narratives.

Luke makes it clear that the Temple authorities were quite aware of the message behind his parables:

> When the scribes and chief priests realized that he had told this parable against them, they wanted to lay hands on him at that very hour, but they feared the people. (Luke 20.19)

This is important. The crowd was on his side. The crowd loved the stories. And the crowd saved Jesus from immediate arrest.

But it was only going to be a matter of time. Jesus was to discover, as many artists, writers and storytellers have found over the centuries, that totalitarian regimes do not like to be ridiculed. Telling stories can get you killed.

'Is it lawful to pay taxes to the emperor, or not?'

So the chief priests leave the arena, but they send some more troops into battle – some Pharisees and Herodians, according to Mark. Having failed to remove his religious authority, the next question seeks to undermine his political authority. Jesus' actions in the Temple protest were linked to the Temple tax, but here the tax question is broadened. Here, the question revolves around the key political issue of the day: the Roman Empire.

> Then they sent to him some Pharisees and some Herodians to trap him in what he said. And they came and said to him, 'Teacher, we know that you are sincere, and show deference to no one; for you do not regard people with partiality, but teach the way of God in accordance with truth. Is it lawful to pay taxes to the emperor, or not? Should we pay them, or should we not?' (Mark 12.13–15)

Christian interpretations of this event have usually suggested that Jesus is encouraging Christians to pay their civic dues. In fact, the whole issue is more subtle. From the moment they assumed direct control of Judaea in AD 6, the Romans demanded tribute money from the Jews. Some Jews (notably the Zealots) refused to give in to such Roman oppression. In this instance, the two groups putting the question to Jesus – the Herodians and the Pharisees – came from differing political positions. The Herodians were members of the Herodian court who had come to Jerusalem with their leader, Herod Antipas, to celebrate the Passover. Some of these were among Jesus' supporters: one of the members of the church at Antioch was Manaean, who is described as a *syntrophos* of Herod Antipas. *Syntrophos* means 'nourished' or 'brought up together with,' 'foster-brother,' 'companion (from one's youth), intimate friend'.[2] Another of Jesus' followers in Galilee was a woman called Joanna, who was married to Herod's steward Chuza (Luke 8.3). The Herodians, unlike the Sadducees and Pharisees, were not a religious group but more of a political party. They supported the interests of the Herodian dynasty and probably longed for some kind of renaissance under a descendant of Herod the Great. This would necessarily have meant a pro-Roman policy: the Herodian dynasty could survive in power only with the support of the Romans. They were, in short, keen fans of the Roman Empire and enthusiasts of Græco-Roman culture.

The Pharisees, on the other hand, were nationalists, albeit in a fairly restrained way. Their attitude to the Empire varied from active opposition to sullen acceptance. Perhaps it is best summed up in the *realpolitik* of Hanina, the Deputy High Priest, who said 'Pray for the peace of the empire, since if it were not for fear of it men would devour each other alive.'[3] However, they did not oppose the paying of taxes.

So why ask the question? Well, clearly, if he answers 'yes', he's going to lose the support of all those who were struggling under the yoke of the Roman tax burden; and if he answers 'no' they will be able to charge him with being a rebel, with opposing Roman authority. So what does Jesus do? He doesn't say 'no'. But nor does he exactly say 'yes'.

The coin that Jesus asks for – the denarius – was most likely the denarius of Tiberius; he was the reigning Caesar and it was to him, ultimately, that Judaean tribute money would go. There were millions of these coins issued and the design changed little throughout Tiberius' reign. On one side was the laurel-clad head of Tiberius; on the other a seated lady, representing peace.[4] The coin that Jesus held up would have made quite a journey; all the denarii of Tiberius were minted in Gaul, in the Lugdunum mint. The question is intended to reveal Jesus' politics. Is he a nationalist, a pious Jew, or a politically realistic Jew? It's a question charged with political menace.

What he does is sidestep their question. By asking them to provide him with a coin, he shows that they are not serious about this. They carry the coins, they have joined the system. If you carry the currency, he seems to say, you have to pay the price. You have taken the Roman Empire's money; you have – literally – bought into their system.

He could have left the answer there, showing how far his accusers had been integrated into the imperial system, but he broadens the issue: 'Give to God what is God's.' Never mind Caesar's slice of the cake, how much are they actually giving to God?

Millions of Christians have had this parable explained as Jesus' policy on paying taxes; with preachers urging the people to pay their taxes because Jesus said 'We should render unto Caesar…' This is missing the point. The point is 'how much are you giving to God?' The hopelessly compromised questioners have got their kingdoms wrong. It's not a conflict between the kingdom of Rome and the kingdom of Israel – both of those use taxes anyway. It's a battle between the kingdom of God and the kingdom of wealth.[5] In this, it ties in with his other teaching. 'No one can serve two masters; for a slave will either hate the one and love the other, or be devoted to the one and despise the other. You cannot serve God and wealth' (Matt. 6.24). The issue of giving money to the Romans pales into insignificance compared to the need to give everything to God.

In that sense at least, the accusation that he 'forbade people' to pay taxes to Caesar has some basis here (Luke 23.2). He has not, in fact, provided any sort of answer. He has presented a problem. How do you live totally for God in a pagan world? It is a problem that his followers have been grappling with ever since.

'In the resurrection whose wife will she be?'

A third tack. They've tried the direct approach; they've tried politics; now his opponents turn to religion. And time for another opponent. We've had the chief priests, the scribes and the elders; we've seen off the Pharisees and the Herodians. Now the Sadducees decide to have a go.

As we have seen, one of the biggest issues separating the Sadducees from the Pharisees was the question of the afterlife. The Pharisees argued for the resurrection of the body. The Sadducees rejected this because they could not find it in the Torah; this world is all you get. Which was fine for them, because they had the comfort in this world. As Goodman has written, 'Sadducaism embodied a smug self-congratulation about the status quo that only the rich could accept.'[6]

And, indeed, there's an air of smugness about this question. It's a theoretical argument, a conundrum, a philosophical and theological riddle. Jesus, in response, simply nukes the argument. He cites the Torah – the Sadducees' own base text – and the implication that by saying 'I am the God of Abraham, Isaac and Jacob', all these were somehow still alive at the time of Moses. In other words he accuses these men – the fundamentalist scripture party – of not having read their scriptures. His argument is partly based on what you might call 'common sense' – in other words, God has the power to sort all this out. What makes you think the resurrected life is going to be like things down here?

There's also another subtext to Jesus' irritation. This is a widow they are talking about, a woman being passed from one man to another. Such people had no power, as we can see. That the Sadducees had turned the plight of a widow into a theological riddle shows just how far they were from the everyday problems of people in the villages and towns of Judaea.

'Which commandment is the first of all?'

Hearing this, Mark tells us a scribe brings his own question. The scribes, who often appear in the Gospel accounts, were, as the name implies, people who wrote things down. Perhaps the best equivalent is our word 'secretary'. Scribes were a kind of religious middle-management: administrators and bureaucrats. In the Græco-Roman world, you could have scribes attached to local councils (e.g. Acts 19.35).

The New Testament tends not to differentiate between different groups of scribes. Often, they are portrayed as a unified group who, generally, are opposed to Jesus. Mark associates the scribes with the Temple and Jerusalem, and, especially, the government of the high priests. So we might think of them as kind of local religious advisory officers: Temple bureaucrats based in Jerusalem. Even where they appear in Galilee, some of them have come from Jerusalem (Mark 3.22; 7.1). At the most basic level, they were literate copyists, who could assist in drawing up legal agreements and writing letters. In smaller villages they might have served as record-keepers, a link between the government and the people; a kind of first-century council official.[7] Scribes could work alongside different groupings and in different roles. Matthew, for example, links the scribes much more closely with the Pharisees, where they are seen as guardians of the traditions and community leaders. Luke, too, shows them as allied to the Pharisees, active in preserving and protecting Judaism.

This questioner, however, is different from the rest. This is not an attack, but a genuine enquiry, and it shows how Jesus was cutting across social and ideological boundaries. This scribe wants to know which commandment is the first – the best. And Jesus, in a moment of magisterial wisdom, summarises the law and the prophets down into a handful of words. It is the scribe's reaction that is instructive. He does what all scribes do: he helps people remember what Jesus has said, by repeating it. But then he adds his own interpretation: 'This is much more important than all whole burnt-offerings and sacrifices' (Mark 12.33b).

This was incredible. For a scribe to stand in the Temple and say that there were some things more important than the sacrificial rites that were going on at that very moment! The scribal position on this can be summed up in the words of Simon the Just: 'The world rests on three things: the law, the sacrificial worship and expressions of love.' Love here means acts of love and generosity; not, perhaps, the deeper commitment that Jesus is calling for.[8] But this particular scribe has made the leap. He has seen through Jesus' eyes; he has written, just for a moment, in a hand that is not his own.

'Beware of the scribes'

Now it's Jesus' turn to ask a question. Following the surprise support of one of the scribes, Mark shows Jesus launching into an attack on the scribes' scriptural expertise. Jesus' question is about the Messiah. How can the scribes call the Messiah 'the son of David', he asks, when David calls the Messiah 'my Lord'? (It's a quote from Psalm 110.1.)

There was a conviction, a hope, a passionate desire, that a Messiah would come to deliver the nation and restore the kingdom. Core to this was the understanding that the Messiah would be a descendant of David.[9] Jesus challenges the idea of that relationship, or, at least, the scribal understanding of it. What do the scribes actually mean when they talk about the Messiah as David's son? In what sense is this true? What's the actual relationship?

Jesus here is doing a number of things. First, he's demonstrating that he can trade scriptures with the best of them; he has already bested the Sadducees, now he takes on the scribes. But this is not just some kind of scriptural arm-wrestling match; what his question does is expose the scribe's understanding of the Messiah. He is, in effect, calling for a redesignation of the phrase 'Son of David'. The scribes' use of the term to describe the Messiah is revealed for what it is: a political designation without any inspired scriptural source.[10] The experts are not so expert after all.

The point, perhaps, is to challenge the idea of a military–political Messiah, an earthly king, claiming the 'throne' by descent.

The scribes, following perhaps their pharisaical or Sadducean leaders, have politicised the role, turned it into a nostalgic yearning for the great days of Israel. But, Jesus is saying, they have no biblical basis for this picture. It's an aristocratic fantasy. There will be no return to the days of David's empire. Jesus is not going to restore the kingdom in the way that the scribes read it. And the battle that he will fight is not going to be with the Romans. There is a deeper and darker enemy to encounter. Having destroyed the scriptural credibility of the scribes – much to the delight of the large crowd (Mark 12.37) – Jesus proceeds to put the boot in. (Or the sandal, possibly.) Given the fact that one of the scribes had only just expressed support for Jesus, we cannot take his comments in Mark 12.38ff. as a blanket denunciation. But evidently there were enough posers within the ranks of the scribes for them to deserve the criticism.

The scribe's uniform was a long robe of white linen, fringed at the bottom. White clothes were marks of distinction and purity – men of eminence wore them, particularly in the Temple. Bright colours were left to the common people. (And to the very common, whatever clothes they could afford).[11] The Mishnah records that scribes were treated with respect: people were supposed to stand when they passed by, with only craftsmen being given exemption. One suspects that this is more what the Mishnah hoped would happen, rather than the reality; either way, status is one thing: pay is another. The evidence shows that these bureaucrats came from the poorer classes.[12] There were some high-status priestly scribes, attached to the Temple, and working in effect for the central government.[13] These would have drawn some kind of income from the Temple treasury, but, for most scribes, it must have been a case of living on subsidies. It was forbidden that scribes should be paid for exercising their profession, so people were encouraged to respect their learning by giving them hospitality.[14] Sometimes this didn't happen: two renowned scholars of Rabbi Gamaliel are recorded as having nothing to eat or wear, while the famous teacher Rabbi Aqiba was forced to sleep in the straw in winter.[15]

But often they were the recipients of charity from pious Jews. It was honourable to support a scribe – and the scribes knew that.[16] Hence the situations that Jesus describes here, where scribes sponge off people with limited means. The widows – the poorest people in society – wanted to do what was right, and how did the scribes repay them? By devouring – by eating them out of house and home. They were the TV evangelists of their day, preying on the pious, taking what little people had and leaving them nothing.

'This poor widow'

For an example of simple piety in action, Jesus points to one of those very widows. Widows were among the poorest and most marginalised people in Jewish society. The concern of the early church to care for these people was evident: 'widow' even became the technical term for women who served in the early Christian community (Acts 9.39).

But here we have a widow with few resources, offering all she can to God. It is significant that Jesus does not point this example out to the crowd, but to his disciples. Was the glamour and glitz of the Temple getting to them? Were they being dazzled by the big amounts that the rich people were throwing into the coffers? Then they should look here. Not at the wealthy but at the totally committed. This woman has given her everything. The episode stands as a poignant example of the real, simple, deep piety that Jesus championed. The piety of the poor was worth much more than the righteousness of the rich. The rabbinic literature also makes this point, telling of a priest who once refused a handful of grain offered by a widow. That night, in a dream, he was reprimanded: 'Do not despise her. It is as if she has offered her life.'[17]

And so the teaching in the Temple draws to a close, with a comparison between two groups of poor people: the scribes and the widows. And the conclusion drawn by Jesus is that the widows were the holier of the two.

The prophecy about the Temple

Where: Outside the Temple

When: Afternoon

> As he came out of the Temple, one of his disciples said to him, 'Look, Teacher, what large stones and what large buildings!' Then Jesus asked him, 'Do you see these great buildings? Not one stone will be left here upon another; all will be thrown down.' (Mark 13.1–2)

The question-and-argument session ends with Jesus and his followers leaving the Temple. In its way, Jesus' teaching and storytelling on this day is as disruptive as his actions had been the day before. By the time he walks down the steps from the plaza, he has taken shots at the scribes, the Sadducees and the Pharisees; he has queried the very financial basis of the Temple, and he has argued that the outsiders – the poor, the lepers, the tax-collectors, the widows – have more understanding of the kingdom than the people in the fine robes.

His parting shot is to have a crack at the Temple building itself. Despite all that Jesus has said, the disciples cannot hold back on their admiration for the building. Jesus' response is abrupt and demoralising. It sounds like a threat – and this is how his opponents chose to report it – but it's actually a prophecy. The building is a figment. Its foundations are built on sand. It's all going to come crashing down. Imagine someone looking at the Houses of Parliament, or the White House, and saying to a group of followers: 'This is all going to be destroyed.' Those words were to come back to haunt him.

In a way, this brief statement summarises where the events, symbols, statements and stories of the past three days have left us. The destruction of the Temple is a consequence of everything that Jesus has criticised through his words and actions. Jesus entered the city on Sunday as an alternative king. His entrance procession proclaimed him to be the Messiah, and at the same time was an implicit put-down of the alternative kingdoms – the wealth, power and prestige which was entering from the other side of the city. The key theme of Jesus' kingdom was peace and love, and the citizens of his kingdom were the outsiders.

On the Monday he attacked the abuses that had become part and parcel of the Temple system. His assault on the moneychangers and the sacrifice-sellers was an attack on the way that money had become central to the cult, on the way that the prophets had been sacrificed for profit. The Temple leaders, like the fig tree, were to be judged for their behaviour.

Now, on Tuesday, the Sadducees, Pharisees, scribes and Herodians have all been shown to be wanting. Their view of Scripture was shallow; their behaviour self-serving and arrogant; their hypocrisy breathtaking; and their vision of the Messiah as an aristocratic king – as, frankly, one of their own class – was inadequate.

Finally, he claims that the very building will come crashing down. This symbol of Israel will be destroyed. You can imagine how his words would have been reported. Those experts in 'whispering', the House of Hanan, would perhaps have had people in the crowd to 'overhear'. (Or maybe they were later given this information by an insider.)

Right back at the Lazarus incident we saw that Caiaphas' main aim was to preserve the Temple and the nation. That was what mattered; that was what had been entrusted to him. And, despite the abuses of power, we should not assume that Caiaphas and his supporters did not hold this as a deeply sincere belief. They really did believe in the Temple and they really were trying to hold the nation together. The trouble is, according to Jesus, that the abuses in their system and the policies that they have been pursuing – both political and religious – will actually result in the very thing that they wish to avoid. Those who seek to save the Temple in that way will lose it. And to those on the other side of the coin, those opponents of Rome, those extremists who would argue for violent revolution, the result for them will be equally catastrophic. The way of violence and the way of compromise will lead to the same destination.

The Temple will be destroyed: root and branch.

Opposite: Temple Mount viewed from the Mount of Olives. The Dome of the Rock stands where the Temple once stood. Beyond the Dome are the two cupolas which mark the Church of the Holy Sepulchre.

The prophecy about the future

Where: Mount of Olives

When: Evening

So Jesus and his followers leave Jerusalem, cross the Kidron Valley and sit on the Mount of Olives looking at the Temple. It's the evening, and, as they look across the valley, the sun is setting behind the Temple, which is glowing white and gold in the twilight. An appropriate time and place for Jesus to talk about how it is all going to end. The conversation runs on from Jesus' statement about the Temple's destruction. 'When will this happen?' ask the disciples. 'What are the signs?'

So Jesus tells them. Whether Jesus actually said all of what is recorded in Mark 13 on the day, or whether it is gathered together from other times and sources, doesn't really change the main thrust. As Jesus sits there, as the sun sets behind Jerusalem, he tells them a tale of death and destruction, of cities besieged, of earth-shattering events and people running to the hills. A tale, in fact, of the apocalypse.

'When will this be, and what will be the sign?'

For most ancient cultures, time, in terms of beginning, middle and end, didn't exist. Seasons came and went, years rolled around, one empire was replaced by another. It was the Jews who invented the idea that time might not be circular, that there might be a moment when things changed. They called this moment 'The Day of the Lord', and it would be the point at which God would step in and restore the proper nature of things. Judgement would be meted out – mainly to Israel's enemies.[18]

So strong was this theme in Jewish thought that it spawned an entire literary genre: apocalyptic. The Greek word *apokalupsis* actually means 'revelation'. An apocalyptic work is something that reveals what will happen. Scholars are divided (as they are on most things) about how to define apocalyptic literature. It's the science fiction of biblical literature – we know it only when we see it.[19] We know, for example, that the book of Revelation is different from the letter of James; the language is different, the story is different – there is an 'otherness' about apocalyptic literature which marks it out.

The language of apocalyptic literature can cause problems, not only because modern readers have difficulty decoding the symbols, but also because we sometimes don't think they are symbols at all. Because apocalyptic literature uses earth-shattering language, we conclude that it must be about the actual shattering of the earth. It must, in short, be about the 'end of the universe'.

This is how we tend to use the word 'apocalypse'; it is equated with disaster and destruction, with tumbling mountains and nuclear explosions, with the end of everything, normally in the far future. Terms such as 'apocalypse' and that other favourite, 'Armageddon', have entered popular culture as a kind of shorthand for destruction. But apocalypse is not just about the end of something, it's also about the beginning of something else. It's about transformation and change, about new things coming into being.[20] And it's not about the far-distant future, but about the imminent present. Just as Orwell's *1984* was actually about 1948 (he just reversed the last digits), Jewish apocalyptic literature is nearly always about what is happening all around, or what will happen in the imminent future.

As a genre, apocalyptic literature was, and still is, favoured by alienated and marginalised groups. Cults are big fans of apocalypse. Many cults live in expectation of transformation (often with the help of aliens.) It's the literature of the outsider, the visions of the oppressed, the imprisoned, the marginalised. 'One day,' it says, 'all this will be changed. And I'll be proved right. You wait and see.'[21]

This is why Christians embraced the genre so readily; apocalyptic literature gave them the vocabulary they needed to really understand what was going on. Early Christianity – a marginalised faith if ever there was one – was an apocalyptic religion. It lived in the expectation of imminent and dramatic transformation and it produced, in the book of Revelation, perhaps the most influential work of apocalyptic literature that has ever been written. Revelation is, it is generally agreed, about the 'end times'. But it was also about seven churches in Asia and what they were going through. It was a letter, written to them, to explain not only what was to come, but also what was happening around them.

Certainly Jesus believed and preached that the times they were a-changing. Traditional Christian interpretation of Mark 13 relates it to the 'end times' – the end of the world, when, Christians believe, Christ will return. It has become one of those passages pored over by zealous scholars, academics, theologians and even cult leaders, to back up their theories about what will happen in the future. Sadly for most of those people, they're some 1,900 years too late. Because, for a start, Jesus is answering a question about the destruction of the Temple. And we know that took place in AD 70. And it's in that light we have to understand it. It's about imminent events, not long-distance events. It's about destruction and also transformation.[22] In that sense the whole of the Longest Week is apocalyptic. One man will be destroyed and then everything will change.

'Wars and rumours of wars'

> When he was sitting on the Mount of Olives opposite the temple, Peter, James, John, and Andrew asked him privately, 'Tell us, when will this be, and what will be the sign that all these things are about to be accomplished?' (Mark 13.3–4)

Mark chapter 13 and Luke 19.42–4 are most often used to determine the dating of the Gospels, because both are descriptions of events in and around the siege of Jerusalem in AD 70. Scholars assume, therefore, that the Gospel writers have invented Jesus' prophecy using details of the actual siege, recorded by later historians, most notably Josephus. This passage describes the fall of Jerusalem so it must have been written after that date.

There are problems with this argument. First, and most fundamental, it assumes that prophecy of this type is impossible, that it's not possible for one man to look at the present and predict what is going to happen in the future. Even leaving aside ideas about Jesus' divine powers, is it really so unlikely that he could see where the political situation was leading? After all, Caiaphas knew that one wrong turn would bring the Jewish way of life and the Temple crashing down; where he and Jesus differed was that Jesus believed that wrong turn had already been taken.

Second, if this 'prediction' was created by Christian writers after the siege of Jerusalem and then put into the mouth of Jesus, then one has to ask why it wasn't even more dramatic. Josephus actually includes a great many more features of the siege than are included here, notably the sickness, the cannibalism and the fire that destroyed the buildings.[23] You'd have thought in such a dramatic reconstruction that these would not have been left out.

Third, and perhaps most tellingly, the details do *not* fit the event perfectly. Although Jesus says not one stone will be left standing, quite a lot of stones were. (And the huge stones in the Western Wall are still standing.) Not only that, but if those in Jerusalem had fled to the hills during the siege, they would have run straight into the Roman army, which was stationed on the Mount of Olives and Mount Scopus. According to early-church tradition, the Christians in Jerusalem fled to Pella, in Perea, which, far from being in the hills, is 285 feet below sea level! So if the writers were turning history into prophecy they did a pretty bad job of it.

So the argument of scholars who claim that this was written after the event runs like this:

▷ The Gospel writers were making it up based on history.
▷ They got the history wrong.
▷ But they were still making it up anyway.

Surely it makes more sense to argue the other way round: that the passage was genuinely predicting what would happen, but talking in a generalised language, which is why some of the details don't match.

Where might Jesus have got this language from? He is drawing on Old Testament descriptions of judgement and disaster. The terror of those who are fleeing with young children is a direct allusion to Hosea 13.16; the saving of the 'elect' to Isaiah (Isa. 65.8–9), while the warnings against false teachers and leaders is a regular Old Testament theme.[24] The exhortation to flee to the mountains is reminiscent of Ezekiel (Ezek. 7.12–16), but is directly comparable to the description of the Maccabaean crisis:

> Then Mattathias cried out in the town with a loud voice, saying: 'Let everyone who is zealous for the law and supports the covenant come out with me!' Then he and his sons fled to the hills and left all that they had in the town. (1 Macc. 2.27–28)

Fleeing to the hills, apparently, was what you did, in times of siege; just as, in later cultures, hiding under the stairs was what you did in times of an air-raid. And very few people in New Testament times who knew anything of the Roman world at large were ignorant of warfare. The Romans had already inflicted siege warfare on Jerusalem once, and some twenty-five years earlier they had marched through Galilee destroying towns and cities after the abortive revolt following the death of Herod. The techniques were well known. So, if one were convinced that a conflict was coming, it would not take a great prophet to know the pattern of things. The description Jesus gives of life in Jerusalem in the coming conflict is common to many cities which were attacked by the Romans. All that differed in Jerusalem was the scale.

Jesus was a prophet, but you didn't necessarily have to be a prophet to see what lay ahead. There's a war coming. Both Jesus and his disciples knew what warfare was like. Cities are besieged, earthworks and ramps are thrown up, starvation and death is everywhere. And those who are able flee to the hills. Just as Caiaphas feared, the Romans will take everything away and they will do it in the way they always do it. They will besiege the city. They will plant their standards in the Temple area. And it will be a judgement of God on the leaders of Israel and their inability to embrace his message.

'Let the reader understand'

It's beyond the scope of this book to look in detail at the theology of Mark 13, but we can draw some inferences from the statements it contains. Jesus' teaching will be distorted by false teachers (Mark 13.6). There will be battles and wars (Mark 13.7-8). Those who follow Jesus will face persecution, trials and even ostracism from within their own family as the good news of Jesus is spread abroad (Mark 13.9–13). Finally, there will be sacrilege on the Temple Mount, similar to that seen in the days of the Maccabees, when a pagan altar was set up in the sanctuary itself (Mark 13.14). That will be the moment to flee, the moment when the hardship is at its worst and when any number of false leaders will arise (Mark 13.14–22).

Thus far, Jesus' description fits well with the eventual revolt and destruction of Jerusalem, a time that saw the Romans take over the Temple Mount and during which a number of false messiahs arose. We know, also, from Acts, that in the years after Jesus' death and before the great revolt those who followed Jesus did face persecution and suffering. So we can see that what Jesus is picturing here are real historical events, which took place in the decades from AD 35–70.

But what about the next bit? What about the darkening of the sun and the moon? What about the falling stars and the Son of Man arriving on clouds? What about the angels and the elect and the ends of the earth (Mark 13.24–27)? Once again we have to recognise that we are dealing with the vocabulary of apocalyptic literature. If we take it at face value it makes no sense. (In what literal sense, for example, can stars 'fall'? In which direction would that be?) Instead, the passage is using a highly stylised language to describe the transformation in the world that will take place when the kingdom of God gets a toehold.

And we still use such imagery today. We talk of institutions being 'rocked to their foundations' when no actual earthquake has occurred. We talk of businesses going into 'meltdown' when no heat has actually been applied. Of course, this may be about the far future; it may be about what is called 'the second coming'. Certainly the early church lived in the belief that Jesus would return. And Matthew follows his version of the apocalyptic discourse with a number of parables and strange tales. However, these all have a common theme of sudden appearance or disappearance. The sudden arrival of the rain in Noah's time, for example (Matt. 24.38–39); of people being somehow 'whisked away' (Matt. 24.40–41); of the arrival of thieves, masters and bridegrooms (Matt. 24.45 – 25.13). These are all warnings to be awake and on guard. And he follows these with stories about doing what's right. There is the parable of the talents (Matt. 25.14–30) and the parable of the sheep and the goats (Matt. 25.31–46). These are judgement parables, certainly, and the parable of the sheep and goats has been interpreted as indicating what will happen 'at the end'. But in this context Jesus' main thrust is to warn his disciples to continue doing the right thing. Being aware of the imminent catastrophe does not mean it is time for hiding their treasure, but for sharing it around: it's a time when the hungry must be fed and the naked must be clothed and the thirsty must be given water.

There is work to be done. There are hard times and painful tasks ahead. And Matthew ends this section with a warning:

> When Jesus had finished saying all these things, he said to his disciples, 'You know that after two days the Passover is coming, and the Son of Man will be handed over to be crucified.' (Matt. 26.1–2)

The apocalypse is closer than they think.

Day Four: The Plot and the Perfume
Wednesday 1 April

The plot to kill Jesus: The Temple, Wednesday morning.
The anointing at Bethany: Bethany, Wednesday evening.
Judas goes to meet the priests: The Temple, Wednesday night.

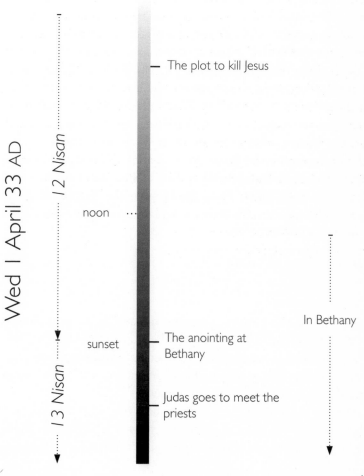

Wed 1 April 33 AD

12 Nisan

13 Nisan

noon

sunset

— The plot to kill Jesus

— The anointing at Bethany

— Judas goes to meet the priests

In Bethany

The plot to kill Jesus

Where: Jerusalem

When: Morning

> It was two days before the Passover and the festival of Unleavened Bread. The chief priests and the scribes were looking for a way to arrest Jesus by stealth and kill him; for they said, 'Not during the festival, or there may be a riot among the people.' (Mark 14.1–2)

Mark begins the next section with another time marker; however, the Greek phrase *meta duo hemeras* can mean 'on the second day' (i.e. 'tomorrow') and that may be the sense in which Mark is using it here. But the more usual translation – and the one preferred by the majority of modern English versions – is 'two days away', which fits better with John's chronology.

By now the festival is fast approaching and this lends a new urgency to the Temple aristocracy's task. Jesus is still protected by the crowd and a direct arrest will lead to a riot, the very thing they want to avoid. Once again, the myth that 'the Jews' killed Jesus is undermined: the leaders of the Temple are unable to arrest him because the Jews do not want him killed.

So they can't risk the arrest happening during the festival itself, the time when Jerusalem was at its most feverish. And they can't do it while he is teaching in the Temple because there will be a riot. They need a plan. And they really need some inside information.

The anointing at Bethany

Where: Bethany

When: Early evening

According to the Gospel accounts, not much happens during the day on Wednesday. It may well be that Jesus didn't go into Jerusalem at all. He knows the temperature is rising, so he stays out of the way. However, he has an engagement – an evening meal at the house of Simon the Leper.

Not the most attractive name: Simon the 'Skin-Disease Sufferer'. Simon the human scab. So, who was this man? Well, obviously he was, or had been at some time, a leper, perhaps one of those whom Jesus had, at some point, healed. The Gospels contain several accounts. However, what the Gospels call leprosy is not what we today would call leprosy. The modern term for leprosy is Hansen's disease. Leprosy in ancient times was a catch-all term for any skin rashes, blemishes or other kinds of disfigurement – a generic term for scaly skin diseases.[1] Such diseases led to ostracism and expulsion. In Job, leprosy is described as 'death's firstborn'.[2] Leprosy turned you into the walking dead, and we have seen how pious Jews felt about touching the dead.

To touch a leper, therefore, was to make yourself unclean. So lepers were kept in a state of almost permanent quarantine. Being under the same roof as a leper made you impure; lying or eating within the house would necessitate a complete change of clothes (Lev. 14.33–47). Even putting a part of your body into the house would make you unclean:

> If a man that was clean put his head and the greater part of his body inside a house that was unclean, he becomes unclean; and if a man that was unclean put his head and the greater part of his body inside a house that was clean, he renders it unclean.[3]

The only houses that could not be made unclean through contact with lepers were those owned by Gentiles – who were unclean anyway.[4] The rabbinical writings, the New Testament and writings from Qumran all presuppose the exclusion of lepers from communities. They were not allowed into cities or towns. The lepers Jesus encountered on the edge of a village in Samaria shouted at him from a distance (Luke 17.12).

And, of course, if you can't enter the city, there is absolutely no chance that you will be allowed near the Temple.[5] Although the accounts of Jerusalem being kept entirely pure may well belong to wishful idealisation of the post-second century, one would have thought that special care would be taken in Jerusalem, since the proximity of lepers to Temple worshippers would have rendered the pilgrims unclean. You come all that way and you bump into a leper and that's the trip ruined. Or, at least, you have to go through yet another purification ritual.

All of which may be why Simon lived in Bethany. There may well have been leper colonies to the east of Jerusalem in the region of Bethany. The Temple Scroll of the Qumran community is a picture of an idealised Temple, but it may reflect the reality, when it talks of making areas east of the city – which is where Bethany was – for lepers.[6] Whatever the case, the fact that Jesus is having a meal at his house reinforces how often Jesus stepped outside the social and religious boundaries of his time. He reached out and touched lepers. He went into their houses and he ate with them. Once again this is an incident that demonstrates how far Jesus was prepared to challenge the taboos of his day in order to include the excluded.

'He was reclining at table'

Jesus was a man who liked a meal. Throughout the Gospels we hear of him sharing a table with people: both the orthodox and the unorthodox, the respectable people and the outcasts. Indeed, such was his delight in meals that he was accused of being a glutton and a drunkard (Matt. 11.19; Luke 7.34). In the ancient world, food held greater symbolism than it does for us today. To share a table with someone was to show them acceptance, to proclaim, in fact, that they were your friends, that they were all right.

As to what they ate, we can make some guesses, even based on very recent history, for, as one historian has written, 'large portions of the rural Arab diets recorded in the 19th century and the beginning of the 20th century included ingredients comparable to those of ancient times'.[7]

The main source of calories was bread. Bread in Palestine was leavened; it had yeast added to it. The grinding of the wheat dominated the day. The housewife and her daughters would need to rise early and grind the daily portion of wheat, then make the dough and bake it. 'A family of six or seven people would grind flour for three to four hours every morning.' (Hence, the 'daily grind'.)[8] There might be pulses, such as lentils, broad beans, chickpeas and peas.[9] Vegetables included garlic and onions, lettuce, kale, radishes, carrots, turnips, squash and cucumber. And there were olives, of course, along with grapes, dates, figs walnuts, almonds, pomegranates and peaches.

And there would be wine. In ancient Israel, and in the Græco-Roman world generally, the inhabitants did not drink the water. Water wasn't safe. Instead they drank wine. Talmudic sources indicate that a family might get through between 330 and 375 litres of wine each year, the equivalent of 440–500 bottles of wine today.[10] But the wine would be mixed half and half with water, or even one-third to two-thirds, depending on strength.[11]

For this meal, as it was a special occasion, perhaps they would have had some meat: most likely lamb or goat (65–70 per cent of the bones found in excavations are goat or sheep), although beef, poultry, fish, pigeons and even songbirds were also eaten.

'Ointment of pure nard'

So much for the menu.

There are different accounts of what happened at this meal. The essence of the tale is this: while Jesus is sitting at the table, a woman comes up to him, breaks open a jar of expensive perfumed ointment, and pours it on his head. The people in the room complain about the action, arguing that the ointment could have been sold to feed the poor, but Jesus defends her. The poor would always be there, he says, but this woman has done something that would be remembered for ever.

That's the basic tale as found in Mark 14.4–9. However, the story flowers in all of the Gospels, each time in a slightly different form. Mark places it in Bethany, on the Wednesday night and in the home of Simon the Leper. Matthew follows suit, but tells us that it was the disciples who complained. John places it in the house of Lazarus in Bethany, with Mary putting the ointment on Jesus' feet and wiping it away with her hair. Luke places it in Capernaum, much earlier in Jesus' ministry, in the house of a Pharisee called Simon, where an unnamed 'sinful' woman anoints Jesus' feet with both ointment and tears.

It seems to me that we're dealing with two stories here, which share similar elements and which become somewhat entwined. Luke tells us of one story where, in Galilee, an unnamed 'sinful' woman comes and anoints Jesus not only with ointment but with her tears, and wipes them away with her hair. The point of Luke's story is forgiveness – the people are scandalised by the very presence of this sinner (most likely a prostitute), but Jesus contrasts her gratitude with the relatively cool hospitality he has received from his host. Mark's story is different. It is not so much about gratitude, but about exclusion and emotion and death.

Can we say who this woman was? Not with any certainty.[12] John tells us it was Mary of Bethany. This may be because he was connecting two traditions: he knew that Jesus was anointed at a meal in Bethany and he knew that he stayed in Bethany with Lazarus' household. So he may have just done the maths: worshipping woman + Bethany = Mary. Having said that, the behaviour of this guest does fit well with the other accounts of Mary's somewhat unorthodox behaviour. After the raising of Lazarus, Mary certainly had reason to be grateful to Jesus. Not only that but Jesus' defence of her actions – 'She has done what she could… wherever the good news is proclaimed in the whole world, what she has done will be told in remembrance of her' (Mark 14.8–9) – is reminiscent of his defence of her when she took on the role of a disciple: 'Mary has chosen the better part, which will not be taken away from her' (Luke 10.42). Nor is it out of character for Mary: pouring the most valuable pot of perfume on the feet of Jesus is exactly the kind of hero-worship you expect from an impulsive young woman.

Whoever it was, we are told that Jesus was reclining, lying on one side, so the inference is that the woman came from behind and poured the perfume on him. Fragranced ointment was in daily use in the ancient world – at least among the moderately well off. People anointed themselves on a daily basis (see, for example, Matt. 6.17). The richer you were, the more exotic the ointment you used, but most people used a fragranced olive oil.

It was the biblical equivalent of aftershave or eau-de-cologne. The use of ointments was medicinal as well as cosmetic, but the primary use was obvious: to make people smell better. In a world without much sanitation this really mattered.

The perfume in this incident is identified as being rare and expensive. Nard was imported from the Himalayan Mountains of India and, according to Pliny, held 'the foremost possible rank among perfumes'.[13] Such perfume would have travelled thousands of miles to reach this village outside Jerusalem, borne along the extensive trade routes that operated in Græco-Roman times. Caravans carried these precious commodities across land routes from either the Arabian desert or the Red Sea ports.[14]

The extent of Mediterranean trade in the Roman world can be seen from this anonymous account:

> Into this trading port [of Barygaza] come wine, principally Italian, but also Laodicean and Arabian, copper, tin, and lead; coral and peridot; all kinds of clothing, plain and patterned; multicoloured girdles a cubit wide; storax, yellow sweet clover, raw glass; realgar, sulphide of antimony; Roman gold and silver money, which is exchanged at some profit against the local coinage; and ointment, inexpensive but not much of it… Exported from this region are nard, costus, bdellium, ivory, onyx… agate; all kinds of cloth, Chinese [silk]…[15]

The roots of the spikenard plant provided the perfume. The finely shaped *alabastron* – or alabaster jar – that the woman owned (Matt. 26.7) was the Græco-Roman equivalent of the fancy perfume bottle. It is significant that she broke the flask to open it, meaning that all of it had to be used. According to the people in the room, it was worth 300 denarii – ten months' pay for an average working peasant. Pliny backs up these high prices, recording that the cost of the most luxurious perfume could exceed 400 denarii per pound.[16]

However, one wonders if they were really that worried by the cost. Complaining about the cost of something is often a cover for another complaint. What made this act really scandalous was not the cost of the ointment, but the person doing the anointing.

'Let her alone; why do you trouble her?'

Independent women – single and apparently unmarried – feature prominently among Jesus' supporters. We have women such as Mary Magdalene, Mary and Martha of Bethany, and Susanna (Luke 8.2–3). Indeed, generally, Jesus gave women a status and a purpose that was rare in the first century. In the Græco-Roman world generally, and in Judaea certainly, women were second-class citizens – and the birth of a girl a disappointment. The Jewish apocryphal work, *Ben Sira*, says 'It is a disgrace to be the father of an undisciplined son, and the birth of a daughter is a loss.'[17]

They could gain a measure of independence. Women could and did have jobs. They could be set up as shopkeepers by their husband.[18] Women could sell olives or serve in the family store.[19] Or they might be innkeepers, providing domestic services for travellers. There are cases in the Mishnah of women preparing dough for sale in the market, or working as garment makers or spinning and weaving. Women, in fact, made the tapestry which served as the curtain in the Temple. (Of course, they couldn't see it, since that part of the Temple was out of bounds to women.) But for the most part women were restricted to the home. Although they could, and did, get involved in the Temple worship, their main role, in the religious custom of the day, was to make it possible for the man to perform the duties. It was women's exemption from having to perform the commandments that allowed men the time to devote themselves to the purity legislation. Women were seen as 'light-headed'.[20] It was the man's role to debate and discuss and learn: the women were there to cook.[21] Women had few rights. They could not initiate divorce, except in the case of impurity. Men, on the other hand, could divorce a woman for virtually any reason.[22]

Most important of all, perhaps, was the conviction that God simply did not talk to women: 'In the name of R. Eliezer b. R. Shimeon: we have not found that the Almighty spoke to a woman except Sarah.'[23]

And women were *dangerous*. They provoked lust. The later Rabbis were emphatic about the danger of even looking at a woman.[24] Jesus too warned about looking at women, but he was clear that the issue was with the man looking, not the woman being looked at. Even in death a woman could be a temptation, which is why men were hanged naked, but women clothed.

In particular, their hair was a source of great temptation. A woman – at least any woman who knew how to behave properly – always went out with her head covered.[25] A woman's hair was considered sexually provocative, much in the same way as her breasts might be considered in Western society today. Going out with your head uncovered was like showing a lot of cleavage: pious women covered their heads in public (and the ultra-pious even kept their hair covered in the home). In the list of offences for which a man may divorce his wife without any financial settlement, the Mishnah includes, 'If she goes out with her hair unbound, or spins *[in the sense of spinning yarn]* in the street, or speaks with any man'.[26] It was an immensely shocking act which had dire consequences for any married woman. In the Babylonian Talmud, Rabbi Meir teaches that it is the religious duty of a man to divorce a woman who does this.[27] This explains the shocked response to the tale as told in Luke and John. The woman's use of her hair was utterly scandalous.

In Mark's story the hair remains in place, but even so the tale is not free from cultural outrage. A woman is stepping out from the role that has been assigned to her, crossing the boundaries. A woman was not expected to engage in debate with men; during the meal, she would be expected to serve the meal but not to speak. But this woman *has* to speak. This woman has to be heard. And the only way that she can be heard is to break open the bottle and fill the house with fragrance. This is not some decorous, careful, polite act: it's the passionate, heartfelt cry of someone whom society has silenced. There were, literally, no words she could say – or she was allowed to say – so she uses her own vocabulary. She makes her own, wordless claims about Christ, using the language of touch and smell.

The disciples rebuke the woman –according to Mark they scold her harshly – but they don't really understand. They don't speak her language. But this woman, she gets it; she sees what is going on. She can see, in the way that only the downtrodden could see, that Jesus was going to be punished. She understands the consequences of breaking social and religious taboos; she understands, as a woman in her position must, that powerful men have no forgiveness for someone who dares to challenge the status quo. Those raised in prison know instinctively what is in store for those who dare to raise the prospect of escape.

This is why Jesus commends her action. He sees in her someone who understands what must happen. What his disciples saw as waste and loss was in fact a priceless deed, whose value would endure as long as the gospel was proclaimed, a beautiful tale that would be told throughout the centuries. She was, in a way, enacting what lay in store. In touch and smell she was writing the first commentary on Jesus' death. By breaking open the jar and anointing Jesus in preparation for his burial, she was paralleling another act of brokenness which would be talked about for ever: the crucifixion itself.

Was it Mary or another woman? Was it on Sunday or Wednesday? Was it at Lazarus' house or at the house of Simon the Leper? We can debate the historicity and the details. But what is startlingly obvious is that this event was another example of Jesus' unique relationship with women. They listened to him; they debated with him; they made statements about him. The formal society offered them no easy route in which to do this. But, like the stones of Jerusalem, they could not be silent.

Judas goes to meet the priests

Where: Jerusalem

When: Late evening

> Then Judas Iscariot, who was one of the twelve, went to the chief
> priests in order to betray him to them. When they heard it, they
> were greatly pleased, and promised to give him money. So he began
> to look for an opportunity to betray him. (Mark 14.10–11)

After the meal, the disciples and Jesus, presumably, return to
their quarters to sleep. Were they all staying with Lazarus?
Possibly not, which would make it easier for one of them to
slip away. Judas Iscariot has made his decision. Maybe the perfume incident was the last straw; maybe it was Jesus' continued
attacks on the religious institutions; maybe it was just that he
could see which way the wind was blowing…

We know little of Judas. His father was called Simon (John
6.71) and he was one of the twelve. Even his identifying name
– Iscariot – doesn't help, since, in the Greek, the Gospels spell
it in ten different forms.[28] The most popular explanation is that
he came from a town called Kerioth, but since we don't know
where Kerioth was that doesn't really help. In some texts the
Greek word is 'Skariotes', which some scholars interpret as a
corruption of the word *siccarius*. Josephus describes the *Sicarii*
as dagger-wielding fanatical revolutionaries and assassins, but
there is no evidence to show that this group appeared until
twenty or thirty years after Judas' death.[29]

However, one wonders whether that was really the motive.
Scholars have debated long and hard over the supposed motive
of Judas. What was he trying to achieve? More to the point,
what had he got to sell?

Some claim that the information Judas sold to the authorities was not the location of Jesus, but the information that he
claimed to be the Messiah, the King of the Jews.[30] But they
could have got anyone to claim that. (Indeed, that's exactly
what they did.) No, what Judas knew was where to find Jesus
when the crowd couldn't get in the way, where the Temple
authorities could send a snatch squad to do the task quickly,

quietly and without attracting attention. They valued what the powerful have always been willing to pay for: discretion.

This is what Judas has to sell. As to his motive, there have been many ideas put forward. One idea – the most charitable perhaps – is that he was actually trying to force Jesus' hand. He believed Jesus to be the Messiah but somehow Jesus kept avoiding the job. Every time there was the chance to start the revolution, Jesus headed off in another direction. Judas knew – he had seen – the power that Jesus had at his disposal. Yet day after day in the Temple he was doing nothing about it.

Or maybe it was the opposite: that Judas was simply disillusioned with Jesus. Perhaps even outraged by his behaviour. Consider when the betrayal happens: immediately after a woman – a woman! – has poured perfume on Jesus' head. And when the disciples remonstrate they are dismissed by Jesus out of hand. Perhaps he had simply had enough of being treated this way. Perhaps he had had enough of Jesus' flagrant shattering of the social and religious mores.

Or perhaps it is more simple. Perhaps it was just a question of money. That's always the chink in the armour. When the disciples talked about feeding the poor, when they reacted to the flagrant use of expensive, luxurious perfume, was it that there was a hint of resentment there? They, after all, were poor. And here they were in the richest city in Judaea, confronted by the wealthy and the powerful in all their finery. It would be surprising if a tinge of jealousy hadn't coloured their vision. As Peter said when they were approaching Jerusalem: 'Look, we have left everything and followed you.' To which Jesus replied:

> Truly I tell you, there is no one who has left house or brothers or sisters or mother or father or children or fields, for my sake and for the sake of the good news, who will not receive a hundredfold now in this age... (Mark 10.28–29)

Jesus seemed to promise his disciples a reward. Yet, so far, they had seen nothing. And the only riches they had seen – an alabaster jar of perfume – had been lavished on the leader. So perhaps the motive of Judas was simply money. The amount offered – thirty silver shekels – was worth about sixty days' wages. This was not a token payment.

It is possible that other motives were involved, but in that case one imagines that they would have been recorded. Judas' notoriety, after all, lay in the act of handing over; the motive was immaterial. But the fact that money features twice in his story, and the fact that it was not a small sum of money, indicates that perhaps he simply saw the way the things were going: he knew this was going to end in disaster and he was going to get out while there was still something to be salvaged from the wreckage.

Day Five: The Arrest
Thursday 2 April

The preparations for the meal: Jerusalem, Thursday morning
The last supper: Jerusalem – the Upper Room, Thursday evening
The arrest: Garden of Gethsemane, Thursday night/Friday morning

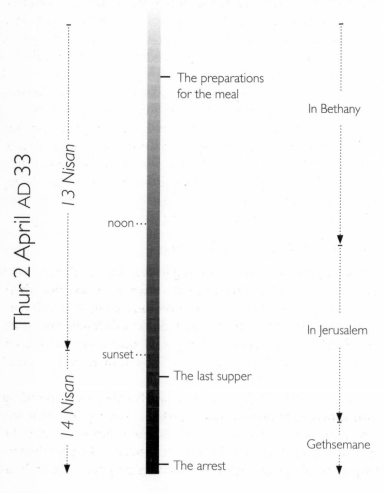

The preparations
for the meal

In Bethany

noon···

Thur 2 April AD 33

13 Nisan

14 Nisan

sunset···

The last supper

In Jerusalem

Gethsemane

The arrest

Preparations for the meal

Where: Jerusalem

When: Morning

> On the first day of Unleavened Bread, when the Passover lamb is sacrificed, his disciples said to him, 'Where do you want us to go and make the preparations for you to eat the Passover?' (Mark 14.12)

Passover was the great festival in which Jews remembered and celebrated their rescue from slavery in Egypt. In the Jewish calendar it was celebrated on 14 or 15 Nisan and was followed by the feast of Unleavened Bread, which began on 15–21 Nisan. These holidays were usually thought of as the week of Passover.

Mark and Luke describe the Thursday as 'the first day of Unleavened Bread (Mark 14.12; Luke 22.7), when the Passover lamb is sacrificed'; Matthew simply calls it 'the first day of Unleavened Bread' (Matt. 26.17). In the Synoptic Gospels, therefore, the Last Supper is a Passover meal. John, however, dates the Last Supper a day earlier than the Synoptics, and puts the crucifixion on the day of Preparation (John 13.1; 18.28; 19.14, 31, 42). He never calls it a Passover meal; he says that Jesus died at the same time as the Passover lambs were being slaughtered in the Temple.

Houston, we have a problem.

'I will keep the Passover at your house'

Some ingenious theories have suggested that the Passover was celebrated by different groups at different times, that there was a different Passover date for Galileans, compared to Judaeans, or that the Pharisees celebrated it at a different time from the Sadducees. It has been suggested that Jesus was following some kind of Essene calendar. None of these have received widespread support.[1]

The simplest solution is just to say that they were recording two different traditions, one of which stated it was Passover and the other which said it wasn't. In this solution, most of the time it is John who gets downgraded, because he uses the iconography of Passover to make theological points about Jesus and his role. It is assumed that John changed the date so that he could use the symbolism of the Passover lamb.

Except that when we look at John's account, it's just *better*. It has a coherence that the Synoptics lack. John seems to know more about Passover – about the way it operated in first-century Jerusalem – than the Synoptics do.[2] He knows, for example, the distinction between the Passover and the feast of the Unleavened Bread. In the verse above, Mark describes the day as 'the first day of Unleavened Bread, when the Passover lamb is sacrificed' (Mark 14.12), but technically, the festival of Unleavened Bread began *after* Passover: the first day of Unleavened Bread is Nisan 15, whereas the Passover lamb was slain on Nisan 14.[3] Now it might be that by Jesus' day the 'festival' was understood to include the day before, just as we might include Christmas Eve in our term 'Christmas', but even so, John is technically correct.[4] At the very least there's a bit of confusion in the Synoptic terminology.

Then there's all the action that Matthew, Mark and Luke include on the day after the Last Supper. If the Last Supper was the Passover meal, then we have to believe that on the next day – a holy day, the day of Passover itself – the Temple authorities sent out soldiers, held a trial and took Jesus to the Roman officials. We have to believe that Joseph of Arimathea was able to go out and buy grave clothes for Jesus (Mark 15.46). All this would have been possible on the eve of Passover but not on Passover itself.[5] In the words of Weiss:

> All the violations of the Sabbath, of which Jesus was accused, would have appeared as trifles in comparison with the actions of the supreme council in sending out armed servants, conducting a troublesome trial, condemning Jesus at an official sitting of the legislature, and finally inciting the complaisant procurator to a desecration of the day by an execution – and all this on such a Sabbatical feast day.[6]

John, on the other hand, includes a number of incidental details which fit perfectly with the idea that Jesus was killed on the day of Preparation. The disciples thought that Judas was going to make a donation to the poor on the night of the meal, which would be possible the night before Passover, but not on the night itself. According to John, the priests accusing Jesus refused to enter the Roman Prefect's headquarters for fear of being rendered impure through contact with Gentiles. This would have stopped them from celebrating the Passover feast later in the day; they would not have had enough time to purify themselves again.[7] And from the point of view of the Temple authorities, the arrest and execution of Jesus on the day of Preparation, when most of the people were getting ready for Passover, or heading towards the Temple on the other side of the city, fits perfectly with their aim of keeping Jesus away from the crowds. It's the moment of biggest distraction.

Even within the Synoptic accounts, there is some confusion. Luke has Jesus saying: 'I have eagerly desired to eat this Passover with you before I suffer', immediately followed by the frankly baffling statement, 'for I tell you, I will not eat it until it is fulfilled in the kingdom of God' (Luke 22.15–16). So is he going to eat a Passover meal or not? Some have suggested that what Jesus is actually saying here is that 'I wanted to share this Passover meal with you, but it's not going to happen, because they're going to kill me.'[8]

Finally, the description of the meal in the Synoptics is not entirely consistent with the Passover meal. It's true that the singing of the Psalm accords with Passover practices (Matt. 26.30, Mark 14.26).[9] And Jesus finds a room inside the city to eat the meal, as commanded by the Passover rules, but he doesn't stay there. Jewish custom demanded that the night, not just the meal, should be spent in Jerusalem: immediately after the meal, Jesus goes out of the city, across to the Mount of Olives.[10] Most noticeably, in the meal itself, there's one crucial element that is conspicuous by its absence: there is bread and wine, as required by the Passover feast (although these were common elements of virtually any meal), but there's no lamb. The lamb – the most important element of the Passover meal – is never mentioned. The Synoptics have no mention of any lamb being slaughtered; the only preparations on their day of

Preparation consist of finding a discreet, almost secret venue. And, during the meal, when Jesus speaks to his disciples, he compares his body not to the lamb, but to the bread. This is an argument from silence, I admit, but it seems improbable that Jesus would have ignored the lamb, with all its associations, and picked up the bread instead.

The final element in this puzzle is the tradition of the early church. The early church never assumed that the Last Supper was a Passover meal; instead they celebrated it weekly, or even daily. There were elements in the early church who believed that the Last Supper was a Passover meal, but they seem to have been a marginal group: Appollinaris of Hierapolis called them ignorant and contentious.[11]

To sum up: Mark, Matthew and Luke say it was a Passover meal, but hardly anything in their account actually looks like Passover. Their accounts, in fact, tally perfectly with a meal held on the night before Passover. John says it wasn't a Passover meal, and his description of events fits much better with the known facts. So, going by the historical accounts alone, we have to go with John. The Last Supper was held on the night before Passover and the meal was not a Passover meal.

Or maybe it was…

'I have eagerly desired to eat this Passover with you before I suffer'

We have already seen that Jesus' attitude to purity laws was one of the things that most angered the religious authorities. If we add to that the belief he had in his divine mission, it is perfectly reasonable to assume that Jesus was using the phrase 'Passover meal' as a generic term, as a description of what they were going to do, even though they were going to do it a day early.[12] It would have been impossible to celebrate Passover a day early in its fullest sense, of course, because the lamb needed sacrificing. But as we have seen, there was no lamb. So perhaps this was a Passover meal of Jesus' own devising, held at his own time and using some of the iconography of Passover. It followed the tradition of eating the meal within the walls of the city and with a small group of up to twenty people, but it did not include the lamb, because no lambs could be prepared. It used, instead, the ordinary elements, because they were going to be something that all families had available to them. Even the poor could have bread and wine. Just as John reinterpreted ritual bathing, Jesus is reinterpreting the Passover meal, investing it with a new significance, reshaping its traditional patterns into a new picture.

There are precedents for religious sects 'doing their own thing'. The most notable is the Qumran community. The documents describing their religious activities do not mention the Passover.[13] But even without those precedents, Jesus' Last Supper – the 'Passover Meal' he was to share with his followers – conforms precisely to his other activities during the Longest Week. He has criticised the Temple, he has pointed to the sacrifice of a widow as being more significant than the other offerings, he taught that loving others and loving God was better than any amount of sacrifice, he claimed that tax-collectors and prostitutes were entering the kingdom of God ahead of the priests.

Now he is simply changing the calendar.

'A man carrying a jar of water will meet you'

To make the arrangements, Jesus sends 'two of his disciples' ahead. It is reminiscent of the arrangements for his triumphal entry: there is a clandestine meeting with a man carrying water, and a cryptic message. The name 'Jesus' is never mentioned, only 'the Teacher'. The anonymity is telling. This is not a miraculous, coincidental meeting, but a carefully pre-planned operation.

The two disciples he sent were not from 'the twelve'. Mark's statement 'when it was evening, he came with the twelve' (Mark 14.17) implies that they remained in Bethany and only entered the city later. Since Passover was celebrated in groups of anything up to twenty people, we don't have to assume that either the Last Supper or the rest of the night's events involved only Jesus and the apostles. A wider group, including women, may have been present, which is why the room is described as 'large' (Mark 14.15).

But why send two anonymous disciples to swap code-words with a stranger? The most obvious explanation is that he doesn't want the twelve to know the location. This meal is important: after the meal, there's a sense in which Jesus feels he's done all that he can do; he then lets events take their course. So Jesus wants to ensure that the meal goes ahead, and the one man who could stop it, the one man who must not know the location ahead of time, was a member of the twelve. Jesus is making sure that Judas doesn't find out.

The upper room was probably on the very top storey of a house, where it was cooler. They were often rooms used for hospitality, as hostels for pilgrims or other social gatherings.[14] The traditional site of the upper room is in the Upper City of Jerusalem. Modern visitors see what's called 'The Upper Room' on the second floor, and beneath it the 'Tomb of David'. Neither is original, but the site may be, for, beneath the existing building, archaeologists have discovered the remains of what may have been a first-century synagogue. This synagogue was probably built by Jewish Christians: plaster fragments were found bearing graffiti, apparently Christian, from the building's original walls and, unlike traditional Jewish synagogues which were oriented towards the Temple Mount, this building points towards the Church of the Holy Sepulchre – the traditional site of Jesus' crucifixion and burial.

Also, the synagogue was built in the late first century, after the Romans had destroyed Jerusalem. At that time, orthodox Jews were not allowed to live in Jerusalem, let alone build synagogues. Christians, however, had fled to Pella (in today's Jordan) shortly before the Jewish rebellion, and were allowed to return. Epiphanius (AD 315–403) wrote that when the Roman Emperor Hadrian visited Jerusalem in AD 130/131, 'a small church of God... marked the site of the [upper room] to which the disciples returned from the Mount of Olives after the Lord had been taken up.' Perhaps the returning Christians built a synagogue on the place where they remembered that the Last Supper had occurred, where the apostles had returned after Jesus' ascension, and where Peter had delivered his sermon at Pentecost.[15]

The Last Supper

Where: Jerusalem – the upper room

When: Evening

> While they were eating, he took a loaf of bread, and after blessing it he broke it, gave it to them, and said, 'Take; this is my body.' Then he took a cup, and after giving thanks he gave it to them, and all of them drank from it. He said to them, 'This is my blood of the covenant, which is poured out for many. Truly I tell you, I will never again drink of the fruit of the vine until that day when I drink it new in the kingdom of God.' (Mark 14.22–25)

Mark's account of the Last Supper is only eight verses long (Mark 14.17–25); Matthew has nine verses – he adds a comment from Judas (Matt. 26.25); Luke follows Mark, but adds the dispute about which disciple is the greatest (Luke 22.24–29), as well as the prediction of Peter's denial (Luke 22.31–33; the other Synoptics place this on the Mount of Olives) and a strange passage about purses and swords (Luke 22.35–38). Even with all that extra material, it still only clocks in at some twenty-four verses.

And then we get to John. 155 verses. Five chapters (13–17). And even with all that, he still misses out the Eucharistic prayer and the bread and the wine, which the others place at the heart of the feast. It does contain some of the elements in the others, but consists mainly of Jesus talking to his disciples. He gets the 'action' of the Last Supper out of the way in chapter 13: the washing of the feet (John 13.1–20), the prediction of betrayal by Judas (John 13.21–30), the new commandment (John 13.31–35) and the prediction of Peter's betrayal (John 13.36–38). After that it's a solid slab of theology: the remaining four chapters consist almost entirely of a long speech by Jesus. Out of the 117 verses in chapters 14–17, 94 per cent consist of Jesus speaking. And the remaining seven verses consist of the disciples asking questions.[16]

It's important to note, however, before we dismiss John's account as unhistorical, that he actually fills in quite a number of the gaps in the other accounts. For one thing, John is the only Gospel that shows Judas actually leaving the room. Nevertheless, John's account is very different. It's beyond the scope of this book – you might be relieved to know – to examine John's account of Jesus' teaching in detail. But if we exclude the teaching material from John, we are left with the following rough outline of the events:

▷ Jesus washes the disciples' feet (John 13.1–20);
▷ Jesus predicts his betrayal and Judas leaves (Mark 14.18–21; Luke 22.21–23; Matt. 26.21–25; John 13.21–30);
▷ They share the bread and wine (Mark 14.22–25; Matt. 26.26–29; Luke 22.15–20);
▷ Jesus talks to his disciples about the future (Luke 22.35–38).

'Lord, are you going to wash my feet?'

Only John records this incident after supper in which Jesus washes the feet of his disciples. However, Luke includes a passage that treats a broadly similar theme – the argument about who is the greatest – so there may well have been a tradition in the early church that an argument about leadership arose during the Last Supper. Indeed, in Matthew's version of the argument about who was the greatest, there is the line 'whoever wishes to be first among you must be your slave' (Matt. 20.27), which is exactly what Jesus is demonstrating here. Because, properly understood, the foot-washing is one of the most radical things that Jesus ever did.

Judaean cities were, as we have seen, filthy. Walking through the streets was a matter of negotiating the dirt and the dust, the excrement and waste matter, ashes from fires, rotten food. At a basic level, then, washing your feet was simply a matter of hygiene. But it was also another piece of purity legislation: anyone entering the Temple was expected to wash their feet and hands at minimum.[17]

No free man washed the feet of others. The task was reserved for slaves, or for wives and children. The lowly nature of the deed can be seen from an episode featuring Rabbi Ishmael. When his mother tried to wash his feet on return from the synagogue he refused to allow her to demean herself. She subsequently asked the court of rabbis to rebuke him for not allowing her the honour.[18]

There was only one group of men who would have to do such a task: slaves.

The Roman Empire relied on slaves. Estimates vary as to how many there were in the Empire, but it was many millions. The majority of these came from the Slavic countries of central Europe – hence the name: slaves were mainly Slavs.[19] Most slaves were trained in domestic duties, or had income-producing skills. Since peasant labour was so cheap, most slaves did not work the land, but, nevertheless, the reality for slaves was a life of unremitting hardship and back-breaking physical labour. Indeed, peasants would have lived at a level of subsistence that might make the life of a domestic slave almost enviable.

In Judaea, there were two kinds of slave: Jewish slaves and Gentile slaves. Gentile slaves, for the most part, arrived in Jerusalem from Tyre. They were mainly Syrian slaves and once in Jerusalem they would have been brought to a special place, a stone, on which they had to stand and be auctioned.[20] Many foreign slaves were forced to become Jewish and be circumcised to protect their owners from coming into contact with a Gentile.[21]

Jewish slaves were not acquired in the same way. A Jewish man could be sold as a slave if he was a thief, and could not afford to pay the necessary compensation. This was the most usual form of Jewish slavery. In other cases he might choose to sell himself, although this was usually the last resort for a man in extreme debt. Israelite girls, under the age of twelve, could also be sold as slaves, but in practice this often meant that they were destined to marry their masters.[22] A Jewish slave would cost you from five to ten minas, while a Gentile slave would cost you anything up to one hundred minas. The reason for this discrepancy was simple: Jewish slaves had a shorter working life.

According to the Torah, a Jewish slave could serve for only six years, whereas a Gentile slave could spend his or her entire life in servitude. And Jewish slaves were 'high maintenance'. As Jews, their life was regulated according to the Old Testament instructions and they were generally treated a lot better. Unlike a Gentile slave a Jewish one could own possessions. His status was protected by the rule in Leviticus which equated a Jewish slave to a 'hired labourer' (Lev. 25.40). That meant they could not be asked to do acts that would make them impure. And one of the things you could not ask a Jewish slave to do was to wash your feet.[23]

Gentile slaves, however, could be asked to do anything – they were impure already.[24] That is why Peter is so shocked by Jesus' action. In the Greek, he splutters incoherently in astonishment: 'Master, you… my!'[25] It's not that he doesn't understand what is going on; he understands only too well. Jesus has descended to the lowest level possible for a human being: the rank of a Gentile slave. This is what is truly shocking about it. It's not just that Jesus is prepared to undress and to clean from the feet of his followers all the crap and the dirt and the dust that they had gathered on the walk in from Bethany; it's that in doing so he assumes the lowest human role possible.

What was his intention in this act? That is a question that has occupied the church for centuries. Was it an image of baptism? Was it an image of forgiveness, by making people clean? I think both explanations reveal only theologians' tendency to overspiritualise. What he was doing was taking on the role of a slave, doing the lowest job that was available. And through it he was showing what the upside-down world of his kingdom was to be like. He was showing how things had to be done.

He was, in essence, starting the church. And, to be fair to them, it was a lesson that the early church learned well. One of the things that distinguished them was their attitude to the lowest levels of society. Paul's claim, for instance, that 'There is no longer Jew or Greek, there is no longer slave or free, there is no longer male and female; for all of you are one in Christ Jesus' (Gal. 3.28) is one of the most astonishingly radical statements of its time. No 'normal' citizen of the Roman Empire could ever have agreed with him. But Paul's radicalism comes straight out of the box marked 'foot-washing'. Without the example of Jesus, I doubt it would have occurred to the early church to claim such a thing.

One more thing. Jesus, here, takes off his clothes in order to put on the uniform of a slave. But this is the only time in the Passion narrative that he voluntarily undresses.

From now on he will be dressed and undressed by others.

'Truly I tell you, one of you will betray me'

Immediately after the washing of the feet, Jesus talks about betrayal. John describes him as 'troubled in spirit'. He dips a piece of bread in a dish of sauce and hands it to the one who will betray him: Judas Iscariot.

It's always slightly worried me, this scene. Because, frankly, how thick do you have to be not to spot the traitor? Especially after Jesus has said: 'It is the one to whom I give this piece of bread when I have dipped it in the dish.' Surely the disciples – or some of them at any rate – must have realised that something was very wrong.

The scene as it's played out in the Synoptics is slightly less worrying, because in those scenes Jesus merely identifies that it's one of the twelve, one of those dipping their bread into the same bowl (Mark 14.20; Matt. 26.23). Or maybe it was never quite as clear as all that. As time went by, there's a sense in which the Gospels focus much more on Judas' betrayal. For example, in the perfume incident in Mark it is merely 'some who were there' who complained (Mark 14.4); in Matthew – written later – it is the disciples who were angry (Matt. 26.8); but by the time we get to John – probably the last of the Gospels to be written – it is Judas Iscariot who is the dissenting voice. What's more, John gives us the information that Judas was a thief who used to steal from the common purse (John 12.4–6). So was John simply correcting the account? Or was he being wise after the event?

And when did Judas leave? In Mark, the passage about betrayal occurs before the meal. In Luke, the betrayer's hand is still 'on the table' after the bread and wine have been served (Luke 22.21). John doesn't include the meal, but he does echo Luke's passage about Peter denying Jesus and by that time Judas has left. If John and Luke were following the same kind of traditions about the passage of events, we might expect Judas to have shared in the bread and wine, and then slipped out.

Whatever the case, John does give us a plausible reason for how Judas slipped from the room without detection. When Jesus tells him to 'Do quickly what you are going to do' (John 13.27), the disciples think that he is going to buy provisions for the festival of Passover the next day, or make a donation to the poor.

The tradition of alms-giving was closely linked with attendance at the festivals. No one was to appear at the festivals without money for alms. This followed injunctions in the Old Testament (e.g. Exod. 23.15; 34.20), which later tradition asserted meant that pilgrims were obliged to give to charity during the festival. Indeed, it may have been that, at ordinary times, the pilgrim could give alms in place of a sacrifice.[26]

As Judas slipped out into the night, the other disciples thought he was going to give money away. How wrong can you be?

'Do this in remembrance of me'

The earliest account of this meal comes not, in fact, from the Gospels, but from elsewhere in the New Testament. Paul, writing to the church in Corinth in AD 54/55, wrote this:

> For I received from the Lord what I also handed on to you, that the Lord Jesus on the night when he was betrayed took a loaf of bread, and when he had given thanks, he broke it and said, 'This is my body that is for you. Do this in remembrance of me.' In the same way he

took the cup also, after supper, saying, 'This cup is the new covenant in my blood. Do this, as often as you drink it, in remembrance of me.' For as often as you eat this bread and drink the cup, you proclaim the Lord's death until he comes. (1 Cor. 11.23–26)

This, then, was the tradition that was circulated among the early church. The church took this symbolic action and turned it into what is known as the Eucharist (from the Greek word meaning 'to thank'). It became the heart of their shared meals, a symbolic action to recall the death of Jesus.

Jesus uses two symbols for this meal that were near universal in the Græco-Roman world. We have seen elsewhere that bread was ubiquitous. The sound of the millstones and the smell of baking filled the streets of every city, town and village. Equally, vineyards were everywhere on the hillsides and in the villages; even in the city we may assume that vines were grown, forming roofs along some of the narrower streets. In that sense, there is nothing exotic about this feast: it's simply the most basic elements of Mediterranean food. And it's delivered in the most basic way. Some scholars, for example, have seen in the breaking of the bread a symbolic picture of violent death, but breaking bread wasn't unusual – it was the ordinary way of starting the meal. This, then, was a meal that could be joined by virtually everybody in the Græco-Roman world.

Attempts to make it exotic miss this point entirely. Its ordinariness was the point. There were no special objects there, no 'holy grail' to hold the wine.[27] It was just a cup. It was just bread and wine, the everyday elements of Palestinian eating and drinking. Indeed, this very ordinariness fits with one of the most distinctive aspects of Jesus' ministry: his love of shared meals. Wherever he went, Jesus had meals with people, meals which satisfied not only their physical hunger and thirst, but also their spiritual hunger and thirst. The outsiders and the marginalised and the impure were welcomed around the table. This meal is the culmination of those traditions. And, indeed, this meal is to be shared with others; it's to be passed on, enjoyed and celebrated from day to day, week to week, generation to generation.

As an event, it also fits alongside the prophetic actions of this week. Like the turning of the tables or the cursing of the tree or the procession into the city, this is a prophecy. With the body and the blood, the bread and the wine, we can see Jesus pointing ahead to his death. He knew, now, what was coming. He knew what fate awaited him. This is a meal that points ahead.

So it fits into both Jesus' symbolic activity and his love of shared meals. But I think it fits into another of Jesus' passions: storytelling. We should not forget that this is Jesus' version of the Passover meal. And the point of Passover was to remember the story of Israel's rescue. The Passover meal, called the *Seder* in Hebrew, tells a tale through the elements. It celebrates the rescue of the Israelites from slavery in Egypt. The unleavened bread symbolises the haste with which they had to leave; the sacrificial lamb is a reminder of the lamb that was slaughtered and its blood smeared on the doorposts for protection (Exod.12.7). Jesus clearly intended that his meal should tell the tale of his sacrifice.

So, then. Outside the upper room, the hot air, the insects buzzing; the very real world of Jerusalem, with its violence and beauty and faith and betrayal. And inside this room, more reality, *greater* reality. Real bread, real wine: the ordinary stuff of life. Yet transformed into the stuff of sharing and story and symbol.

'Lord, look, here are two swords'

John has a lengthy speech – or series of speeches – in which Jesus warns his disciples about what faces them in the future. Luke, too, has a warning, but it's shorter, although, in its own way, no less cryptic than John's mysticism. In Luke's version there is conflict among the disciples about importance and then Luke puts the warning to Peter (see below). There follows a curious passage about purses, bags and swords.

The point seems to be that things are about to change. When Jesus sent them out before (Luke 10.4) they experienced God's miraculous provision. Now things are different: now purse and bag will be needed, and cloaks must be sold in order to buy weapons.[28] It all sounds very un-Jesus-like. The point, surely, is not that they should start to fight, but that they will be in the position of outlaws, numbered among the wrongdoers. Jesus is speaking symbolically here, a point that is underlined by a grim note of ironic humour at the end. The disciples, taking him literally, rustle up a couple of swords between them. (Although where they came from is never made clear.) 'Is that enough?' they ask. 'That'll do,' he replies.

We shall see one of these swords in action soon.

And with that they leave for the Mount of Olives.

Gethsemane

Where: Garden of Gethsemane

When: Late night/early morning

> After Jesus had spoken these words, he went out with his disciples across the Kidron valley to a place where there was a garden, which he and his disciples entered. (John 18.1)

The Passover meal had to end by midnight or by 2 a.m.[29] So it was probably some time in the early hours that Jesus' version of the Passover finished and the disciples made their way out of the city.

It was a moonlit night. A full moon. From the Upper City, they made their way down the steps, into the maze of alleys of the Lower City and out through the charmingly named Dung Gate. Beyond this gate lay the Valley of Hinnom, Gehenna, the place that Jesus often used as a synonym for hell. This place, where the refuse and rubbish of the city was brought to be burnt (or simply discarded) was dotted with the glows of the fires that burnt there day and night. From there he and the disciples went up and across the Kidron Valley, where the tombs would have been clearly visible in the moonlight.[30] There was death everywhere you looked.

Jesus was going, Luke tells us, 'as was his custom, to the Mount of Olives' (Luke 22.39), John tells us it was across the Kidron Valley (John 18.1), Mark tells us the name: Gethsemane.

The Kidron Valley looking south. On the right is the wall of Temple Mount. To the left are the remains of monumental tombs, dating from the second century BC.

The site of the Garden of Gethsemane, today marked by an olive grove and the Church of All Nations, has a considerable claim to authenticity. Of course, we can't be sure where Jesus stopped, but the traditional site must be very close to the first-century route from the Mount of Olives to the eastern entrance to the Temple. Beneath the Russian church further up the hill archaeologists have discovered a flight of stone steps, indicating the ancient route.[31] John's description of the place as 'a garden' means not a flower garden, but a market garden; a plot of land, enclosed by a wall, with an olive trees and an oil press. The name 'Gethsemane' probably comes from the Aramaic *Gatsemani*, meaning oil press. The press was probably housed in a cave and, indeed, there is a cave at the traditional site.[32]

It is close to Jerusalem, but far enough away to avoid the crowds. However, it is not far from the Temple. You could see it in the moonlight, just across the valley. Look the other way and you could see the road to Bethany, and then east to Jericho. This is the thing about Gethsemane: it wasn't just outside the city; it was on the way east. To escape, all Jesus had to do was crest the hill and keep going.

But he didn't. He stopped.

The Garden of Gethsemane

'Before the cock crows'

Peter said to him, 'Even though all become deserters, I will not.' Jesus said to him, 'Truly I tell you, this day, this very night, before the cock crows twice, you will deny me three times.' But he said vehemently, 'Even though I must die with you, I will not deny you.' And all of them said the same. (Mark 14.26–31)

By reporting that he told Judas to go, the Gospels make it clear that Jesus knew what was going to happen. The disciples, of course, don't share this insight; certainly they don't show any anxiety here. Jesus warns them of what is coming, but here, outside the city, they are confident that they will remain faithful.

It's important to note that Jesus' prophecy about Peter, and his subsequent denial, is recorded in all the Gospels. Luke and John place it in the context of the Last Supper (Luke 22.34; John 13.38), Mark and Matthew put it here, in Gethsemane (Matt. 26.34; Mark 14.30). This was a core story for the early church, one of their most important. Peter is adamant that he will never deny Christ. And the disciples are generally adamant that they will never desert Jesus. But none of the disciples escape the blame; three times they too are found to be sleeping when they should be awake.

They have failed the test, and now it is too late: the betrayer is at hand.

'As though I were a bandit'

Who arrested Jesus? Not the Romans, certainly; thus far all he had done that could possibly anger them was the procession on Sunday. They might have registered some kind of disturbance in the Temple courtyards but that didn't warrant an arrest, either.

No, the people who came to arrest Jesus were the people with whom Judas had been negotiating: the Temple authorities. The actual arresting party is described variously in the Gospels: Mark has a crowd, accompanied by the chief priests, the scribes, and the elders (Mark 14.43); Matthew doesn't include the scribes, and Luke has the crowd, the chief priests, the officers of the Temple police and 'the servant of the high priest' (Luke 22.50, 52). John has 'a detachment of soldiers together with police from the chief priests and the Pharisees.' It's difficult to see why the Pharisees would be there, as they held no civil power in Jerusalem, and the word that John uses for the soldiers is *speira*, which usually means a cohort. Since a cohort of soldiers consisted of 500–600 men, this is unlikely to be accurate. I'm not convinced, in fact, that this is what John meant. Whatever else he was, John wasn't stupid, and the idea that the Roman commanders emptied the Antonia fortress of troops just to arrest one man is simply ridiculous. It's probable that what John is implying is that there were some Roman troops accompanying the Temple police, perhaps including a kind of liaison officer with the troops in the Antonia. (John also has the assembled arresting party falling to the ground (John 18.6) when Jesus says the words 'I am he'. Rather than all collapsing in a heap, it's more likely that he means they were taken aback by the power of the occasion. There are other accounts of Romans being awestruck by events in the Gospels, after all.)

However, even if there was a Roman liaison officer there, two considerations lead one to believe that the Temple police were the main arresting force. One is the geographical proximity of the Temple. It would have been relatively simply for a snatch squad to emerge from the eastern entrance to the Temple and cross the Kidron Valley to Gethsemane. Jesus' statement that he has been teaching in the Temple courts and they have not arrested him there makes much more sense if the Temple police formed the main part of the arresting party.[33] The party was probably the same kind as that which later arrested the apostles and brought them to face the Sanhedrin: 'some priests, the captain of the Temple [guard], and some Sadducees' (Acts 4.1).

As we have seen, the Romans preferred to let the local forces do the work wherever possible. The Temple police, like the priesthood, were formed from the Levite tribe. They served as gatekeepers at the entry to the sanctuary, patrolled the Temple courts, and stood guard on the rampart around the Court of the Gentiles. This force was at the disposal of the Sanhedrin and would have formed the arrest party sent to fetch Jesus from Gethsemane.[34] The leader or captain of the Temple guards was known as the 'man of the Temple Mount'. It was his job to inspect the guards every night; every guard had to give a special greeting to prove that he was awake.[35] With them came some Temple servants, whose normal duties included such tasks as helping the high priest on and off with his vestments, sweeping the porches and open areas (except the Court of the Priests, where non-priests were allowed only if making a sacrifice.) And heading them up were the chief priests, including the high priest's representative – his 'servant' – who would no doubt report back to his master.

'He approached Jesus to kiss him'

The fact that Judas kisses Jesus is one of the most shocking moments of that shocking night. Even Jesus seems baffled by it:

> Jesus said to him, 'Judas, is it with a kiss that you are betraying the Son of Man?' (Luke 22.48)

So why did Judas kiss Jesus? The idea that Judas used the kiss as an identifier is odd. This, after all, is not a covert operation and, although it's at night, there is a full moon, not to mention the presence of torches. So Jesus does not need to be identified. And it can't have been to preserve the element of surprise: it's not as if the disciples don't realise that something is up, the moment all those police enter the garden.

In general the culture of the time rather frowned on such displays of public affection. By Jesus' time, the public kiss was probably not practised among Jews.[36] The same was true of the wider Græco-Roman world. The Romans did not use what we would call the 'social' kiss – except among the aristocracy.[37] Yet, within Jesus' followers, and in the early church, kissing seems to have been the normal sign of greeting. Jesus rebukes Simon the Pharisee for not welcoming him with a kiss, unlike the woman who kissed his feet (Luke 7.45). Paul often urges his correspondents to 'greet one another with a holy kiss'.[38] Kissing seems to have been such a feature of the early church that it was adapted into part of the liturgy. What we have, therefore, is a distinctively Christian act which would be shared between Christians, not just in their meetings but at other times as well.[39] For the first Christians, therefore, the kiss was a distinctive practice which showed that they were a family, that 'in Christ there is neither male nor female, Jew nor Greek, slave nor free' (Gal. 3.28). It was a sign of discipleship. It was one of the things that the followers of Jesus did.[40] The kiss was 'an expression of revolutionary social bonding and or radical equality'.[41]

Perhaps, then, Judas kissed Jesus because that was the normal sign of greeting: that was the special thing that Jesus' disciples did. This is why Jesus is so shocked. He's not shocked by the betrayal – he knows that is going to happen. But using one of the things that identified Jesus' followers as a way to single out their leader is not just a betrayal of Jesus; it's a betrayal of their rituals, their unique habits. He's breaking the fellowship apart, using the one act that was supposed to bind them together.

Or perhaps it was not, in the end, as pre-planned as that. What seems a callous act on Judas' part was, perhaps, more instinctive. He'd greeted Jesus this way for three years. Perhaps in that garden, on that night, the one thing he could not betray was the force of habit.[42]

'All of them deserted him and fled'

Immediately after the kiss, a scuffle breaks out and Peter cuts off the ear of the High Priest's slave. John gives us the slave's name – Malchus. This is one instance – like the anointing in Bethany – where John reveals names that are otherwise anonymous in Mark. He also tells us that it was Peter who did the deed. Bauckham has argued persuasively that one of the reasons why John gives names where the earlier writers don't is that the Synoptics were concerned with protective anonymity. In other words, while Peter was still alive it was a risk to have him publicly associated with acts of violence. But, by the time John is writing, Peter is long dead, so there is no risk to him.[43]

And if John is based at least partly on eye-witness accounts from Jerusalem, then it was probably well known around Jerusalem who the parties were in this incident.

Whatever the case, Jesus' ironic comment about the swords back in the upper room is lost on Peter, who lashes out. Nevertheless, Jesus heals the wound; they are not to resist. Non-violence is the path from now on. Once the possibility of resistance has been extinguished, the disciples evaporate. 'All of them deserted him and fled,' says Mark (which is hardly surprising when your leader has forbidden you to fight back.) It must have been terrifying. A moment ago they had barely been able to stay awake; now there were footsteps and shouts and torchlight and swords, and one of their own destroying everything that they had hoped for.

They flee, leaving everything behind. Literally in one case, for Mark gives us a further story – of a young man who could escape arrest only by leaving his clothing behind. He was wearing just a simple garment – a *sindon* in Greek – which was a sleeveless rectangle of cloth wound round the body.

Who was he? Various names have been suggested, including Mark himself, although the testimony of the early church was that Mark had never met Jesus. The fact that Mark doesn't name the man probably means it wasn't one of the twelve. We do know that he was young, and that, unlike the rest of the followers, the snatch squad seem to make a concerted effort to get him. None of the others seem to have had problems escaping, even Peter, who had been involved in a violent act. Indeed, Peter was not followed at all, since in a little while he was able to turn round and follow the arresting party back through Jerusalem. But this young man was grabbed.

Why? Well maybe the answer lies with the other person whom the Sadducean leaders were particularly keen to get hold of. We saw right at the start that Lazarus was marked down for execution as well, for the apparent crime against theology of being raised from the dead. And I have argued elsewhere that he was a young man. The High Priest's servant could well have had instructions to catch both Jesus and Lazarus, if possible.

If it was Lazarus, why not say so? Well, perhaps for a reason that we have already explored: the idea of protective anonymity. As we saw with Malchus, characters unnamed in the other Gospels are sometimes named by John. Lazarus doesn't actually feature in any of the other gospels, only in John. At the time when Mark was writing his Gospel, Lazarus may still have been in Judaea, and even still a wanted man. His resurrection – more than the others that Jesus performed – had political ramifications. Mark probably wrote his Gospel in the mid-60s AD. Around the same time in Judaea, James the brother of Jesus was killed on the orders of Ananus. So the political climate in and around Jerusalem was still boiling. This may be why Mark keeps the names anonymous and doesn't even include the Lazarus episode. By the time John comes to write his Gospel the Temple has fallen, the Sadducean powers have dispersed and the true story can be told.[44]

The real point of the episode is to show that people were so desperate to escape that they left even their clothing behind. Whatever the identity of the young man, the followers of Jesus disappeared from the garden as fast as they could. In the end, only Jesus and Judas of their number are left. The arrest is effected; the snatch squad have their man. Jesus is bound and taken back across the valley and up into the streets of Jerusalem.

Day Six: The Execution
Friday 3 April

Interrogation by Annas: Caiaphas's House, early hours of Friday morning

The night trial: Caiaphas's House, early hours of Friday morning

Peter in the courtyard: Caiaphas's House, before dawn

Morning council meeting: Caiaphas's House, 5.30 am

The first hearing before Pilate: The Palace of Herod the Great, 6.30 am

Interrogation by Antipas: Hasmonaean Palace, 7.00 am

The death of Judas: Temple treasury, 7.30am

The second hearing before Pilate: The Palace of Herod the Great, 7.30 am

The flogging: The Palace of Herod the Great, 8.00 am

The crucifixion: Golgotha, 9 a.m.

The darkness: Golgotha, 12 noon

The death of Jesus: Golgotha, 3 p.m.

The burial of Jesus: Near Golgotha, 4 p.m.

First-century steps leading from the Upper to the Lower City. Jesus would have used this route or similar to get from the Upper Room to the garden of Gethsemane, and may have been brought back this way after his arrest.

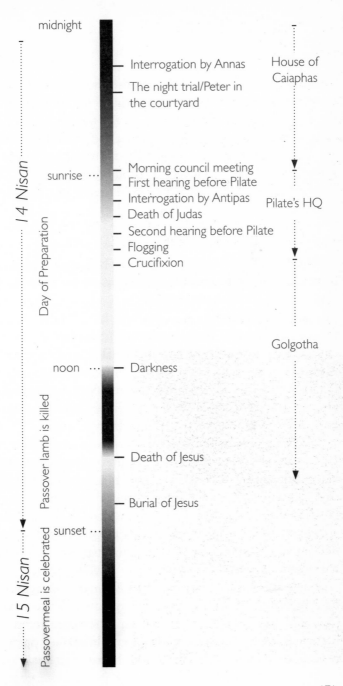

Fri 3 April 33 AD

14 Nisan

15 Nisan

Day of Preparation

Passover lamb is killed

Passover meal is celebrated

midnight

Interrogation by Annas

The night trial/Peter in the courtyard

House of Caiaphas

sunrise

Morning council meeting
First hearing before Pilate
Interrogation by Antipas
Death of Judas
Second hearing before Pilate
Flogging
Crucifixion

Pilate's HQ

Golgotha

noon

Darkness

Death of Jesus

Burial of Jesus

sunset

Interrogation by Annas

Where: Caiaphas' house

When: Early hours

Which way was he taken? Through the western gate of the Temple, across the plaza and over the bridge? Or, more likely, down the Kidron Valley, through one of the south-eastern gates of Jerusalem and up the steps? Whatever the route, the destination was clear: he was going to the Upper City, to the house of the High Priest. The first meeting, though, is not with Caiaphas. Instead, Jesus is interrogated by his father-in-law, Annas:

> So the soldiers, their officer, and the Jewish police arrested Jesus and bound him. First they led him to Annas, who was the father-in-law of Caiaphas, the high priest that year. (John 18.12–13)

Only John describes this scene, and its historicity has frequently been challenged. Critics usually centre on the fact that Annas – or Ananus, as Josephus calls him – was not High Priest at this time and therefore had no legal jurisdiction. Apart from the assumption that the arrest, trial and execution of Jesus had anything to do with conventional legality at all, the picture of Annas that emerges from history chimes exactly with John's portrait. He was an elder statesman, a political grandee, the founder of a dynasty; exactly the kind of man to retain influence and power, even when his official role is over.

John parallels the meeting with Annas with the story about Peter's denial, implying that the interrogation actually took place at the house of Caiaphas. There is little problem in locating this scene in Caiaphas' house: it's likely that the high-priestly families lived in the Upper City quite close to one another; it is also likely that Caiaphas, busy with preparations for Passover, delegated the arrangements of the arrest to his father-in-law; a man with considerable experience in Jewish politics.

Annas asks Jesus about 'his disciples and his teaching'. Perhaps he is already sensing that there is more to this movement than just one charismatic leader. Jesus, however, refuses to tell him anything he doesn't already know. He's talked openly. He's been in the Temple. 'Ask those who heard what I said to them;

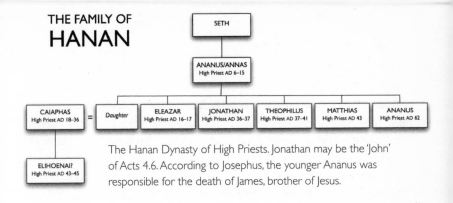

THE FAMILY OF
HANAN

SETH

ANANUS/ANNAS
High Priest AD 6–15

CAIAPHAS High Priest AD 18–36	=	*Daughter*	**ELEAZAR** High Priest AD 16–17	**JONATHAN** High Priest AD 36–37	**THEOPHILUS** High Priest AD 37–41	**MATTHIAS** High Priest AD 43	**ANANUS** High Priest AD 62

ELIHOENAI?
High Priest AD 43–45

The Hanan Dynasty of High Priests. Jonathan may be the 'John' of Acts 4.6. According to Josephus, the younger Ananus was responsible for the death of James, brother of Jesus.

they know what I said' (John 18.19–21). His lack of 'respect' for Annas is rewarded with a punch in the face and the question, 'Is that how you answer the high priest?' Jesus' complaint 'If I have spoken rightly, why do you strike me?' tells us all we need to know about this scene. We are in the shadows of the law here. This is not a legal hearing; it's an interrogation by one of the major players in the close-knit world of Jewish Temple politics. Perhaps, indeed, *the* major player. Annas, or as he is named by Josephus, Ananus, had been appointed High Priest by the Romans and served as High Priest from AD 6–15.[1] As we saw earlier, he founded a dynasty of high priests (see chapter 3). He was the Joseph Kennedy of his day, creating a political dynasty – the House of Hanan – that held power for decades. Five of his sons were to hold the office of high priest: Eleazar (AD 16–17), Jonathan (AD 36–7), Theophilus (AD 37–41), Matthias (AD 43) and Ananus (AD 63). Caiaphas, who held the office from AD 18–36, was his son-in-law. (There may even have been other relatives as well. Elionaeus ben Cantheras, who was High Priest under Agrippa, may be the same as the Elihoeni son of ha-Kayyaph mentioned in the Mishnah. That would make him Caiaphas' son and Ananus' grandson.)[2] The fact is that from AD 6 to AD 43, there were only two years when the position of high priest was not held by a son or son-in-law of Ananus.[3]

And it's not just John's Gospel that records the continued involvement of Ananus in the events of his day. Luke writes, for example, that John the Baptist's ministry began 'when Pontius Pilate was governor of Judaea, and Herod was ruler of Galilee... during the high-priesthood of Annas [Ananus] and Caiaphas' (Luke 3.1–2). Luke also records that when Peter stood before the council 'Annas [Ananus] the high priest, Caiaphas, John, and Alexander, and all who were of the high-priestly family' were present (Acts 4.6). So there are three accounts of Ananus' continued involvement in political issues in the New Testament: two of them are independent of John's account. What Luke and John are recording, it seems to me, are the realities of the political situation. A high priest might always be a high priest, even when he left office, much as an American president is always referred to as 'Mr. President'.[4] And if that high priest were actually the head of the dynasty in power, then he would continue to play a significant part in the political decisions of his day. If anyone was working behind the scenes during the Longest Week, it was Ananus, the head of the family.

But why would Ananus be so interested in Jesus? Perhaps the answer lies in the Temple protest which, as we saw, may well have caused specific offence to the House of Hanan. The name of Hanan or Ananus is not an uncommon name, so, as we saw earlier, the mentioning of them in the rabbinic literature does not mean that they are necessarily from the same family, but there is no doubt that when it comes to Jesus and his followers and family, the House of Hanan has a bit of history. As we have seen, Peter was dragged before a council that included Annas, Caiaphas, John and Alexander. The 'John' mentioned here is probably Ananus' son, Jonathan. Faced with such a 'jury', Peter's statement – 'Jesus Christ of Nazareth, whom you crucified, whom God raised from the dead' (Acts 4.10) – is much more pointed and more powerful. On the face of it, after all, none of the people he's talking to did crucify Jesus. But if he was speaking to the family who arrested Jesus and handed him over to the Romans, then this is not some kind of early creed, or statement of faith: it's an accusation against the whole House of Hanan – *you* crucified this man.

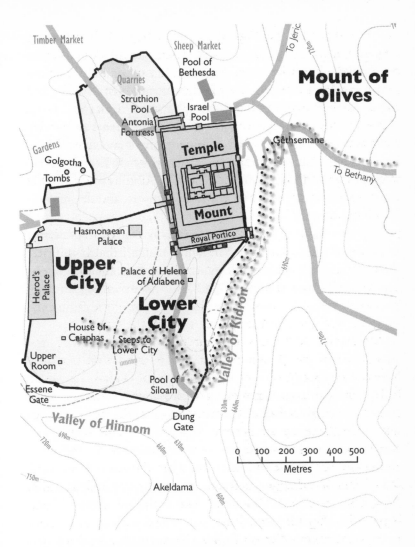

Same route, different destination: the journeys of Jesus on Thursday/Friday.

- •••••• 1. From Bethany to the Upper Room, Thurs afternoon
- •••••• 2. From the Upper Room to Gethsemane, Thurs night
- •••••• 3. From Gethsemane to the House of Caiaphas, Thurs night/Fri morning

But the grudge goes further than that. In AD 62, Ananus, son of Ananus became High Priest. During a power vacuum between Roman governors, Ananus Jr convened the Sanhedrin and brought before them James, the brother of Jesus – 'and certain others'. He accused them of having broken the law and had them stoned to death. Fair-minded inhabitants of the city, it is recorded, were outraged at this treatment and sent to King Agrippa to complain, and went to meet the new Roman governor, Albinus, on his way to the province. Albinus was furious at the high-handed action and wrote to Agrippa, and Ananus was hastily removed from office.[5]

This then was the family who were in charge of Jerusalem at the time of Jesus. Talk of a Sanhedrin which decided things, a council, is clearly wide of the mark. Jerusalem was run by one family: the House of Hanan. And Jesus' first meeting was with the elder statesman, the clan leader, the head of the family.

Night trial

Where: Caiaphas' house

When: Early hours

From the hearing with Annas, Jesus is taken before a wider group of people. Mark calls this meeting a meeting of 'all the chief priests, the elders, and the scribes' and 'the whole council'. Luke seems to cover everyone with 'the assembly of the elders of the people, both chief priests and scribes' and the 'council' (Luke 22.66). Matthew has 'Caiaphas the high priest, in whose house the scribes and the elders had gathered' (Matt. 26.57) and John has just 'Caiaphas the high priest' but no other details of either what was said or who was there (John 18.24, 28).

We should be wary of thinking that the council constituted an official body. It's not even clear what Mark and the others mean by chief priests. Was this an official designation of rank in the Temple? Most likely Mark means the group in power – the supporters and adherents of the Sadducean House of Hanan.

The Gospel writers also differ in the order of events:

▷ Mark: Meeting with High Priest (14.53, 55–64); Mockery and beating (14.65); Peter's denial (14.66–72); Morning council meeting (15.1);

▷ Matthew: Meeting with High Priest (26.57–65); Mockery and beating (26.67–68); Peter's denial (26.69–75); Morning council meeting (27.1–2);

▷ Luke: Peter's denial (22.54–62); Mockery and beating (22.63–65); Morning council meeting (22.66–71);

▷ John: Meeting with Annas (18.13–14, 19–24); Peter's denial (18.15–18, 25–27); Meeting with High Priest (18.24).

Leaving aside the hearing before Annas, we can detect a similar pattern. Although Luke doesn't record details of the first late-night/early-morning meeting with the High Priest, he does record that Jesus was taken to Caiaphas' house at night. And he does record that Peter was in the courtyard for some time. (The time between the first challenge of Peter and the second is 'about an hour' (Luke 22.59), which gives plenty of time for Caiaphas' interrogation.)

So, broadly, we can see the following pattern of events:

▷ Jesus is arrested and taken to the High Priest's mansion;

▷ He has an initial interrogation with Annas, former High Priest and elder statesman of the House of Hanan, the leading family;

▷ He is then interrogated by Caiaphas and his group of advisors, who charge him with wanting to destroy the Temple and accuse him of blasphemy;

▷ While this meeting is going on, Peter denies knowing Jesus;

▷ Jesus is taken back through the courtyard, where he sees Peter (Luke 22.61);

▷ He is subjected to humiliation and some physical abuse, then held in custody (Luke 22.63);

▷ At daybreak, Jesus is taken before a second group from the Temple, possibly a hastily convened 'Sanhedrin', including those who were not present at the night-time meeting.

There he is accused of blasphemy and it is agreed to send him to Pilate.

'The chief priests, the elders, and the scribes'

There has been a massive amount of analysis of the trial, questioning the Gospel accounts because they depict legal irregularities. 'It couldn't have happened like that,' say the critics. 'It would have been illegal.' Objections to the legal procedures within the trial are as follows:

▷ It was a night session;
▷ There was a trial on a feast day;
▷ The accounts omit the statutory second session;
▷ The blasphemy conflicts with the regulations in the Mishnah; [6]
▷ The meeting in the house of the High Priest is illegal.

First, we have to point out, again, that the regulations from which this analysis comes were written after AD 200 in the Mishnah. There is absolutely no proof that they were in force at the time. The Mishnah's view of the Sanhedrin is, in fact, seriously misleading.

Second, and perhaps more fundamentally, the whole idea that the hearing should follow a legal pattern shows a touchingly optimistic faith in the rule of law in the first century. Ancient cities were not democratic places. There was no independent judiciary or media; no Geneva Convention or UN Charter on Human Rights. The idea that there could not have been a night-time meeting of the council because 'it doesn't say so in the manual' is ludicrous. In this world of murky politics the manual was ignored. Nor is this a particular criticism of the Sadducean ruling family; it's just a statement of fact: fair trials were a rarity in the ancient world. Even under the much-celebrated system of Roman law, when politics was involved, the verdict was generally decided before the trial took place. The trial itself was a mere formality.

The first meeting with Caiaphas does at least try to keep up appearances. Witnesses are brought forth and testimony is presented (Mark 14.56). The major charge is that Jesus sought to destroy the Temple (Mark 14.56–61). He was charged, in effect, with planning a terrorist act. After that Caiaphas asks about Jesus' Messianic pretensions (Matt. 26.63–66; Mark 14.62–64). This is the only point where Jesus answers, and the answer he gives is self-condemnatory, at least in their eyes.

> But he was silent and did not answer. Again the high priest asked him, 'Are you the Messiah, the Son of the Blessed One?' Jesus said, 'I am; and "you will see the Son of Man seated at the right hand of the Power", and "coming with the clouds of heaven."' (Mark 14.61–62)

It is the final statement of Jesus' destiny. He is the Messiah and he will usher in a new kingdom. It is not, we should note, Jesus' claim to be the Messiah that is blasphemous; the Jews did not view the Messiah as a divine figure. It is more likely the claim that he would one day be seated at 'the right hand of power' that meant, in their eyes, that Jesus was equating himself with God. And his statement that he would come with the clouds of heaven, his picture of a new kingdom, was obviously a judgement on their present regime. Jesus' statements about destroying the Temple and rebuilding it are clearly Messianic metaphors. But metaphor is a dangerous weapon to play against dictators and the powerful – especially when they have no imagination. And anyway, the decision to kill Jesus had been taken days, even months, ago. After his actions this week, whatever he said would have been taken as blasphemy.

Again, as at the hearing before Annas, the mockery and the beatings are what give the game away. This is the language of power, not justice. The mockery, it has to be said, is characteristically Sadducean. The Sadducees did not believe in angels or in the spirit of prophecy. Their challenge to Jesus to 'prophesy' and indicate who struck him is theology dressed up as brutality (Mark 14.65).

To sum up, the hearing before Caiaphas has all the hallmarks of a show trial hurriedly organised by Sadducean chief priests. It was not a formal meeting of the entire Sanhedrin – it didn't need to be. It was a late-night kangaroo court. This, as Jesus always claimed, was how the leaders of Jerusalem treated their prophets.

Peter in the courtyard

Where: Caiaphas' house

When: Early hours

While Jesus is facing his accusers inside, Peter has managed to make his way into the courtyard of the High Priest's house.

The story of Peter's denial in the courtyard is one of the best-known episodes of the Longest Week. It's also one of the relatively few episodes that appear in all four Gospels. It falls into the category of Gospel stories that we might call 'so bad, it has to be true'. A story like this reflects so badly on Peter – at least initially – that one would hardly expect the Gospel writers to invent such a thing. After all, if you were inventing the history of Jesus' week, would you invent a story in which the key leader of your new movement actually betrays his master?

But if it's true, there's one troubling aspect: how did Peter get into the courtyard in the first place? Houses in the city were not easily accessible, certainly not at night. Mostly, the wall of the building facing the street had no windows, just a gate, in this case manned (or womanned) by a servant. Courtyards were not open to all and sundry, but carefully guarded. For example, archaeological excavations of the palatial mansion in Jerusalem show that the courtyard was not at the edge of the house, but right in the centre of the building. To gain access a visitor would have to go through the door, down a flight of steps through a kind of hallway, and then out into an open courtyard in the centre of the mansion.[7] Whether the palatial mansion was the site of the High Priest's house is impossible to decide for sure – even though the four ritual baths might imply it. There was another mansion nearby with a more open, colonnaded courtyard, which might be a more likely venue from the description.[8] But the point is that this was not a case of nipping over the garden hedge. Once Peter was in, he was in.

Any entry would have been carefully guarded, especially at a time of heightened tension like this, and especially in the light of the arrest of the charismatic teacher and preacher. The Temple aristocracy are concerned that nothing should get in the way of a swift execution. So how was it that a supporter of Jesus was allowed through security?

John, in fact, tells us how Peter got in. He was accompanied by 'another disciple':

> Simon Peter and another disciple followed Jesus. Since that disciple was known to the high priest, he went with Jesus into the courtyard of the high priest, but Peter was standing outside at the gate. So the other disciple, who was known to the high priest, went out, spoke to the woman who guarded the gate, and brought Peter in. The woman said to Peter, 'You are not also one of this man's disciples, are you?' He said, 'I am not.' (John 18.15–17)

Peter, we are told, had someone to vouch for him, someone who knew the High Priest and who was assumed not to be a security risk. And note that the woman at the gate says to Peter, 'You are not also one of this man's disciples, are you?' The person with Peter, then, was known to be a follower of Christ.

'A disciple', as we've seen, doesn't have to mean one of the twelve. And it seems unlikely that any of those would have known the High Priest, coming as they did from Galilee. The disciple was almost certainly a male: the Greek word is a male one and, although Jesus had women followers who were every bit as committed and courageous as the men, they were not described as disciples. In the culture of the time, that word could not be used.[9] And whoever this disciple was, he knew the High Priest well enough to gain immediate access to the residence. He was known to be a follower of Jesus but not perceived to be a threat. (The fact that Peter denied being a follower shows that any other follower of Jesus would have been barred from entry.) Finally, and importantly, I believe, John does not identify this person either because he doesn't know who he is, or because he has decided not to.

I think we can rule out the author of John's Gospel being the 'mystery' disciple. Although he is never explicitly identified, the author continually describes himself as 'the beloved disciple'. In his five other appearances in the Gospel he always makes it clear that he is the 'beloved', but here, there's no 'beloved' in sight.[10]

As to the other high-ranking Jerusalem-based disciples, such as Nicodemus or Joseph of Arimathea, they are mostly characterised by secrecy. Their allegiance to Jesus is not made clear until after the event. Joseph of Arimathea was a secret disciple 'because of his fear of the Jews', that is, the Jewish authorities (John 19.38). It's unlikely their sympathies would have been common knowledge. So we have to find someone who is known to be a follower of Jesus, but not perceived to be a threat.

There is one disciple who fits the bill, one follower who would have had the freedom to enter the High Priest's house and who would be known to the woman on the gate. One person who would definitely not be seen as a threat. And that person was Judas Iscariot.

We know he was present at the arrest, but the New Testament doesn't say what happened then. Indeed, after that, Judas seems rather to be discarded. He has served his purpose; he can now be ignored. Certainly the implication is that he was not part of the arresting team. And he passes each of our criteria. He's a known disciple of Jesus, but not one who is a threat. The woman may even have seen him just a short while earlier, when he came to inform the High Priest of the whereabouts of Jesus. And how could he be a threat? He was on their side.

But if this is so, then why doesn't John name him? I think John couldn't name him. Once again, as we saw in the case of Mark not naming Lazarus, it's a case of protective anonymity. But this time the person being protected is not Judas, but Peter.

Because, by the time John was writing his Gospel, Judas was a byword for treachery and betrayal. The Gospels, as we shall see, preserve two different accounts of his death, but later writers turn him into an almost inhuman monster of depravity.

Here's a legend preserved by Papias, an otherwise reliable source from the late first century:

> Judas walked about in this world a sad example of impiety; for his body having swollen to such an extent that he could not pass where a chariot could pass easily, he was crushed by the chariot, so that his bowels gushed out.[11]

This increasing hatred for Judas can even be detected in the Gospels, where stories about him get steadily darker in Matthew, Luke and John. So John isn't protecting Judas here, but he's protecting Peter from association with this 'monster'. It is Peter's reputation that John is concerned for. It was all very well to have the disciples associate with Judas before the event – they didn't know what he was going to do. But *after* the event? That's a different matter.

Logically, I think all this fits together. The shocking nature of Peter's denial argues strongly for its historicity. If that happened, he had to be in the courtyard. And to get into the courtyard he had to be let in.

Why should Judas have done it? Well, perhaps he didn't care any more. Perhaps he was hoping to see another disciple fail as he had done. Or perhaps he was already regretting what he had done. Perhaps he was trying, in this small, futile way, to make amends.

'I do not know this man'

Once in the courtyard, of course, the full reality of the situation must have hit home to Peter. Always impetuous, always brave (or nearly always, anyway) he suddenly finds himself in the heart of enemy territory. And every time he opens his mouth, his accent gives him away.

All the Gospels use the dramatic contrast in this story: while Jesus is being tried above, Peter is denying him below. He is standing by the fire, warming himself, when the questions start. Luke's depiction is wonderfully evocative: a female servant of the High Priest 'seeing him in the firelight, stared at him and said, "This man also was with him"' (Luke 22.56). Peter denies this, but a little while later someone questions him again, and again he denies it. Then an hour goes by and they question Peter again and this time he curses and swears and denies all knowledge. And then the cock crows. There are minor differences between the stories, but broadly the story is clear: three denials before dawn.

What gave Peter away? One of his interrogators is a relative of the man he attacked in the garden (John 18.27). Perhaps this man had been one of the arresting party and had seen Peter escape in the gloom. The major factor, though, was his accent. The Aramaic dialect of the Galileans was a topic of much mirth in sophisticated Jerusalem. Galileans did not speak 'proper'. There is an anecdote about a man from Galilee in a Jerusalem market trying to buy something that sounded like 'amar'; the market traders mock him mercilessly because they don't know if he wants a donkey to ride on [*hamâr*], a drink of wine [*hamar*], a dress [*'amar*, meaning wool] or a lamb for sacrifice [*immar*].[12] This is why the sophisticated elite in Jerusalem cannot believe in a Galilean Messiah (John 7.41, 52). To them, Galileans are idiots, ignorant of the Torah. Messiahs don't, apparently, speak in the wrong accent. The same kind of bigotry can be found in many cultures today. For readers in the UK, it would be like Jesus, Peter and the other Galileans coming from Birmingham or the Black Country. According to one survey, it was 'found that people with the distinctive nasal tones of the Birmingham region are considered far less intelligent than those with other accents'.[13] Jesus was a first-century Brummie.

Significantly, Mark records the first and second denials as happening in different places. The first denial happens in the courtyard (*aule*). The second denial happens in the *proaulion*, or forecourt. This was further away; Peter has retreated.[14] He is still trying to live up to his boast that he would never desert Jesus, but the fear of being discovered has kicked in; physically and mentally he is beginning to distance himself from his leader. The story of Peter has taken us through to nearly dawn. Luke then includes a detail that is difficult to fit: he shows Jesus turning and looking at Peter (Luke 22.61). Was this a piece of poetic licence by Luke, underlying the depth of Peter's betrayal? Or does it mean that Peter was still in the courtyard, still in the heart of the High Priest's house, and that, as Jesus is led out from the hearing to a place of imprisonment, their eyes meet?

If so, no wonder Peter went out. No wonder he wept bitterly.

Morning council meeting

Where: Caiaphas' house

When: 6 a.m.

As daybreak came, Jesus was taken from whatever temporary cell he'd been held in and dragged before another meeting of the Temple hierarchy.

Mark describes the participants as the 'chief priests', the 'elders and scribes and the whole council'. And the word he uses for council is 'Sanhedrin' (Mark 15.1).[15] The Sanhedrin was the supreme court of the Jewish nation. There is a lot of uncertainty about the nature of the Sanhedrin, how often it met, and what powers it had. The description of the Sanhedrin in the Mishnah is an idealised version – a lofty, formal, supreme court, where all the members were Torah scholars and the president of the Sanhedrin was the leading rabbinic sage.[16]

In fact, both the New Testament and Josephus record that the High Priest presided and that the influence of the Pharisees in the body was marginal. It was not some kind of independent supreme court staffed by Torah scholars, but a tightly controlled council, convened at the request of the High Priest, serving at best as an advisory body and, at worst, as a bunch of yes-men. The Romans liked the province to have some kind of ruling council, if only to collect the taxes and rule in legal matters, and the Sanhedrin may have served this purpose, but it was never an independent body.[17]

And even assuming this was a 'proper' meeting of the Sanhedrin, you would not have needed many of them for it to be quorate. It consisted normally of seventy-one members, but only twenty-three were needed to pass a death sentence. It would have been perfectly possible for Caiaphas to convene twenty-two of his supporters, which would explain how someone like Joseph of Arimathea could be part of the council and yet not part of the verdict. He wasn't there; he wasn't invited.

Along with the council, Mark's account mentions scribes and elders. We should note that the Pharisees are not mentioned. Jesus' old sparring partners were probably not involved in the trial at all.[18] The scribes were there to give the proceedings some kind of quasi-legal verisimilitude; the 'elders' probably means the city's elder statesmen. The picture is of a hastily convened meeting of the people with influence, the people who need to be kept in the loop. It's a cabal of the High Priest and his closest allies. Indeed, this morning meeting has all the air of a rubber-stamping exercise. In Luke's account, no mention is made of the threat to the Temple; instead, the charges focus on Jesus' claims of Messiahship and in particular his claim to be the son of God.

But in order to kill Jesus, to remove him permanently, the Temple aristocracy are going to need some help. It's not that they didn't have the means: they had swords; they could have stoned him. No, they had the weapons, but they weren't allowed to use them. There has been a lot of debate over the limits of power, but the line in John seems to be accurate. It was the Prefect who had the *ius gladii* – the right of life and death. Josephus states quite clearly that Coponius, the first Roman prefect of Judaea, had delegated power from the emperor to inflict capital punishment. And this was a power he did not allow the Jews.[19]

We can see this at work in a case involving another Jesus, which took place in AD 63, four years before the rebellion. During the feast of Tabernacles, a man called Jesus ben Ananus began wandering around Jerusalem, prophesying:

A voice from the east, a voice from the west, a voice from the four winds, a voice against Jerusalem and the holy house, a voice against the bridegrooms and the brides, and a voice against this whole people!

According to Josephus, the eminent members of the populace took him and beat him, but still he would not desist. So they sent him to Albinus, the Roman procurator, where he was 'whipped till his bones were laid bare'. Despite this, with every stroke of the whip, all he would say was 'Woe, woe to Jerusalem!'

What is illuminating about this account is the resemblance it bears to Jesus' situation. Ben Ananus is summarily beaten by the leaders or the people, but only the Roman Prefect, Albinus, has the power of life and death.

Another clue is found in the *Megillat Ta'anit*, a Jewish chronicle which lists thirty-five significant dates for Jewish celebration. On 17th Ellul, in the Jewish calendar, it records that the Romans were forced to leave the city, which in all probability refers to the expulsion of the Roman garrison in AD 66. Five days later it says 'we regained the right to execute criminals'.

This implies that it was only with the expulsion of the Romans that they regained the ability to execute criminals. At the time of Jesus, then, the Jewish leadership were not allowed to execute people.

No, for that you needed the Romans.

A copy of the inscription found in 1961, commemorating the building of a Tiberieum by 'Pontius Pilatus'

The first hearing before Pilate
Where: The Palace of Herod the Great
When: 7 a.m.

In 1961, in Caesarea, an Italian archaeologist brought to light the only physical evidence we have for the rule of Pontius Pilate. It's a dedication inscription to a *Tiberieum*, a temple built in honour of Tiberius, the Emperor of Rome. It tells us two things: first, that Pilate's proper title was *Praefectus Iudaeae* – Prefect of Judaea; and, second, that he was very keen to please the Emperor.

The fact that Judaea was under the rule of a prefect shows where it stood in the great scheme of things. Pilate was an equestrian, from the second layer of the Roman class system. The equestrian class or *equites* were originally those Romans with enough money to serve as cavalry officers in the army. (Knights, in other words.) By the time of Augustus they had developed into a distinct class, gained the title *eques* and allowed to wear a special gold ring and to sit in the front row at the theatre. They could also wear a toga with a purple border. There was a property qualification of 400,000 sesterces or more.[20] Many of them were content to be big fish in smaller ponds, part of a local elite, with power in the provinces or cities. But they were not from the upper class of Roman society; they were not senators. The prefects of Judaea were not of high social status. At least one – Felix – is known to have been an ex-slave. An ex-slave governor is remarkable, but it says something about the low status of Judaea that if any province could be ruled by an ex-slave, that would be the one.[21]

His name gives us some clues about his origin. Roman names have three constituent parts: *nomen, praenomen* and *cognomen*. *Nomen* signified your tribe; *cognomen* your family, and *praenomen* your individual name. We don't know Pilate's *praenomen*; later traditions record the *praenomen* of Lucius, but that is just a myth. However, his *nomen* – Pontius – indicates that he came from the Pontii tribe, who were Samnites, living in the territory of the south-central Apennines in Italy. The Samnites had always been a tough, warlike people. Centuries earlier, they had almost brought Rome's rise to power to a halt. In 82 BC, the Roman dictator Lucius Cornelius Sulla marched on Rome and defeated the Samnite forces of another Pontius: Pontius Telesinus. Sulla slaughtered many Samnites and inflicted a wave of destruction on the region. Strabo wrote that:

> Sulla's proscriptions did not end until he had destroyed or driven from Italy all who bore the Samnite name. When asked the reason for this terrible anger, he explained that experience had taught him that no Roman would ever know peace as long as they had the Samnites to deal with. So the towns of Samnium have become villages and some have even vanished altogether.[22]

So Pilate was a man whose people had suffered in the past. An outsider, perhaps, whose family land had been absorbed into the Roman state.

His *cognomen*, or family name, was Pilatii, which comes from *pilatus* or spear. A warlike family, perhaps; a family of soldiers. Certainly Pilate, as an equestrian prefect, would have been a career soldier, a military man through and through, serving in battle, gaining promotion, until finally he was given command of Judaea. His job was simple: to collect taxes and keep the populace subdued and maybe to maintain the infrastructure of his area.[23] To help him he had a small staff of attendants (*lictores*), messengers, some Roman soldiers as bodyguards perhaps, his slaves and his family. His role involved overseeing the collection of taxes and the administration of justice, although only the most important cases would have been brought before Pilate.

As we have seen, the prefect had the power of life and death. Josephus confirms that the first governor, Coponius, was from the equestrian ranks, and was granted extensive powers.

> And now Archelaus's part of Judaea was reduced into a province, and Coponius, one of the equestrian order among the Romans, was sent as a procurator, having the power of [life and] death put into his hands by Caesar.[24]

Judaea might have been a small place; it might have been stuffed to the gills with religious nutters and zealots. It might have been far from Rome, dry, dusty and arid. But it did give you the chance to make a name for yourself. It gave you the chance to exercise power; absolute power.

And, of course, it was an opportunity to make money. The governors of the Roman provinces were rapacious, greedy and incompetent. And that's not my opinion: that's what the Romans themselves said. Writers such as Tacitus and Juvenal portray provincial officials as greedy bloodsuckers, while Josephus blamed the brutality and stupidity of the Roman governors for revolts not only in Judaea, but in Gaul and Britain as well.[25] As long as the money taken from the provinces was not overly excessive, governors were allowed a free hand. It is said of Emperor Tiberius that 'once he ordered a governor to reverse a steep rise in taxes saying: "I want my sheep shorn, not skinned"'.[26]

In other words, it was *expected* of a governor that he would take all he could from his province. He was not there to improve the life of the people he governed; he was there to serve the interests of himself and his political masters in Rome. Even when a governor had gone too far, if he still had support at Rome, he would not suffer too badly. Here's the Roman poet Juvenal:

> A provincial governor, exiled
> For extortion, boozes and feasts all day, basks cheerfully
> In the wrathful eye of the Gods; it's still his province,
> After winning the case against him, that feels the pinch.[27]

In practice, as long as the governor enjoyed the favour of his superiors, he was safe. It was only when he fell out of favour, or when he was worried about what was happening 'back in Rome', that the governor became vulnerable.

And Pilate's problem, in AD 33, was that events in Rome had left him very vulnerable indeed.

'The rulers of the Gentiles lord it over them, and their great ones are tyrants over them'

Pilate was appointed prefect of Judaea in AD 26. But he was not appointed by the Emperor, because, at that time, Emperor Tiberius had retired from public life to spend his days in his villas in Campania and Capri. For the first twelve years of his reign Tiberius never left Rome. Then, in AD 26, he decided to go and dedicate a temple in Campania and on his way passed the isle of Capri. He stayed there, built a villa and began a kind of government by remote control. He left control of Rome and the government of the Roman Empire largely in the hands of his trusted lieutenant, L. Aelius Sejanus.[28]

Sejanus was an outsider to the Roman political system. He was not, indeed, a Roman but an Etruscan, and, like Pilate, from the equestrian, rather than the senatorial, rank. He had been a commander of the Praetorian Guard, the elite special-forces unit created by Augustus as a personal security force, which developed under Sejanus' command into the most significant military presence in Rome.[29] Sejanus was basically the head of the secret (or not so secret) police. He had an army of professional informers – known as *delators* – who kept him informed of every rumour that circulated in Rome.

According to Philo, Sejanus was a notorious anti-Semite who wished to 'do away with the nation' and so invented false slanders against the Jews. Certainly there is some evidence of Sejanus' violently anti-Jewish behaviour. In AD 19 he forced the Jews in Rome to burn their religious vestments, and expelled them from the city. It was under Sejanus' rule that Pilate was appointed. While Sejanus remained in power, therefore, Pilate could do pretty much as he liked. If Philo's description is true, Sejanus was not likely to listen to the complaints of the Jews.

Pilate's freedom was further helped by the fact that his 'line manager' was not around.

The Prefecture of Judaea was subordinate to the Legate of Syria, based at Antioch. The Legate was a member of the senatorial class, with some 30,000 troops under his command. However, for the first eight years of his rule, the Syrian Legate was not actually in Syria. Instead, the Legates stayed in Rome, where Sejanus, presumably, could keep an eye on them.

We can see this sense of security reflected in coins. From the start of Pilate's rule, he had been careful not to mint coins with images that might offend the Jews. But in the years AD 29–31 he had coins minted which, for the first time in Judaea, depicted Roman objects and images of power, such as the *simpulum* (a ladle used for pouring wine on sacrificial animals) and the *lituus* (a wand used in augury).[30] These coins must have occasioned disquiet among the Jews, but Pilate was evidently in a strong enough position to ignore it. He didn't have to worry about reports reaching the Emperor, because everything went through Sejanus who had appointed Pilate and hated the Jews anyway. Obviously Pilate had to show some sensitivity, but the Jewish leadership would have known that there was not much use complaining. Sejanus was unrivalled in power: golden statues of the general were being put up in Rome, the Senate had voted his birthday a public holiday, public prayers were offered on behalf of Tiberius and Sejanus and, in AD 31, he was named as Consul with Tiberius.

Then it all began to unravel.

The exact cause of Sejanus' downfall is not known, but somehow Tiberius became aware of the threat. Secretly, Tiberius transferred command of the Praetorian Guard to another officer. Then Sejanus was invited to the Senate. He went willingly, thinking he was going to be promoted to Tribune; instead, a lengthy denunciation was read out. Sejanus, the most powerful man in Rome, found himself in a dungeon, while outside the people celebrated his downfall by pulling his statues over.[31] The same evening he was summarily condemned to death. He was led from prison, strangled, and his body cast onto the Gemonian stairs, where the crowd tore it to pieces.

Sejanus' downfall released a flood of cruelty and revenge. Tiberius used the occasion to purge not just Sejanus and his family, but all of his opposition in Rome. There were riots throughout Rome as mobs took revenge on anyone even suspected of being associated with Sejanus. His children – Strabo, Capito Aelianus and Junilla – were all executed over the following months and his wife, Livilla – Tiberius' own daughter – committed suicide. Junilla was a virgin at the time of her death.

According to ancient sources she was raped while the noose was actually around her neck.[32] Tiberius began pursuing all those who could have been involved in the plots of Sejanus.

Meanwhile, in Judaea, Pilate must have been badly shaken. He was a Sejanus appointee. One can imagine him pacing the palace at Caesarea, wondering what was happening back in Rome. Were his friends and family under suspicion? Would he be purged like the others? Worse news was to follow. The new governor of Syria – L. Pomponius Flaccus – was actually sent to Syria; he arrived in Antioch in AD 32.[33] Imperial attitudes to the Jews changed as well. Philo records that Tiberius 'charged his procurators in every place to which they were appointed to speak comfortably to the members of our nation in the different cities, assuring them that the penal measures did not extend to all but only to the guilty, who were few, and to disturb none of the established customs but even to regard them as a trust committed to their care, the people as naturally peaceable, and the institutions as an influence promoting orderly conduct'. [34]

So Pilate had lost his supporter at the top, his new boss was on his doorstep, and there had been a change of policy regarding the very people he was in charge of.

He would have to watch his step.

'I also am a man under authority'

Which brings us back to the *Tiberieum*. Roman emperors were deified after their death, but Pilate is the only known official who built a temple to a living emperor.

Why did he do it? Given the political situation, the *Tiberieum* may have been the first move in Pilate's PR offensive to redeem himself in the eyes of the emperor. Pilate was attempting to curry favour with the emperor, to prove his loyalty. And what better way than to build a temple in his honour, a temple that recognised his deity? Well, lots, actually. Because it is doubtful whether Tiberius was impressed. He was sceptical of such honours and, according to Suetonius, did not allow the consecration of temples to himself. [35]

So the move may well have backfired. At the very least it would have been a waste of Pilate's money.

Then there was the incident with the aqueduct. Pilate decided to build an aqueduct to bring water into Jerusalem. On the face of it this seems a perfectly reasonable thing to do: Jerusalem was a big city with a need for water and an aqueduct that brought the water some 'two hundred furlongs' would help. But the Jews complained bitterly about this design, because, to pay for it, Pilate took money from the 'sacred funds' in the Temple. When Pilate arrived in Jerusalem to see the work, a crowd gathered to complain. Pilate stationed soldiers around with concealed weapons and, at his signal, the men set on the unarmed crowd with 'much greater blows than Pilate had commanded them', punishing both the protestors and the innocent alike. Many Jews were killed in the indiscriminate slaughter, the 'sedition' was brought to a halt and the aqueduct was completed.[36]

The offence, then, was that Pilate had taken 'holy' money. But there is no hint that any force was used, no troops sent in to take the cash. So either the High Priest agreed with this scheme, or he didn't object when Pilate asked. If some people believed the use of the Temple money to be sacrilegious, that was a feeling which was not, apparently, shared by the Temple authorities.[37]

'We do not want this man to rule over us.'

Then there was all the trouble with the shields. There are two tales that have Pilate involved in incidents connected with votive shields – shields which bore an effigy of the emperor. One is recorded by Philo, the other by Josephus. They may, indeed, be the same incident, although there are some major differences.

As with coins, images of the emperor were considered by Jews to be blasphemous, an affront to the scriptural command to make 'no graven image'. Previous Roman prefects had ensured that troops stationed in Jerusalem did not carry these images, but Pilate sent troops armed with the offensive shields.

According to Josephus, he had the deed done at night, meaning that the Jews woke up to find 'posters' of the emperor in their holy city. Outraged Jews rushed to the Prefect's HQ in Caesarea to complain. Pilate, initially, refused to back down, but, as their complaints continued, he arranged a meeting in a large open space in the city, where he would hear their petition again. Many Jews filled the square, unaware that Pilate had stationed troops with concealed weapons around the perimeter. At his signal, the soldiers stepped forward and drew their swords and Pilate warned that the protestors would face immediate death if they didn't return home immediately. The protestors, however, simply lay down on the ground and, according to Josephus, 'laid their necks bare, and said they would take their death very willingly, rather than the wisdom of their laws should be transgressed'. Pilate realised that he couldn't win this one and ordered that the shields be removed from Jerusalem and brought back to Caesarea. [38]

The story demonstrates that the one thing that really outraged the Jews was the status of Jerusalem, the Holy City. The shields, apparently, were no problem in Caesarea, but in Jerusalem they were an outrage. It also shows that the one thing Pilate could not cope with was non-violence. It was not a fight that defeated him, but the prospect of mass, voluntary suicide. This incident probably took place early in Pilate's career. But Philo records another version – or another incident – which has a very different ending, and which must have taken place later:

> [Pilate] not more with the object of doing honour to Tiberius than with that of vexing the multitude, dedicated some gilt shields in the palace of Herod, in the holy city; which had no form nor any other forbidden thing represented on them except some necessary inscription, which mentioned these two facts, the name of the person who had placed them there, and the person in whose honour they were so placed there.

More shields, then, but this time containing no image, just an inscription. Nevertheless, rumours get out about them. 'The multitude' hear that the shields are back and all of a sudden there are complaints. This time, according to Philo, the Herodian royal family are involved:

> But when the multitude heard what had been done, and when the circumstance became notorious, then the people, putting forward the four sons of the king… and those magistrates who were among them at the time, entreated him to alter and to rectify the innovation which he had committed in respect of the shields.

As with the first story, Pilate refused their petition (Philo describes him as 'a man of a very inflexible disposition, and very merciless as well as very obstinate'). Significantly, the leaders threaten to complain to Tiberius, which alarms Pilate. Philo was not exactly Pilate's greatest fan, but, according to him, Pilate feared that if an embassy was sent to the emperor, other facts would emerge, such as 'his corruption, and his acts of insolence, and his rapine, and his habit of insulting people, and his cruelty, and his continual murders of people untried and uncondemned, and his never ending, and gratuitous, and most grievous inhumanity'.

In the end, the leaders wrote a letter to Tiberius who immediately replied, ordering Pilate to remove the shields to Caesarea and set them up in the Temple of Augustus. Philo dates this event late in Pilate's office.[39] Certainly it must have taken place after the fall of Sejanus. If the Jews had sent an embassy to Rome in the days of Sejanus they would have been sent packing.

Significantly, it's hard to see what Pilate had done wrong this time. Assuming this is a different incident from the first shield episode (and most of the details do differ considerably), the inference is that Pilate had learnt his lessons. After all, it's not as if Pilate was doing anything that the Jews themselves didn't do. The Temple complex itself had dedicatory inscriptions showing who had donated money to various parts of the building and even Philo admits there were no images on the shields. So he must have thought that he was on safer ground. Here was a way of demonstrating his loyalty to the emperor and his control of Jerusalem. But as soon as the rumours spread, Pilate was in trouble.

The involvement of the Herodian princes – the 'four sons of the king' – in this episode is interesting. The fact that they were together indicates that this was probably at the time of a festival. And the fact that they even got involved indicates that they sensed Pilate's weakness. This, for them, was unlikely to be about the shields. Antipas was not exactly an orthodox Jew. No, this was a chance to make a point, to reassert their own power. The fact that Pilate was forced to back down cannot have helped relations between Pilate and the princes. Perhaps it explains the statement in Luke: 'That same day Herod and Pilate became friends with each other; before this they had been enemies' (Luke 23.12). If so, we can infer that the argument between the Herodian princes and Pilate occurred before the trial of Jesus and after the fall of Sejanus, which leads us to a festival somewhere in AD 32.[40] The previous year, in fact.

The story shows a man walking a political tightrope. Pilate is trying to please the emperor and placate the Jews. He is a man at the mercy of rumour, rather than fact. He is a wounded beast; and the pack are circling, waiting to bring him down. At Passover AD 33, therefore, the one thing that Pilate could not afford was any trouble. Another complaining letter sent to Tiberius, and that would be it. Suddenly he needed people who were on his side. Suddenly, he needed to placate the Jews rather than ignore them. He changed the coinage. No coin in Palestine after AD 30/31 shows the pagan *lituus* or simpulum symbol. He had learnt his lesson.[41]

And even allowing for Philo's over-the-top description, the charges against Pilate must reflect his reputation at least. He was known among the Jews in Alexandria as a man who was corrupt, cruel and arrogant. And who was renowned for 'continual murders of people untried and uncondemned'.

'The Galileans whose blood Pilate had mingled with their sacrifices'

Finally, there was the incident with the Galileans. This is recorded only in Luke, who writes that 'at that very time there were some present who told him [Jesus] about the Galileans whose blood Pilate had mingled with their sacrifices' (Luke 13.1–2). We don't know any more about this event, but the context suggests that it was during Passover.[42] Given that this event is not reported by Josephus, the numbers involved were probably small, leaving resentment in Galilee, but not really registering much elsewhere. There are no chronological clues in Luke – the reference is set in the midst of a large block of teaching. But it seems to refer to a contemporary event and, given its general placement in Luke, we can easily imagine that it took place the year before Jesus' death. Sometime, then, at a major festival in AD 32, Pilate had quelled a riot at a festival by force, and blood had been spilt.

All of this means that, in AD 33, Pilate does not want any more trouble. His efforts to impress the emperor have failed, he has had one complaining letter sent about him already and his previous protector has been executed.

This Passover, he doesn't want any difficult problems to deal with.

Fat chance.

'Then they took Jesus from Caiaphas to Pilate's headquarters'

Jesus was sent to Pilate first thing in the morning, on the day when Passover was about to reach its climax. John records that the priests accompanying him would not enter the Palace itself, for fear of being contaminated by coming into contact with Gentiles (John 18.28).

This is not exactly the kind of attitude that would make Pilate well disposed towards you. It may well be this, rather than any particular support for Jesus, that makes Pilate initially refuse to go along with their desires. It was not far from the High Priest's house to Pilate's quarters in Herod's old palace. But it was far enough for the main charges against Jesus to have been altered completely.

> We found this man perverting our nation, forbidding us to pay taxes to the emperor, and saying that he himself is the Messiah, a king. (Luke 23.1–2)

No blasphemy, then; no threat to the Temple; Pilate would hardly be swayed by that. Instead, there is direct challenge to Roman rule. Jesus' accusers are framing the charges in the two terms that would be most likely to elicit a fierce response from the Romans: the refusal to pay taxes and the claim to be the real ruler. You could not be a king unless you had the permission of Rome.

But evidently the man before him didn't look much like a king. Pilate's question – 'Are *you* the King of the Jews?' – can hardly be serious. Jesus has been knocked about. He has been spat on and slapped. He has not slept for twenty-four hours. Pilate's sarcasm is met by Jesus' deadpan response: 'You say so.'

So Pilate's immediate assessment of the situation is to dismiss the accusation (Luke 23.4). But the Temple authorities persist: 'He stirs up the people by teaching throughout all Judaea, from Galilee where he began even to this place' (Luke 23.6).

There's a strong sense of irritation in Pilate's words in this first encounter. It's clear he doesn't want to have to deal with this problem. Then he hears a word that offers him a way out of the situation. 'Galilee'. It's Passover time and those annoying Herodian princes are in Jerusalem, as all leaders of the Jews have to be. He has a score to settle with the Herodians. Jesus is from Galilee, so let the king of Galilee deal with it. Send the man to Antipas.

Interrogation by Antipas

Where: Hasmonaean Palace

When: 7.30 a.m.

Some scholars argue that, as this appears only in Luke, it is a fabrication. The reasoning goes that the story is a Lucan invention, based on verses from Psalm 2, as quoted in Acts 4.25–6:

> ...The kings of the earth took their stand, and the rulers have gathered together against the Lord and against his Messiah.

In other words, Luke knew that the early church interpreted these words as referring to Herod and Pilate (the 'kings' and 'rulers'), so he invented a scene to bring Herod into the story.

But this doesn't make sense. For a start, the 'invention' isn't particularly inventive. If you were going to invent an appearance by Herod, you'd have him do more than just ask a few questions and look foolish. Nor, as we shall see, is Herod actually 'against' Jesus. It is more likely in fact that it happened the other way round. It was because the early church knew that Jesus had been sent to Herod that they interpreted Psalm 2 in this way. The early church took it for granted that Herod had been involved in Jesus' death in some way.[43]

If that's so, then why doesn't the story crop up in the other Gospel accounts? Probably because they didn't know enough details. They might have been aware of the tradition that 'Jesus met Herod', but without enough information to make it worth mentioning. Luke, however, had some unique information. Luke had his own sources. One might have been Joanna, a follower of Jesus, whose husband Chuza was a steward – a kind of a finance minister – in Antipas' court (Luke 8.3). Perhaps a more likely source for the Jerusalem story is Manaen (Acts 13.1), a man described as a close friend of Herod the Tetrarch. Manaen was a prominent member of the church at Antioch, a city with which Luke had strong links. So Luke might have included this story simply because he had spoken to Manaen, a man who was there at the time.

Luke was also writing for 'Theophilus', a Roman, who may have been more interested in the behind-the-scenes diplomacy of Roman rule in Judaea. And if this story is about anything, it is about diplomacy and intrigue.

'He sent him off to Herod, who was himself in Jerusalem at that time'

The Gospels tend to portray Herod Antipas, one of the many sons of Herod the Great, as a dithering, uncertain, even slightly ridiculous figure. Like his father, he was not Jewish. He was a half-Idumaean, half-Samaritan who had been raised in Rome. Hardly the most auspicious background for a Jewish leader.

Although he was initially named in his father's will as successor, that will was revoked at the last minute, leaving Antipas only Galilee and Perea. This disappointment stayed with him all his life, for the Romans did not allow him to be king, but called him instead 'tetrarch', which literally means 'the ruler of a fourth part of the kingdom'. He was Herod-Lite, a quarter-king, a twenty-five-per-cent monarch.

Antipas was married to the daughter of Aretas IV, King of Nabatea, but while on a visit to Rome he fell in love with Herodias, the wife of his half-brother.[44] She agreed to elope with him, provided he divorced his first wife. (His first wife got wind of what was happening and fled to her father in Nabatea.) This marriage was illegal in Jewish eyes: Antipas was, in effect, sleeping with his sister-in-law (Lev. 18.16; 20.21), for which he was vehemently criticised by John the Baptist. Clearly Antipas' lifestyle, and that of his court, was not 'orthodox' in the eyes of his Jewish subjects. Their ruler was ritually impure.[45] Despite this fierce criticism, Antipas was fascinated by John. His wife Herodias shared no such fascination. A thoroughly scheming and manipulative individual, it was she who insisted on John's arrest and who manoeuvred the drunken Antipas into executing the prophet, using her twelve-year-old daughter Salome as a lure.[46] The descriptions we have of Herod Antipas and his court show a distinctly un-Jewish character. Perhaps diplomacy, rather than piety, was really why Antipas was in the city. For a ruler whose subjects were predominantly Jewish, it was important to 'do the right thing'. But in AD 33, there were even more compelling diplomatic reasons why Antipas was there, and why Pilate asked him for a second opinion about Jesus of Nazareth.

As we have seen, relations between Antipas and Pilate must have been frosty at this time, after the complaint to Tiberius. From Pilate's point of view, this background also explains why he might have sent Jesus to Herod. Partly, no doubt, it was because he was keen to hand the problem over to someone else. However, Pilate may also have been making a shrewd diplomatic move. He was paying Antipas a compliment by keeping him in the loop. More to the point, if Pilate consulted Antipas, then Antipas could not possibly complain to Rome about the decision.

The venue for this meeting is unknown, but it was probably the old palace of the Hasmonaeans in the Upper City, just across from the Temple Mount. Of the palace itself, little is known. Josephus records that it stood in an elevated position, giving it excellent views of the city. The remains of the Hasmonaean palace at Jericho show it consisted of an open courtyard surrounded by elegant rooms with colonnades and bathrooms with bathtubs. Even though it was dwarfed by Herod's palace, the Hasmonaean palace must have been an impressive building on a commanding site.[47]

Jesus would have been marched the short distance east from Herod's palace to the palace of the Hasmonaeans. He was accompanied on the journey not only by a few guards – either Pilate's troops or Temple police – but also by some of those accusing him as well.

Antipas, we are told, was eagerly anticipating the meeting; he had heard about Jesus and had wanted to see him for some time (Luke 9.9). Perhaps he was hoping for debate and discussion, the kind of discussion he had enjoyed with John the Baptist. Perhaps he was merely hoping to be entertained, that Jesus would act like a court magician. Certainly he must have believed that he would be treated with the respect due his rank.

None of these things happened. Jesus refused to perform, refused to debate, refused even to speak. There was just a kind of embarrassing silence, which Antipas allowed Jesus' accusers to fill with their vehement attacks. The interview ends in mockery and contempt. Powerless to make Jesus speak, Antipas exerts his power in a much more trivial way: by mocking Jesus and dressing him up like a doll (Luke 23.8–11).

And this is where it gets intriguing. Luke describes how Jesus is dressed in robes, literally in a 'bright or shining' garment. It is frequently assumed that this is Luke's version of the mockery scene in Mark 15.16–20, but the differences are vast: there is no purple robe, no crown of thorns, no whipping of Jesus, just some bullying at the hands of Herod's bodyguards. Luke clearly hasn't condensed a scene from Mark; this is an entirely different event.

So what's going on here? The clue, perhaps, lies in the clothing. Several suggestions have been made regarding these garments. Some have suggested that they were the clothes worn by candidates for office, others that they were splendid clothing as befits a king; in each of these interpretations, the 'joke' is the contrast between the clothing of this 'king' and the clothing Jesus finds himself in. But there is another interpretation. Antipas, we are told, dresses Jesus in these clothes and then sends him back to Pilate. When Jesus returns, Pilate takes one look at Jesus and says to the chief priests:

> I have examined him in your presence and have not found this man guilty of any of your charges against him. Neither has Herod, for he sent him back to us. Indeed, he has done nothing to deserve death. (Luke 23.14–16)

Now how did he deduce that? Antipas himself does not accompany Jesus. He could have sent a message via the accompanying guard, but there is no mention of it. What is more likely is that the robes themselves were the message; that for bright clothes, we should understand 'white', the colour of innocence. Antipas mocks Jesus, ridicules the pretensions of this dumb prophet. But his verdict is that Jesus is not guilty; he dresses Jesus in the colour of innocence.[48]

Undoubtedly Jesus' silence was insolent and irritating, but Antipas was not going to make the mistake he had made with John. He was not going to have another innocent man killed. He was not going to be haunted by another prophet. In Antipas' eyes, Jesus may have been insolent, he may have lacked respect, he may have been the butt of jokes. But he was not guilty.

Antipas plays only a small role in the drama of the Longest Week. But this walk-on part, this short cameo, opens a window on to the diplomatic manoeuvring of the time. And the mockery of Jesus, while cruel, has an underlying message. Pilate inter-prets it as a confirmation of Jesus' innocence.

There is one final detail to this story; Luke says that, from that day on, Pilate and Antipas were friends. Pilate's diplomacy has worked. The decision to send Jesus to Antipas does not solve the immediate problem for Pilate, but it does solve a longer-term problem. The two leaders were reconciled, united in the opinion that Jesus was innocent.

The death of Judas

Where: Temple treasury

When: 8 a.m.

> Then when Judas, his betrayer, saw that Jesus was condemned, he changed his mind and brought back the thirty pieces of silver to the chief priests and the elders, saying, 'I have sinned by betraying innocent blood.' They said, 'What is that to us? See to it yourself.' And throwing down the pieces of silver in the temple, he departed, and he went and hanged himself. (Matt. 27.3–5)

Meanwhile, back at the Temple...

There are two accounts of the death of Judas. The only thing they have in common is a place – *Akeldama*, or the field of blood. According to Luke, Judas bought the field with the money he had earned for betraying Jesus. In the field he seems to have exploded: '...falling headlong, he burst open in the middle and all his bowels gushed out' (Acts 1.18).

Matthew's account is no less shocking, although somewhat less dramatic. Matthew depicts Judas as bitterly regretting what he had done. When he saw Jesus condemned he threw the money back into the Temple and went and hanged himself. It was, in Matthew's account, the chief priests who took the money and bought the field with it, on the grounds that it was now impure, so could not be returned to the Temple. Matthew links this event with a prophecy in Jeremiah.

How are we to reconcile these two accounts? I'm not sure that you can. What they indicate, it seems to me, are that different traditions about the death of Judas circulated in the early church. What they knew was that he died, in a violent manner, and close to the time of Christ's death.[49]

The horror of what Judas had done would not have been lost on Jewish readers. 'Cursed be anyone who takes a bribe to shed innocent blood,' it says in the Torah (Deut. 27.25). It's a curse that doesn't seem to affect the Temple aristocracy, whose response can be paraphrased as 'Not our problem'. To Judas, who cannot feel so callous, their response is like a slap in the face. He casts the money down and leaves. It is not likely that Judas threw it into the Temple sanctuary itself. Apart from anything else, one cannot imagine him meeting the chief priests there to discuss such an issue. Far more likely is that the meeting took place in the Temple treasury, where the money came from to pay Judas in the first place. It may be that he threw the coins into the kind of receptacle that held the widow's contribution (Mark 12.41–44).[50]

To ancient readers, Judas' remorseful suicide may well have been seen as an additional sign of disgrace, rather than viewed with compassion. Jewish attitudes to suicide were harsher than in our day. For suicides, one did not mourn openly. A suicide's body was not buried – it was exposed until sunset.[51]

This is what links the two stories. For *Akeldama* – the field of blood – was also a burial ground for 'strangers'. The traditional site is outside the present walls, to the south, in the Wadi Kidron. In Old Testament times this was the burial ground of the common people (2 Kings 23.6; Jer. 26.23), where objects or people rejected by the kings of Israel were cast down. In the times of the Temple it was where the water that rinsed away the blood from the sacrifices was supposed to flow. [52]

At the Last Supper, in Matthew's account, Jesus gave three predictions about his future, all of which have come to pass. Peter has denied him (Matt. 26.69–75); the disciples have fled (Matt. 26.56). The third prophecy was that someone at the table would betray him. And, for that person, there was to be the feeling common to so many desperate, despairing suicides: it would have been better had he never been born (Matt. 26.24).

The second hearing before Pilate

Where: Herod's Palace

When: 8 a.m.

The Gospels are universal in stating that Pilate knew the whole thing was a set-up. Although Mark never says that Pilate found Jesus innocent, he does realise that he has simply been accused 'out of jealousy' (Mark 15.10). The accounts differ only in the level to which the Prefect was prepared to go in order to avoid executing him. Mark shows Pilate offering Barabbas instead of Jesus, then asking two questions: 'What do you want me to do with the man you call the King of the Jews' and 'Why, what evil has he done?' (Mark 15.12, 14). Then he hands over Jesus to keep the crowd happy (Mark 15.15). Matthew has the same series of events (although Pilate calls Jesus 'Messiah', rather than king of the Jews). Luke has a simpler version. Pilate offers Barabbas, then asks 'What evil has he done?' (Luke 23.22) and then grants the wishes of the crowd.

John has much more interaction, with Pilate first arguing that the Jews should try him (John 18.29–32); then offering Barabbas (John 18.38b–40); then beating Jesus and putting him on display (John 19.1–5); then telling the crowd that they should do the job (John 19.6–7); then offering the crowd one final choice – "Shall I crucify your King?" (John 19.15) – before doing what the crowd wants.

So, as far as Pilate's involvement in the death of Jesus goes, the broad outline of events included:

▷ Interrogating Jesus (Matt. 27.11–14; Luke 23.13–16; John 18.29–38a);

▷ Offering Barabbas in exchange (Matt. 27.15–18; Mark 15.6–14; Luke 23.18–19; John 18.38b–40);

▷ Declaring Jesus innocent (Matt. 27.24–25; Luke 23.20–23; John 19.6–12);

▷ Having Jesus beaten and crowned with thorns (Matt. 27.27–31; Mark 15.16–20; John 19.1–5);

▷ Sending Jesus to be crucified (Matt. 27.26; Mark 15.15; Luke 23.24–25; John 19.12–16a).

Luke has no crown of thorns (and John places it before the sentence has been given); all the Gospels agree that Pilate ordered Jesus to be crucified.

Clearly, Pilate does not want to execute Jesus. But we need to realise that Pilate's overriding concern throughout this is not that an innocent man would be killed, but that he, Pilate, would be blamed. The Gospels are often understood to portray Pilate as weak-willed in the face of popular pressure. This, I would suggest, is far from the truth. Pilate was afraid at points, and he was, to a certain extent, manipulated. But, as we shall see, he too did a fair bit of manipulating throughout this hearing. John depicts Pilate as a man moving between two spaces: the inside of the Palace, where he talks to Jesus, and the courtyard, where he addresses the mob. And that is, indeed, symptomatic of the whole event: it sways back and forth; it is a battle, a context, a football match. And guess who gets to play the ball?

In John's account, Pilate's dialogue with Jesus consists almost entirely of questions: 'Are you the King of the Jews?' (John 18.33), 'What have you done?' (John 18.35); 'So you are a king?' (John 18.37); 'What is truth?' (John 18.38).

The last question is, of course, the most pertinent. What is the truth? The cynicism of this statement – or perhaps it's simply *realpolitik* – shows us beneath the skin of Pilate's world. It's not about the truth; it's about the perception of the truth. It's about what his superior up the coast in Syria gets to hear. It's about keeping everyone happy while still being seen to be in charge. It's about not making a decision that would cause you to lose your job.

This, more than anything, is what motivates his actions. He doesn't care about Jesus, whatever his wife may have dreamt (Matt. 27.19). If Pilate had wanted to release Jesus, he could have done. He could have held him in custody until after the festival. He could have ridden out the storm. But what good would that have done?

So, what Pilate has to do is test the ground. He has to find out whether this man Jesus has any popular support. And the way to do that is to give the people in the courtyard a choice.

'Which of the two do you want me to release for you?'

Now a man called Barabbas was in prison with the rebels who had committed murder during the insurrection… (Mark 15.6–15)

There is no known precedent for this: provincial governors don't seem to have had the right to grant a pardon.[53] However, amnesties are not unknown in the Græco-Roman world. Pilate may have considered the release of a relatively minor offender a worthwhile price to pay for a bit of Jewish goodwill. Matthew and Mark suggest that it was a regular custom at Passover, but, significantly, John implies that it was a Jewish custom.[54] In that case it may be a custom dating back to Herod's rule or even before.

The strongest argument for the historicity of the event is that it is in all the Gospels. I don't mean the simplistic argument that 'just because it's in the Gospels it must be true'. I mean the argument that says historical details in the Gospels must, at least, have been credible to their readers and listeners. If prefects never, ever, released a prisoner on amnesty, if such a thing was impossible in Roman law, then one would have thought that the story would not appear so prominently in all the Gospels. One of the sources would have known it to be impossible. But the fact that it is there means that it was not impossible.

We don't know much about this man. We don't even know his name – the name 'Barabbas' is a patronymic, meaning 'son of Abba or Abbas'.[55] Nor is it entirely clear what Barabbas has done. Mark describes how he is in prison with 'the rebels who had committed murder during the insurrection'. Which insurrection, we are not told. Matthew says he was a 'notorious prisoner' (Matt. 27.16). John says he was a bandit (John 18.40) and

Luke says he was in for insurrection and murder (Luke 23.25).

Clearly, Barabbas was part of a group of political revolutionaries. John's word for him – bandit (*lestes*) – means not just an everyday robber, but a class of thief that is part highwayman, part political guerilla. The word is used by Josephus to indicate a political revolutionary, a guerilla, a first-century terrorist.[56] Bandits were not complete outcasts from the society around them – many kept links with the peasants in the villages, and villages could be punished for complicity with the *lestai*.[57] Pilate is offering the crowd a choice between two political prisoners: Jesus of Nazareth, a man who has advocated non-payment of taxes and claims to be king, and Barabbas, a bandit who has been involved in terrorism and who may or may not have committed murder.

In any case, what Barabbas has done isn't the key issue. He is just a kind of political litmus test. This is not, as it has so often been portrayed, a heroic attempt to release Jesus in the face of a frothing load of savages; it's Pilate's version of an opinion poll. He's simply attempting to find out which execution is going to be more popular. He knows that the Temple aristocracy have handed Jesus over 'out of jealousy' (Mark 15.10). What he doesn't know is whether doing what the High Priest wants is going to cause him trouble.[58] The answer is clear: in this crowd, Jesus has no popular support. This crowd want Barabbas.

And that, in turn, tells you all you need to know about the nature of the 'crowd'.

'But the chief priests stirred up the crowd'

One of the most pervasive of all the myths and misinformation about the Longest Week is that the 'Jews' wanted to crucify Jesus.

And it's all to do with our understanding of this scene. So often it is depicted as though the 'Jews' have suddenly turned against Jesus en masse. We hear all the time that the people who cheered him into the city on Sunday were chanting for his death on Friday, but no one ever tells you why they changed their minds. What happened to turn the crowd around? Why did they suddenly turn against Jesus? The answer is simple: they didn't.

The charge comes mainly from the verse in Matthew that runs 'Then the people as a whole answered, "His blood be on us and on our children!"' (Matt. 27.25). The word Matthew uses for people is *laos*, which is often used to mean the people as a whole, i.e. the Jewish nation. Yet standing on its own it can also mean 'crowd'. This is especially true when it follows the normal Greek word for 'crowd', *ochlos*. So this might be why Matthew uses the word. In Matthew 27.24 we have Pilate washing his hands 'before the crowd' (*ochlos*) and then in 27.25 we have 'the people (*laos*) as a whole...' A better explanation is that Matthew means not only the crowd in the courtyard, but all who were there, including the representatives of the Temple leadership – i.e. the leaders of the Jews.[59] What he cannot, logically, mean is 'all the Jews' because we know that there were many Jews who were opposed to this verdict. He can't even mean 'all the Jews in Jerusalem' since that would go against Matthew 26.5 where the leaders could not arrest Jesus because there would be a riot among the people. (And the word that Matthew uses for the people in 26.5 is, wait for it, *laos*.)

It's perfectly clear from the Gospel accounts that the people were on Jesus' side, or, at least, enough of the people to make the Temple authorities unable to arrest him. Jesus' popularity was his shield. They were able to arrest him only in the early hours of the morning at an isolated place.[60] Jesus had widespread popular support. This is emphasised not only by the verses that attest to the support of the people, but by the timing of the events. The trial, such as it was, was pushed through quickly precisely to avoid the crowd getting wind of what was happening. The execution was timed, as we shall see, to take place when the attention of the vast mass of people was elsewhere. So the idea that the entire Jewish population of Jerusalem somehow switched allegiance is just stupid.

So what was the nature of this crowd? There are two clues: the place and the time.

The place is the courtyard of the prefect's HQ. Now do you really think that a large crowd of the general populace is going to be let in there? Imagine a crowd of angry protestors gathering outside the American or British Embassy in a Middle Eastern country. Is the Ambassador likely to fling wide the gates and invite them all in? Not likely. And anyway, although we know that Herod's Palace was large, it wasn't so vast that it could contain a huge, baying mob.

Then there's the timing. Here we are, very early on the day of Preparation. The day of Preparation was a very busy day for the festival pilgrims. At three in the afternoon the sacrifices would begin, but before then everything has to be got ready. The food has to be obtained, the lamb brought into the city, their houses searched for yeast. Frankly, the vast majority of pilgrims and citizens would be otherwise engaged at this time.

So this is a carefully controlled mob. This is a riot by invitation only. Mark describes it as 'the chief priests, the leaders, and the people', but the key lies in the first two groups. The chief priests and the leaders are the Temple aristocracy. They have not come this far to see their plans fall apart at the last minute. They have not spent a week waiting to catch Jesus only to have the crowd ruin everything at the last moment. Instead we're in rent-a-mob territory. This is a crowd of supporters. This was not unusual for the Temple factions.

An account, for example, of the High Priest, Ishmael ben Phiabi, who was appointed in the late forties or early fifties AD, tells of how the ruling classes tried to defeat their political rivals using gangs.[61] The civil unrest during the time of revolt was marked by the different factions and their own followers warring among themselves. Josephus describes them as behaving like brigands. Especially significant are the household servants of the ex-High Priest Ananias, whose bullying tactics secured his power, while two other ex-High Priests – Jesus ben Damnaeus and Jesus ben Gamalas – used their gangs.[62]

It was not 'the Jews' who bayed for Jesus to be killed. It was not 'the Jews' who chose Barabbas. They were busy elsewhere.

In the streets of the Upper City and the tenements of the Lower City, in the towns and villages of Galilee and Judaea, in the Jewish quarters of cities throughout the Roman Empire, the Jews were getting ready for Passover. But in the former palace of Herod the Great there were the gangs of the chief priests and leading families of Jerusalem. This is why the chief priests were able to stir up the crowd to do what they wanted (Mark 15.11): they were issuing instructions to their gangs. And the gangs decided that they would choose Barabbas.

How far Pilate fully understood the nature of this crowd is open to debate. I doubt he would have been able to tell the different factions apart and his track record at understanding the minutiae of Jewish religious politics shows that he never was one to grasp the subtler distinctions. And anyway, occupying powers are always insulated from the reality on the ground.

Pilate thought that this would act as an opinion poll. What he didn't know is that they had already had their opinions decided for them. That was why they were there.

'No friend of the emperor'

The different Gospels have different points that, in the end, decide Pilate's course of action. For Mark and Luke he simply satisfies the crowd (Mark 15.15; Luke 23.23). Matthew puts it more strongly, with Pilate fearing that a riot was about to start (Matt. 27.24). But John has Pilate still uncertain, especially when Jesus claims to be from God (John 19.8). This may be no more than John's tendency to show Gentiles in awe of Jesus – along with the arresting party staggering back and the centurion looking at Jesus on the cross. Or it may have been a sudden realisation by Pilate that there was more here than met the eye; that maybe there really was something special about this man.

Whatever the case, it doesn't work. Because it's at that point that the Temple leaders play their trump card:

If you release this man, you are no friend of the emperor. Everyone who claims to be a king sets himself against the emperor. (John 19.12)

At this point in Pilate's career, these words must have really struck home. The last thing Pilate needed was another letter to the emperor. Especially one that accused him of not being the emperor's friend. This was not just a general threat, either, but a calculated use of a specific term. Caesar's Friends – *amici Caesaris* – were an informal grouping whose membership was reserved for senators and those equestrians, high in government service, who were specifically called to this status. Loss of the rank *amicus Caesaris* led to political and social ostracism, even suicide.

This decides it for Pilate. As far as he can tell, Jesus has no popular support and the Jewish leadership are threatening to turn this minor event into a major crisis that could bring him down. All he has to do is make sure that no one can ever blame him. And so we come to one of the most famous events of the Longest Week. Pilate, having polled the crowd, washes his hands.

> So when Pilate saw that he could do nothing, but rather that a riot was beginning, he took some water and washed his hands before the crowd, saying, 'I am innocent of this man's blood; see to it yourselves.' (Matt. 27.24)

Note what Pilate is actually saying here: it is Pilate who is claiming innocence. It was nothing to do with me, guv. My hands are clean.

At the end of this messy process, we're not really sure who has won. The Jerusalem Temple leadership have flexed their muscles and reminded Pilate of his position. Pilate, on the other hand, has secured his relationship with Antipas, maintained order and avoided the blame. Not only that, having given the 'crowd' and the Temple leadership what they wanted, Pilate has time to wring out two more rather significant victories.

John locates the first of these on 'The Stone Pavement' also known as Gabbatha. This probably refers to the main paved area of the palace, an area where the prefect sat in judgement. The meaning of 'Gabbatha' is unclear. It's an Aramaic word, one of John's local Jerusalemite details. It probably means raised place, or even hump.[63] It may have been a specific raised area of paving, or simply refer to the fact that Herod's Palace was in the highest part of the city. Pilate sits there, on his judge's bench, to deliver the verdict. He gives them one last chance: 'Shall I crucify your King?' The question is deliberately mocking. That's the point, he's *not* their king. Pilate is taking a small revenge here for their threats; he's winding them up. And it works, for the chief priests answer, 'We have no king but the emperor' (John 19.15).

Now that's brilliant. That's gold dust. Because, despite the precariousness of his position, despite the fear that he seems to have felt at times, Pilate has secured from the chief priests a proclamation of loyalty to Rome and the emperor.

It is possible, therefore, to read these accounts and see in Pilate not the weak, compliant figure of myth, nor the decent Roman doing a difficult job, but a cunning, highly attuned political manipulator. There are times when the situation looks as though it is going to go away from him; there are times when he does realise that he is in danger of being outgunned. But he turns it all round and by the end of the trial Pilate's authority is actually strengthened. He has given the Temple authorities what they wanted, without giving in. He has secured from them an admission of loyalty. He has distanced himself from the sentence should it blow up in his face, and he has headed off a potential riot.

And all it took was the execution of one Jewish peasant.

The flogging

Where: Herod's Palace

When: 8.15 a.m.

> Then the soldiers led him into the courtyard of the palace (that is, the governor's headquarters); and they called together the whole cohort. And they clothed him in a purple cloak; and after twisting some thorns into a crown, they put it on him. And they began saluting him, 'Hail, King of the Jews!' They struck his head with a reed, spat upon him, and knelt down in homage to him. After mocking him, they stripped him of the purple cloak and put his own clothes on him. Then they led him out to crucify him. (Mark 15.16–20)

In John's account Jesus is flogged and humiliated before being presented to the crowd one last time. In the other accounts, the order to flog Jesus follows the decision to have him crucified.

It is, therefore, the first stage of the punishment. The first steps down into hell.

If we want to really get a grip of the extent to which the twenty-first century differs from the first century, then all we have to do is look at the punishment that Jesus took. To us it is a scene of almost unimaginable horror and degradation, but to the soldiers it was entertainment.

Flogging was a punishment that the Romans frequently used on lower-class or foreign offenders. It's hard to realise the full extent of the pain, and I don't want to appear to wallow in horror, but it was a savage beating, which removed the flesh of the victim. We saw, in the account of the hapless Jesus ben Ananus, that he was 'whipped till his bones were laid bare' (see earlier in this chapter). During the flogging, the victim would lose control of his bodily functions. Indeed, Jewish law – which also allowed flogging – made this one of the differences in punishment between men and women. According to one Rabbi, the flogging should be stopped after the man soiled himself with excrement, but for a woman the flogging was stopped after she urinated. In their own, brutal, way, they were advocating a more lenient punishment for women.[64] The Romans wouldn't have cared about such things. No ritual uncleanness for them. All that mattered was the beating, the softening-up.

It would have been harsh; it would have been unrelenting. And, when we examine who was actually doing the beating, it would have been motivated by hatred as well as contempt.

Jesus was killed by the Roman army. It was soldiers who carried out the death sentence. In Rome, numerous executions ordered by Claudius and Nero were carried out by military personnel – and often by high-ranking officers. The Gospel portrayal is clear that soldiers beat Jesus and crucified him and that there was at least one high-ranking officer present.[65]

But that word 'Roman' can be misleading. It brings to mind the idea of Latin-speaking Italians, far from home and pining for their vineyards. There were, in fact, very few Romans in Pilate's small entourage, probably just the officers and administrative officials. The rest were locals.

Mark talks about the 'whole cohort' being in the Prefect's headquarters (Mark 15.16), which would indicate that, at Passover, there were probably no more than 1,000–1,200 troops present: one cohort in the Antonia, and one in the Palace. We have seen that Judaea was not garrisoned with Roman legionaries but with five cohorts of auxiliaries. Whereas legionaries had to be Roman citizens, auxiliary troops were local recruits (although they might gain citizenship at the end of their twenty-six-year military service). And they were not Jews; Jews were exempt from military service because of their inability to fight – or do anything very much – on the Sabbath. Instead, the force was made up of local provincials, non-Jewish residents of Samaria and Caesarea.[66] We know the name for one of those cohorts: the name that Josephus gives to one of these units is *Sebastii* – the Augustans – from *Sebaste*, the Greek word for Augustus. And Sebaste was the Greek name for the city of Samaria.[67]

So the soldiers who were carrying out Pilate's orders were neither Italian nor Jewish; they were Greeks from Caesarea, or Samaritans. We have the distinct possibility that some of those guarding Jerusalem and accompanying Pilate into the city were Samaritans. Samaritans were not exempt from military service as Jews were.[68]

And the Samaritans *hated* the Jews.[69]

'Love your enemies'

The hatred between Jews and Samaritans went back centuries. Nehemiah, when rebuilding the Temple, considered Sanballat the Samaritan to be a Gentile and refused to have any contact with him. When Sanballat's daughter married the grandson of Eliashib, the High Priest, Nehemiah returned to Jerusalem and banished the pair immediately (Neh. 13.28).

During the inter-testamental period, even though both Samaritans and Jews suffered at the hands of Antiochus IV, it never occurred to them to join forces to fight him. And during the Maccabaean era, John Hyrcanus burned their temple to the ground and destroyed the town of Shechem. The destruction of their temple forced the Samaritans to the conclusion that they were a separate sect and they would always be a separate sect. In their religion the holy city was Shechem and not Jerusalem and the holy temple was on Mount Gerazim, not on Mount Moriah. This was the key cause of conflict. In later rabbinical teaching the 'problem' of the Samaritans is addressed: 'When shall we take them back? When they renounce Mount Gerazim and confess Jerusalem and the resurrection of the Dead.'[70]

When Pompey captured Palestine he took the city of Samaria, and the region surrounding it, out of Jewish control, gave control back to its inhabitants and attached it to the province of Syria.[71] The area returned to Jewish control during the reign of Herod the Great, who, in a shrewd diplomatic move, invested heavily in the infrastructure of the city. Herod the Great's building projects included a temple to Augustus. Herod settled the city with his veteran soldiers, with people from the neighbouring ethnic groups. According to Josephus, some 6,000 colonists were settled in Sebaste. One of Herod's wives, Malthrace, may have been Samaritan. At any rate she came from the area and she was a Gentile.[72]

Herod's efforts did nothing to lessen the divide. Neither side ever missed an opportunity to take pot shots at the other. Josephus records that during the early years of Roman rule some Samaritans infiltrated the Temple and put dead bodies in the courts, an act which rendered the building unclean.[73] Because of their hatred of the Samaritans, the Jews kept as far away as possible. Samaritans were Gentiles; therefore they were unclean. Unlike Jews in Galilee, who had to travel through Samaria regularly, for most people in Jerusalem – certainly for most of the Temple aristocracy – the only time they saw a Samaritan he would have been dressed in a Roman army uniform and staring down at them from the ramparts of the Antonia fortress.

If the soldiers were Samaritans it makes the mockery of Jesus all the more poignant. Jesus, of course, had an entirely different attitude to the Samaritans. These were people whom, at other times, he might have encountered on the roads of Judaea, or in his journeys through Samaria; these were people whom he had used as examples of people who were entering the kingdom ahead of the pious Jews.

The idea, then, that Jesus was crucified by a load of Latin-speaking Italians is far from the truth. He was crucified by local squaddies, recruited from people who hated the Jews with a passion.

'The soldiers wove a crown of thorns'

This, then, is one reason why the soldiers relish the beating and the humiliation so much. 'Hail King of the Jews'! What a joke. It's not just humiliating one pathetic peasant: it's mocking the pretensions of the whole Jewish nation. Their 'king' is entirely at the mercy of the Romans. The Samaritan troops can do with him – and with them – exactly as they wish.

Jesus, already bleeding and broken, is brought back into the main square, where the entire cohort join in the fun. They have the power over him now: they will dress him and undress him like some kind of grotesque doll. They dress him in a coloured robe. Although the translation says purple, the word can mean a range of colours from blue to red, and it's unlikely that they would have had a purple robe handy, that being the most expensive dye.[74] Anyway, it's all part of the 'let's pretend' joke. Jesus is dressed in a mockery of imperial clothing. And a crown of thorns is pressed onto his head.

The crown of thorns is part of the iconography of the Longest Week. It is usually portrayed as a standard Western crown, a broad circle of thorns pushed down around Jesus' head. However, it may well have been a different sort of crown entirely. Images of kings from that time, which have been found on coins, depict crowns that radiate out from the head, like the rays of the sun. And with regard to the thorns, it's reasonable to suppose that the soldiers used whatever thorny plants they could find nearby. The most common would have been the date palm, *Phoenix dactylifera*, which has ferociously sharp and vicious thorns that stick upwards.[75] Since these would have been the palm branches waved just a few days earlier when Jesus entered Jerusalem, the soldiers' use of them may be significant. Had the story of his alternative procession reached them? And was this the revenge for his mockery?

So Jesus is beaten savagely, humiliated, mocked, spat upon and struck repeatedly. And then, in the chillingly plain words of Mark, 'they led him out to crucify him' (Mark 15.20).

The crucifixion

Where: Golgotha

When: 9 a.m.

The Græco-Roman world didn't talk about crucifixion. They knew about it, of course. There were permanent crucifixion sites in most of the cities. But crucifixion was a death reserved for the lowest classes; it was a death for slaves or rebels. It was not a subject for polite conversation.[76]

This is why we don't really know a great deal about the process. The Gospels themselves are probably the fullest accounts of crucifixions in ancient literature, and even they skim over the details. However, they do describe the general process. After flogging, the victim had the crossbeam of the cross strapped to his arms, across his shoulders. Since wood was so scarce in Jerusalem, he was probably allocated a crossbeam that had been used before.[77] He would then be led out to the place of execution.

It was not a long journey. Although pilgrims today in Jerusalem commemorate the event by following the stations of the cross along the *Via Dolorosa*, that is a mediaeval invention which probably starts from the wrong point. As we have seen, Pilate was in Herod's Palace, not in the Antonia Fortress, and Herod's Palace is just a few hundred metres south of the place where Jesus was to be killed.

So the journey could not have taken long, yet even those few hundred metres were too much for Jesus. The Romans co-opted a helpful 'volunteer'. The Synoptics simply identify him as 'Simon of Cyrene, the father of Alexander and Rufus' (Mark 15.21). That he had come in from the country (Mark 15.21) may mean that he had been working in the fields, or it may mean that he was a supporter of Jesus who had just heard the news. Because, by now, a group of supporters have gathered – a great number, according to Luke.

Mark, after all, mentions Simon's sons, in a manner which suggests that they would have been known to his readers. There was a Rufus in the church in Rome (Rom. 16.13) and there was a church in Cyrene from a very early date (Acts 6.9; 11.20; 13.1). A burial cave discovered in the Kidron Valley revealed a first-century ossuary with the bones of 'Alexander, son of Simon' and in Hebrew '*Alexandros Qrnyt.*' Some scholars read these letters as *qrnyh*, which means '*qireniyah*', or Cyrene. The names are all very common, but it may be that we have the grave of the son of the man who carried Jesus' cross.[78] Did Simon and his family become followers? Was he the first follower of Jesus to literally take up his cross? All guesswork and connections. Per-haps more significant is the fact the Jesus cannot carry it himself. So harsh was the beating that he can hardly walk.

Behind him and around him, however, is a crowd. Once again the description of the people following Jesus belies the myth of the 'Jews' turning against him. A great crowd of people – wom-en mainly – are wailing, broken-hearted, banshee-voiced and beating their breasts in the full pain of sorrow. Some of these would have been there out of curiosity, others out of mercy. It was common for women to witness executions and provide pain-killing opiates for the victims.[79] But some of them we know were Jesus' followers. And the grief expressed here seems to go beyond the formulaic requirements of official mourning.

Otherwise, why would Jesus address them? Jesus' words to them, as recorded by Luke, are words of judgement, taking us back two days to the hill overlooking Jerusalem. 'If they do this when the wood is green, what will happen when it is dry?' (Luke 23.31). There is a fire coming; the green wood has already been caught up in it – imagine what will happen when the dry wood catches light.[80]

'They brought Jesus to the place called Golgotha'

The place of execution was known as Golgotha, or the Place of the Skull. It was just outside the city, as all such sites were. With typical Roman efficiency it was about the nearest point outside the city to the Herodian Palace – a graveyard in an old quarry.

Today, there is a church on the site, one of the most ancient and famous churches in the world. The Western church calls it the Church of the Holy Sepulchre. The Eastern church, showing perhaps more of a 'glass-half-full' optimism, calls it the *Anastasis* – the Church of the Resurrection. The church is a divisive place: you either love it or hate it. Many Christians are put off by the endless arguments, the obscure ritual and the interior, which is a mixture of bling and submarine. To others, there is a sense of mystery there, a sense of rootedness. *This* – this is where it all began.

But is it the place? Well, there are good reasons for assuming that Jesus was executed here and buried nearby. First, at the time of his death, this site was outside the city walls. Second, it is a short distance north of the site of Herod's Palace, making it convenient for the Roman troops. The church does, indeed, stand above a first-century graveyard: graves have been found beneath the building. And the tradition that this was the site dates back to before Christianity became the official religion of the Roman Empire, so the likelihood is that the early church remembered the place, even when it was dangerous to do so. So, if it was not the place, it was near the place. If the rock within the church is not Golgotha, then it is something very near to it.

The soldiers offer Jesus wine mixed with myrrh, but he refuses it. Normally this is seen as a refusal to take sedatives: whatever Jesus is going to go through he is going to experience it awake and conscious. However, myrrh is neither an analgesic nor a

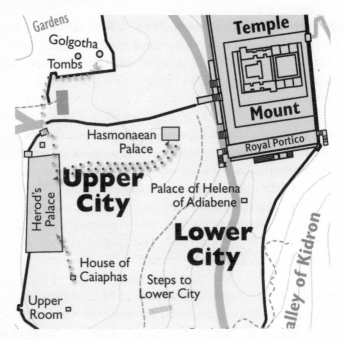

Trial and execution: the journeys of Jesus on Friday morning.

•••••• 1. From Caiaphas' House to Pilate
•••••• 2. From Pilate to Herod Antipas, and back
•••••• 3. From Pilate's HQ to Golgotha

sedative. In fact, wine mixed with myrrh was a delicacy. Unlike the nard with which Jesus was anointed in Bethany, myrrh was a local product, from the balsam groves in the Jordan valley, where the desert climate and the low altitude made the perfect growing conditions.[81] Pliny wrote, 'The finest wine in early days was that spiced with the scent of myrrh.'[82] This, then, is not a gesture of help from the soldiers, but another piece of mockery: the king of the Jews, drinking the 'finest' wine. Indeed, the soldiers were probably lying about the wine; later on they drop the pretence and offer him ordinary soured wine instead.

Then they stripped off his clothes and at nine o'clock in the morning, they crucified him.

As for how it was done, the details are difficult to define, since crucifixion itself could take a variety of forms. Crucifixion was not a Roman invention, but like many Roman practices it was something that they perfected. Like their roads and bridges, there was something horribly efficient about the Roman way of crucifixion. As Hengel has put it, 'Crucifixion was a punishment in which the caprice and sadism of the executioners were given full rein.'[83] Josephus tells how Roman soldiers besieging Jerusalem 'amused' themselves by crucifying their victims in different poses and positions:

> Scourged and subjected before death to every torture, they *[the captured prisoners]* were finally crucified in view of the wall...The soldiers themselves through rage and bitterness nailed up their victims in various attitudes as a grim joke, till owing to the vast numbers there was no room for the crosses, and no crosses for the bodies.[84]

Seneca reported on a mass crucifixion that he saw: 'I see crosses there, not just of one kind but made in many different ways: some have their victims with their head down to the ground, some impale their private parts, others stretch out their arms.'[85] Evidence from a crucifixion victim found near Jerusalem – the only crucifixion victim discovered by archaeologists – indicates that the crossbar was set in place and the victim's hands nailed, then his legs were lifted up and he was sat on a small peg. A single nail was then either driven laterally through his ankles, or his feet were nailed into the side of the main beam.[86]

This means that the victim would not have been raised up high on the beam (that, after all, would have required a lot of effort), but was most probably just above eye level. The Christian traditions record that the site of Jesus' crucifixion was on a rocky outcrop – a place that would have meant that lots of people could see it. But the cross itself was not high. Jesus would have been able to look his executioners in the eye.

Pilate had had a sign written to put on the cross, which read: 'Jesus of Nazareth, the King of the Jews'. It was written in all the major languages of Jerusalem: Hebrew, Latin and Greek – and it was Pilate's last snipe at the Jewish leaders who had asked him not to use the phrase 'King of the Jews' on a public sign. Despite their complaints, Pilate refused to change the wording (John 19.22) and this was the 'charge sheet' that was hung on the upright beam, just above Jesus' head.

'They crucified Jesus there with the criminals'

Crucifixion was a shameful death. That, indeed, was the point. It was a death designed to shame you, to humiliate and terrify. It was a death designed to frighten people into obedience. Because the primary target group for this kind of death were slaves. Crucifixion was 'the slaves' death'. With so many millions of slaves in the Empire, it was crucial that they should never be allowed to get out of control. So they had to be terrorised into obedience, and one of the main ways of doing that was through crucifixion. The slave rebellions of the second century BC culminated in mass crucifixions; the victorious Crassus had six thousand slaves crucified, lining the main road into Rome. But a slave could expect this terrible punishment for all manner of offences.[87]

Crucifixion was also the punishment for rebels. At the slightest hint of rebellion in the provinces, Rome hit back with terrible force. Crucifixion was one of their methods. It was a public humiliation and degradation. Often the victims were not allowed burial. It was, in the words of Borg and Crossan, an act of 'imperial terror'.[88]

It is a cruel irony that for so many years the Jews have been somehow held responsible for the cross, when it was so often the punishment that was inflicted on them. Few people suffered more from crucifixion than the Jews themselves. Josephus describes how the Hasmonaean ruler, Alexander Hannaus, had 800 men crucified in 88 BC.[89] In the days preceding the Jewish revolt, the Roman Procurator, Florus, used crucifixion as a punishment for those who mocked him. He had a large number of Jewish citizens and members of the Jewish aristocracy picked at random, put in chains and then crucified. This was despite pleas for mercy from Queen Bernice.[90] According to Josephus,

The Crucified Man

In 1968 the bones of a crucified man were unearthed in an ossuary found at Giv'at ha-Mivtar, near Jerusalem. His name was Yehohanan ('Jonathan'). He had been nailed through the heel bone (*calcaneum*) and his legs had been broken – probably to hasten his death.

Two theories have been put forward as to the manner of his death. The first suggested that his wrists were nailed, then his legs lifted and a nail driven through the ankle bone, leaving the victim in a foetal position (Fig 1.).

A revised theory argued that the victim 'straddled' the cross, and that two nails were used, one through each ankle. His arms were put over the cross and secured by ropes. (Fig 2.)

According to the gospels Jesus was nailed through the hands, in which case his arms were probably bound to the cross. Crucifixion victims were also supported either by a **sedile** – a small peg sticking out of the cross on which the victim sat – or a **suppedaneum** – a ledge on which the victim stood.

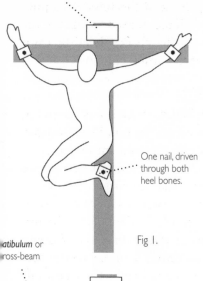

One nail, driven through both heel bones.

Fig 1.

atibulum or ross-beam

Sedile

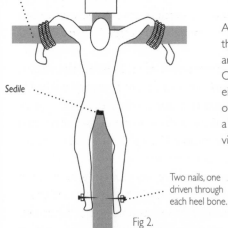

Two nails, one driven through each heel bone.

Fig 2.

The earliest known depiction of the crucifixion of Jesus. From a fifth-century door panel in the church of Santa Sabina, Rome.

Quintillius Varus had 2,000 Jewish people crucified after the revolt in the wake of the death of Herod the Great.[91]

So when Jesus talked about his followers taking up their crosses he was referring to a practice that was common. It was understood by the Jews that, if they stepped out of line, that was what the Romans would do to them. Jesus knew the fate that awaited him would be at the hands of the Romans.[92] Indeed, it was seen as a likely reward for obedience, as much as rebellion. In a commentary on Exodus 20.6, Rabbi Nathan wrote:

> 'Why are you being led out to be decapitated?' 'Because I circumcised my son to be an Israelite.' 'Why are you being led out to be burned?' 'Because I read the Torah.' 'Why are you being led out to be crucified?' 'Because I ate the unleavened bread.'[93]

In other words, faithfulness to the Torah would lead to conflict with the Romans. And conflict with the Romans could only ever have one outcome.

The use of crucifixion as a punishment for rebels lies behind the deaths of the other two prisoners who were crucified alongside Jesus that day. They are often called thieves or robbers, but they belong in the same class as Barabbas: bandits, *lestai*. They were political insurgents as well as robbers, people who targeted the rich and the powerful and, especially, supporters or members of the pro-Roman governments of Galilee and Judaea.[94] For Josephus, what made someone a bandit, rather than a thief, was that the motivation for the act was political from the first.[95] The *Syriac Sayings of Menander* produced a chilling epigram: 'Stealing is the carpenter of the cross.' But by 'stealing' they did not mean petty theft or burglary. What the cross punished was banditry with a political agenda.[96]

The aim of such banditry was not only to get money, but also to cause disruption and fear. It was about disturbing the *pax Romana*, one effect of which was to increase travel. 'You may be in control of the city,' says the bandit, 'but, out here, it is a different matter.' So Jesus wasn't crucified between two pickpockets, or two housebreakers. He was crucified between two political bandits, two terrorists – at least in the eyes of the Romans.

And, from the Roman point of view, Jesus wasn't much different from them. He, too, was a political prisoner, a man charged with insurrection, with claiming to be a king. One criminal, at least, seems to recognise that Jesus is in a class of his own. 'Remember me,' he says to Jesus, 'when you come into your kingdom.' Jesus' reply is an extraordinary statement of faith and hope: 'Today you will be with me in Paradise' (Luke 23.42–43). 'Paradise' is a word borrowed from the Persians, a word meaning a walled garden, a place of trees and shade and coolness and rest.[97] This is what Jesus, this dying peasant, promises. Here, amidst the blood and the dust and the heat of a Roman execution site in a disused quarry, he promises a criminal a different ending.

Something is happening here that is out of the ordinary, something that is to do not with the Roman world, but with a different vision of kingdom entirely (Luke 23.43). The whores and the tax-collectors are already beating the pious frauds into Paradise; now the bandits are at it as well.

'They divided his clothes among themselves'

The soldiers who crucified Jesus got to keep his possessions. Which is not saying much. Just the clothes he stood up in, in fact. Soldiers were not well paid. The officer class were OK. An auxiliary centurion received around 3,750 denarii per year – over ten times the annual wage of a peasant.[98] But down among the squaddies, down among the grunts, it was a different matter.

The yearly wage of an infantryman in an auxiliary cohort was 750 sestertii a year – around 187 denarii.[99] Their accommodation and food was subsidised, but the charges for it were deducted from their pay at source. Legionaries who mutinied in AD 14 complained of the arbitrary deductions from their pay. Along with deductions for food, clothing, equipment and tents, there were other charges as well, miscellaneous costs, which basically amounted to bribes to centurions. The lower ranks of soldiers may have lost anything from forty to seventy-five per cent of their stipend to these deductions. This meant that, although they were looked after at a very basic level, they had little money to support any dependants.[100]

They had to make up this money in other ways, notably by doing some 'moonlighting' in trade, or engaging in extortion.[101] This is why, when soldiers ask John the Baptist what they should do after baptism, he replies: 'Do not extort money from anyone by threats or false accusation, and be satisfied with your wages' (Luke 3.14).

So when the time came to grab some loot, they went for it. Jesus had always said that if someone asked for your coat, you should give them your shirt as well (Luke 6.29). Here, his clothing was being given away.

Luke also records that the soldiers joined in the general mockery of Jesus, offering him sour wine and challenging him to save himself. All the Gospels record the general mockery of Jesus; it is attributed to passers-by (Matt. 27.39), to the soldiers (Luke 23.36), and to the chief priests, elders, scribes and other leaders (Matt. 27.41; Mark 15.31). (The latter cannot have been high up in the Temple hierarchy; otherwise they would have been occupied in the preparations for Passover on the other side of the city.) But their mockery and that of the 'passers-by' is consistent with the charges that the Temple aristocracy brought at the first hearing: Jesus threatened the Temple, now look at him! He said he was the Messiah but he can't save himself (Mark 15.31–2).

'Meanwhile, standing near the cross'

There were other people among the bystanders, people who had no reason to mock: Jesus' family. At least, the female members of his family. His father, Joseph, was probably dead by this time, but his mother, Mary, was present.[102] In fact, the Gospels list different groups of women around the cross.

▷ Mark: Mary Magdalene, and Mary the mother of James the younger and of Joses, and Salome (Mark 15.40);

▷ Matthew: Mary Magdalene, and Mary the mother of James and Joseph, and the mother of the sons of Zebedee (Matt. 27.56);

▷ John: Jesus' mother and his mother's sister, Mary the wife of Clopas, and Mary Magdalene (John 19.25).

Some of these are probably the same person, but identified by different relationships. So Matthew puts in 'the mother of the sons of Zebedee', whereas Mark has 'Salome'. Matthew, aware that his readers didn't know who Salome was, prefers to explain her status. This raises the possibility that she is present in all three lists; she may be the woman John calls 'his mother's sister.' If this is so, it would make the apostles John and James, Jesus' cousins on his mother's side.[103] Obviously they could be different women; the sheer number of women called Mary shows how popular a name it was, and the Gospel writers say that these women were 'among' those standing there. But this identification would explain why John and James' mother asked Jesus for preferential treatment. After all, they were family (Matt. 20.20–23).[104]

For the moment, the question is: where are the men? None of Jesus' brothers are there; nor, apparently, are any of his disciples (apart from the author of John). We know his brothers' names: James, Joses, Judas and Simon (Mark 6.1–4), but the Gospels imply that they were not convinced of Jesus' mission until after the crucifixion. John says that 'not even his brothers believed in him' (John 7.3–5) and they even tried to stop him (Mark 3.21). At this point they must have felt that he had brought utter shame on his family.[105] At the cross, therefore, Jesus entrusts the care of his mother not to a brother, but to John. His family, for the most part, have deserted him and it will be left to a stranger to lay him in the grave.

Darkness at noon

Where: Golgotha

When: 12 noon

From twelve noon till three o'clock, the Synoptic Gospels record that there was an unnatural darkness over the land. Some have argued that this was an eclipse, but that is astronomically impossible. Passover was scheduled to take place at the time of a full moon, and you can't have a total eclipse during a full moon. Many theories have been put forward, everything from sun spots to sand storms.[106] Certainly, eclipses were signs of doom.[107] The darkness is also linked with Old Testament prophecies, such as Amos 8.9–10:

> On that day, says the Lord God, I will make the sun go down at noon, and darken the earth in broad daylight. I will turn your feasts into mourning, and all your songs into lamentation… I will make it like the mourning for an only son, and the end of it like a bitter day. (Amos 8.9–10)

I think this is the first indication of something that, increasingly, is going to push us out of history and into something darker, deeper and altogether mysterious. This is a cosmic phenomenon: inexplicable, strange. From now on, in the Gospels, the weirdness begins to kick in.

It captures the way in which this story has been getting progressively darker. The shadowy world of Judaean politics has led to this: three hours of pain and humiliation and casual, gratuitous mockery. Three hours of women weeping at the death agonies of their son, their nephew, their rescuer. The darkness has been gathering since dawn.

'The day of Preparation'

During the afternoon the screaming began.

If there is one noise that must have been associated with that day, it must have been the screams of terrified animals as they were taken to the Temple to be slaughtered, as they were crammed together to await their fate.

Because this was the day of Preparation. At 3 p.m., the

slaughter started and the city began to smell of blood.

The evening before, while Jesus was eating the meal with his disciples, the households in the city would be carefully searched for yeast, so that it could be removed and set aside. Then, on the day of Preparation itself, the crowds would begin to gather around the Temple and in the Temple precincts. Each man – or group of men – would be carrying a lamb which had been carefully selected (and for the most part purchased) four days before. During the afternoon of Nisan 14, through the strange, unearthly gloom, the celebrants had made their way to the Temple, where, at the appointed time, they would enter the Court of Priests in three groups. After each group had gone in, the gate was shut behind them. The celebrant would then slit the lamb's throat and flay the carcass, while a priest collected the blood in a basin. These basins were passed back from priest to priest, until they reached the altar, where the blood was dashed against the steps. Meanwhile the celebrant also had to skin the lamb, and then remove the entrails, which were taken away and burnt on the altar. While the rites were being performed, the Levites played music and psalms were sung or recited.

The sheer numbers of animals given by Josephus are staggering – and quite probably completely exagerrated. Josephus puts the number of lambs killed, during one festival, at 256,500.[108] If we are to believe that the sacrifice only took place over a two-hour period, this would mean that there had to be a slaughtering of 2,000 lambs a minute and that, with one lamb to every twenty people there was a population of over five million. Jeremias suggested a figure of between 80,000 and 125,000 pilgrims to the festival, along with some 30,000 in the population of Jerusalem, yet even that seems suspiciously high.[109] That would still require at least 5,000 lambs: a throughput of forty-two lambs a minute, each lamb requiring its blood be collected, its skin to be removed and its entrails to be taken out.

A lamb with its throat cut can take up to two minutes to die.[110] Add at least another two minutes to skin and prepare the animal and it would take a total of 333.33 man hours to kill 5,000 lambs. So you could just about do that number if you had 170 priests, but they'd have to be working at peak capacity for two hours.

It seems unlikely, especially as the area in which all these people were crowding – the Court of the Israelites – was only some seventy metres wide and twenty metres deep. The only inference we can make is that the numbers in Jerusalem were smaller, the slaughter took longer than the two hours, the groups were bigger or – and this seems most likely – not everyone in Jerusalem got involved. Out of the inhabitants of Jerusalem there must have been many who simply did not or could not participate. Indeed, the Mishnah implies that those who could not afford a lamb could join in with one of the many groups who would be celebrating in the city.

Whatever the case, the slaughtering of that many animals would require an industrial-scale production line. Today, the Hajj is the only comparable event. At the Hajj today, an estimated 800,000–1,000,000 sheep, goats and camels are ritually slaughtered over three days. The meat is intended to be a gift to the poor and not a blood sacrifice. Today the slaughter can take place only in a designated area, and the pilgrim is not allowed to take away from there more meat than he and those with him can eat in three days.[111] However, even with modern methods, the sacrifices can cause enormous problems. In 1972 the slaughterhouse area was blocked with carcasses, and bulldozers had to be employed to open emergency gates.[112]

In the much smaller area of the Court of Israelites, the crush must have been enormous. The stench of the blood and the plaintive screams of distress from the animals, the mess of the hides and the dung, all set against the bright white marble and gold of the Temple, must have been an almost physical, visceral assault on the senses.

At Golgotha, just across the city, the sounds and the smells must have been only too apparent. And there, too, at 3 p.m., the screaming started.

'It is finished'

Where: Golgotha

When: 3 p.m.

A 3 p.m., according to Mark, Jesus gave a 'loud cry'. The Greek indicates that this was a scream of urgency, a cry for help: a prayer, in fact.[113] The translation of *phone megale* is literal, but cannot possibly capture the intensity of a man screaming out from the cross.

Mark says that Jesus screamed out a verse from a psalm in Aramaic: *Eloi, Eloi, lema sabachthani?* which means, 'My God, my God, why have you forsaken me?' (Mark 15.34). The quotation comes from Psalm 22, and is the only statement uttered by Jesus on the cross that Mark records. It is a cry of utter isolation and alienation, and is almost certainly authentic. One cannot imagine a later writer, a follower of a triumphant Christ-figure, making up a cry of such utter despair. There is something touching about the language, something heart-rending. One of Jesus' most characteristic habits was the use of the familiar Aramaic word *abba* to describe his relationship with God. Here, too he lapses back into his mother tongue. At this moment, though, '*Abba*' seems almost incomprehensibly distant. The people standing by mistake the words, thinking that the Aramaic *Eloi* is the same as the Hebrew word for Elijah.[114] It has been questioned whether Roman soldiers would have understood about Elijah; but this is one more indication that the auxiliaries were local. Italian legionaries would not have known about Elijah, but Samaritan recruits would have spoken Aramaic.

Was it a cry of failure, or a cry of recognition? Traditional theology argues that this was the point of abandonment, when Jesus was suffering for all mankind, but we should remember that it was a prayer, and prayer always implies the hope that someone, despite appearances, is listening. And Psalm 22 ends with vindication and restoration.

All the Gospels record Jesus being offered sour wine, or wine mixed with vinegar. Luke places it earlier in his narrative, John and the Synoptics just before the end, but there's no reason to think that he was offered it only once during the ordeal. John's account is the most detailed. Jesus says, 'I am thirsty' and someone puts a sponge on a branch of hyssop, dips it in sour wine and holds it to Jesus' lips. The use of a branch does not indicate that Jesus was out of reach, it was merely a tool for transferring some of the liquid from the jar to Jesus, without using a cup.

The offer of sour wine may have been a continuation of the mockery, although by now I think mockery would have been a bit pointless. The wine that was standing there in a jar (John 19.29) was simply the commonest sort of drink, the red peasant wine drunk by the ordinary soldier. Immediately after taking a drink, Jesus dies. In Matthew and Mark he gives a loud cry; in John he says 'It is finished'; in Luke he says 'Father, into your hands I commend my spirit' (Luke 23.46). (Matthew follows Mark's description.)

And with that, it was finished. Just another death of a failed revolutionary; just another ritual killing on this day of ritual killings; just another daily sacrifice for the well-being of the Empire.

'It is finished'

The death of Jesus raises the question of exactly *how* he died. Because, horrific though it is, crucifixion does not puncture any major arteries: having nails driven through your hands and feet does not kill you.

Many doctors have offered opinions on how, exactly, crucifixion killed its victims. At least ten different theories have been proposed, with many writers suggesting a combination of these different theories.[115]

The most frequent explanation is that the victim dies of asphyxiation. Accounts of prisoners who have been suspended by their arms with their feet off the ground show that their muscles go into spasm, and, unable to raise themselves to exhale, they die quickly. However, ancient accounts of crucifixion imply that victims survived for a long time, sometimes even days. Indeed, that was the purpose: crucifixion was, as we've seen, a graphic, visible warning to anyone thinking of rebelling. So, from the Romans' point of view, the longer the victim stayed alive and suffering, the better.

The reason they were able to survive for so long, is, in fact, that they weren't just suspended by their arms. Crucifixion victims generally sat on a small peg or block of wood fixed to the main upright beam, and called a *sedile* ('seat'). We can see this reflected in the unusual speed of Jesus' death.

> When evening had come, and since it was the day of Preparation, that is, the day before the Sabbath, Joseph of Arimathea, a respected member of the council, who was also himself waiting expectantly for the kingdom of God, went boldly to Pilate and asked for the body of Jesus. Then Pilate wondered if he were already dead; and summoning the centurion, he asked him whether he had been dead for some time. When he learned from the centurion that he was dead, he granted the body to Joseph. (Mark 15.42–45)

Jesus, then, died much more quickly than was expected, which indicates that he was actually badly injured before he even came to the cross. We have seen that he was unable to carry his own crossbeam to the site of execution, despite the distance from Herod's Palace to Golgotha being reasonably short. The implication, therefore, is that he was already seriously weakened by the loss of blood. When the loss of blood reaches a certain level, victims enter what is termed hypovolaemic shock, where the blood loss is so great that there is simply not enough to deliver oxygen to the organs.

We normally have around five litres of blood in our bodies. Hypovolaemic shock can be caused by both external and internal bleeding. A loss of more than 10–15 per cent can start to drive the body into shock; at 30 per cent the shock will be severe. For someone whose body is undergoing the extra trauma of crucifixion, a much smaller volume might have a proportionately greater effect. The external bleeding from the whips and the nails, and the internal bleeding from the beating, would have been more than enough. He died of blood loss from the beating he had taken earlier. This is, indeed, what happened to many crucifixion victims. Many actually died during the beating.[116]

Jesus died on the cross; that is certainly true. But the cross was just the *coup de grâce*, the final slash of the knife. The cross was for display purposes. It was a display of power, a grotesque human billboard advertising the consequences of rebellion.

Jesus had essentially been beaten to death by soldiers that morning. Just as he had been convicted long before the sentence was pronounced, he was dead long before they drove the nails in.[117]

'They did not break his legs'

Because it was a holy day, and also the Sabbath, the Jews did not want the bodies of the crucifixion victims left out after sunset, i.e. the beginning of Passover and Sabbath. This was one of their religious rituals. So they asked that the legs of the victims should be broken, an activity which may have served to increase the speed of death. The usual theory about this practice of breaking the legs – what the Romans called *crurifragium* – is that the victims would no longer be able support themselves by their legs and would, therefore, asphyxiate. As we have seen, however, they were supported on the peg, so *crurifragium* must simply have been a brutal way of inducing more trauma into an already savagely traumatised body. It was shock, more than anything, which must have sped up the process of dying.

The bandits either side of Jesus were dispatched in this way. But Jesus was already dead and, to make sure, a soldier stabbed him through the side. John reports that he was actually there, and that 'blood and water' emerged. John makes theological conclusions out of this death, linking it with two Old Testament prophecies (John 19.31–37).

Physiologically, various suggestions have been made, for example the idea that the blood came from the heart and the water from the pericardial sac. However, another theory fits better. Victims of severe 'non-penetrating' chest injuries have been shown to have 'haemorrhagic fluid' in the space between the ribs and the lung – as much as two litres – which can separate into two layers, red blood and a clearer, pale serum. The proponent of this theory, A. F. Sava, suggests that 'the brutal scourging of Christ several hours before his death upon the cross, was sufficient to produce a bloody accumulation within the chest, so that the settling by this fluid into layers and its ultimate evacuation by opening the chest below the level of separation must inevitably result in the "immediate" flow of blood followed by water'.[118]

In Mark, the centurion, seeing the way that Jesus died, declares 'Truly this man was God's son!' (Mark 15.39). In Luke, he declares, 'Certainly this man was innocent' (Luke 23.47). In Matthew, he sees the earthquake, and says 'Truly this man was God's Son!' (Matt. 27.54). Whether he was saying 'the son of God' or 'a son of God' is difficult to determine, for the Greek has no definite article. There's no need to see it as a sudden 'conversion', necessarily. It could be a response to the manner of Jesus' death, a soldier standing by and declaring, 'This was a divine man!'

Again, the centurion is often portrayed as a Roman but, given that he would have been in charge of auxiliaries, he may have been Samaritan or Greek. Auxiliary units were under the command of a tribune, from the equestrian class. For many such officers, these units would have been their first command, a way for them to get some experience. Probably, then, these tribunes came to rely heavily on their centurions – who may well have risen from the ranks. So this is not a cultivated Roman, but a local appointment: either a member of a well-respected provincial family who has entered at centurion level, or, more likely, a humble soldier who has risen through the ranks, a career soldier.[119] He may have been Pilate's appointment: certainly the Prefect of Egypt appointed the centurions in his auxiliaries.[120]

The centurion recognised that there was something

compellingly, unaccountably different about Jesus. He was a singularity, an uncommon man, even when he died the commonest of deaths.

'The curtain of the temple was torn in two'

With Jesus' death, we go further into the twilight world of strangeness that began with the darkness. Once again, there are some significant differences between the accounts. Mark and Luke have the tearing of the veil in the Temple and the proclamation of the centurion. Matthew has the curtain, the centurion, an earthquake, tombs open, and the dead walking. John, whom we might expect to be the most cosmically attuned and mystical, is, in fact, the most prosaic. No curtain, no earthquake, no dead men walking. (Not even, in fact, any mysterious darkness.)

What are we to make of this? And what, historically, are we to do when faced with tombs opening? With earthquakes? And with a twenty-five-metre embroidered curtain being torn from top to bottom?[121]

Let's start with the curtain. The Synoptic Gospels record that, with Jesus' death, the curtain in the Temple was torn from top to bottom (Matt. 27.51; Mark 15.38; Luke 23.45). This event is often questioned, as it's not recorded anywhere other than in these Gospels. Surely such a momentous event would have been recorded by Josephus?[122] There were two curtains in the Temple; one separating the Holy of Holies from the holy place, and one separating the sanctuary from the courtyard. The likelihood is that the writers are referring to the inner curtain, if only for symbolic reasons.

In Christian theology, the tearing of the curtain has been taken to mean that Christ's death now allows anyone access to the Holy of Holies; that the place where only the High Priest could go is now open for all. In fact, it may have other layers of meaning. One is that it's an image of exit, rather than entrance: the implication that the spirit of God has actually left the Temple.[123] But if we look at contemporary descriptions of the curtain we may discern another meaning – one that might fit slightly better with Matthew's earthquakes. For Jews such as Josephus and Philo, the Temple had a kind of cosmic significance: it was the centre of creation. For Josephus, the seven branches of the candlestick represented the planets, while Philo believed that the high priest's vestments represented heaven and earth: the emeralds on each shoulder the sun and the moon.[124] The curtain was woven from Babylonian cloth, and embroidered in blue, scarlet and purple. According to Josephus this represented creation:

> ...for the fine linen was proper to signify the earth, because the flax grows out of the earth; the purple signified the sea, because that color is dyed by the blood of a sea shell fish; the blue is fit to signify the air; and the scarlet will naturally be an indication of fire. [125]

Matthew, who is a contemporary of both Philo and Josephus, shares the same kind of cosmic understanding. He links the tearing of the curtain with the earth shaking and rocks splitting (Matt. 27.51). He uses the same verb to describe both the tearing of the curtain and the ripping-open of the rocks. So, although later Christian tradition sees this as symbolising access to the Holy of Holies, in contemporary Jewish belief it just as likely symbolised a rupture in creation. That great symbol of creation, the curtain – which hung in the heart of the Temple, itself the centre of the universe – had been torn. To Jews such as Josephus and Philo, it would have been a sign that something had gone badly wrong with creation.

Indeed, it is in the light of this ground-shaking, cosmos-tearing event that Matthew reports that the tombs were opened. His description is rather odd:

> The tombs also were opened, and many bodies of the saints who had fallen asleep were raised. After his resurrection they came out of the tombs and entered the holy city and appeared to many. (Matt. 27.52–53)

So, although the tombs were opened – presumably by the earthquake, which would have rolled away stones and lifted the lids – the dead were not seen in the city until days later. They had to come into the city, of course, because the dead

A typical first-century tomb. The stone is set into a grooved channel, and rolled across the face of the cave.

were buried outside the city walls and away from habitation. It would certainly not have been unusual for an earthquake to open up tombs. But the appearance of these walking dead has not been recorded anywhere else in the New Testament, let alone outside the New Testament. In the light of the absence of such information, we have to view the event as a theological statement more than a historical one.[126]

'The women who had followed him from Galilee'

The different Gospels preserve different traditions; even where they reflect the same traditions, they often do so in a different order. Nevertheless, there is one thing that ties all the accounts together: the presence of the women.

We have already looked at some of the women who would have been at the crucifixion. It is not hard to imagine the scene. If the crucifixion of Jesus took place on the rocky outcrop of

Golgotha, we can imagine the women and the crowd down below, on the floor of the disused quarry.

Luke paints the picture, as the scene ends. Jesus is dead; the bodies are being taken down from the crosses; the crowd, which had had such hopes for Jesus, begins to drift away. Only the faithful few remain:

> And when all the crowds who had gathered there for this spectacle saw what had taken place, they returned home, beating their breasts. But all his acquaintances, including the women who had followed him from Galilee, stood at a distance, watching these things. (Luke 23.48–49)

It will be the acquaintances who take charge now. And it is the women who will be the witnesses of the final dramatic act.

Joseph of Arimathea

Where: Tomb

When: 4 p.m.

It was getting late and there wasn't much time. Joseph of Arimathea had to move quickly.

No point in worrying about the fallout; what had to be done, had to be done. Having seen the death of Jesus, he made his way south, through the gates and down to Herod's Palace. There, pulling whatever strings such a wealthy and influential man could, he persuaded Pilate to let him have the body of Jesus and give it a decent burial.

There is no reason to think that he would have had to tug very hard on those strings. Pilate, we know, had been ambivalent about whether or not Jesus had deserved such a fate.

At this time, according to Mark, Jesus' body had not yet been taken down from the cross. Given that Joseph also had to arrange for the purchase of a linen cloth, we can presume that Jesus died pretty soon after three o'clock. Otherwise, people would have been shutting up shop for the Passover.

Joseph had just had a new tomb dug. He was a man of means, but then you'd expect that from a member of the Sanhedrin. As we've seen, just because he was on the Sanhedrin doesn't mean that he agreed with – or was even consulted about – the death of Jesus. Pilate, having checked that Jesus was already dead, grants permission for Joseph to bury Jesus.

It's particularly striking that Jesus is not buried by his family (at least, not the male relatives), nor, as was the case with John the Baptist, by his disciples (Mark 6.29). Instead, the burial arrangements are made hurriedly, and by an apparent stranger.

For those who deny the historicity of the burial stories, Joseph of Arimathea is a complete fabrication, invented to explain how a crucified man who would normally be denied burial ended up in a grave (from which he subsequently disappeared). But it seems to me that the strength of the tradition (Joseph appears in all four Gospels) means that we have to take it more seriously than that. We know he was wealthy, and we know he was a member of the Sanhedrin, although not one with a massive amount of power and influence. A prominent backbencher, perhaps, in the language of modern politics. Arimathea, his town of origin, is unknown. It was not in Galilee, since Luke calls Arimathea 'a Jewish town' (Luke 23.51), meaning that it was in Judaea. Several sites have been proposed. Eusebius, the early church historian, suggested Rempthis or Rentis, northeast of Lydda.[127] Whatever the case, Joseph was now permanently domiciled in Jerusalem, which is why he had bought a tomb there. Some have argued that his burial of Jesus has more to do with Jewish piety than with being an actual follower, especially since Mark does not call him a disciple. However, John and Matthew call him a disciple, and, as we have seen, John, in particular, seems to have had a source of information about the followers in Jerusalem.

That Joseph needed 'boldness' (Mark 15.43) may simply mean that approaching the Roman Prefect for anything required a bit of courage. Or that Pilate was not inclined to welcome any of Jesus' sympathisers.[128] Or, indeed, it may be that the boldness was not for fear of Pilate, but for fear of his colleagues on the Sanhedrin. John says that he had kept his interest in Jesus quiet for 'fear of the Jews', i.e. the Jewish leadership (John 19.38).

But, at this point, they were all on the other side of the city, in or around the Temple, active in the Passover preparation; they would have had little idea that, late in the day, one of their own was giving a decent burial to the heretical rebel they'd just rid themselves of. So Joseph needed courage, not least the courage to proclaim himself a sympathiser of Jesus.

Pilate's first response is to check whether Jesus is really dead. Since crucifixion victims could linger for days, he wants to be sure that this isn't a rescue attempt. People could recover from crucifixion.[129] Once the death was confirmed, Pilate agreed to let Joseph have the body. As for the reason why Pilate granted permission to a man who was not, after all, any relative of the deceased, I think, given the political manouevring of the morning, that it may be as simple as this: he wanted to annoy the Temple leadership. Like the sign that he had made to hang over Jesus' head, like the repeated questions about 'your king'. Pilate knew that the Temple aristocracy wanted Jesus dead, and he knew that, for political reasons, he had to comply. But, having done so, he was free to find other ways to remind them who was really in charge. For Pilate, then, just as much as for Joseph of Arimathea, the burial of Jesus was worth doing. A small victory is still a victory.

Although the accounts talk of Joseph 'taking the body down', there's no need to view that literally. Nor is there any need to get over-analytical about the lack of involvement of the women. Joseph was a rich man, and rich men have servants and slaves to do things for them; they have workers and employees who will move stones and even corpses. Perhaps he had Gentile servants who would not be concerned about corpse impurity. Or maybe he paid the soldiers – as we've seen, they were always open to a bit of extra duty. This, I think, is quite likely, since the soldiers appear to know where the tomb is when they are sent to guard it the next day (see below). The women who were there – the 'women who had come with him [Jesus] from Galilee' (Luke 23.55) – would simply have to have followed. So they knew where the corpse was.

There was no time for the usual rituals. Burial ritual could be quite complex: the corpse would be washed and anointed, the body wrapped or clothed, the chin bound up and the eyes closed.[130] But there was no time for ritual. Jesus wasn't even washed – the minimum one would expect, since blood on a corpse was considered unclean.[131] John mentions that the corpse was bound and anointed, but it still reads like a rushed job.

'A Pharisee named Nicodemus'

And John mentions another who was involved – Nicodemus, who had come to meet Jesus before, by night (John 3.1–21). He was a Pharisee who was also 'a leader of the Jews', (John 3.1), which presumably means he was another member of the Sanhedrin. The fact that he appears several times in John's Gospel may indicate that he was one of John's special sources of information (John 3.1, 4, 9; 7.50; 19.39). He may have originated from Galilee (John 7.52), although the question 'Are you from Galilee too?' reads more like an insult than anything else. And he, too, was wealthy, judging by the spices and ointments he brought with him to anoint the corpse. John says he brought 100 Roman pounds of myrrh and aloes – about thirty-five kilos in modern measures. This is another of John's big numbers, like the 600 troops sent to arrest Jesus. Thirty-five kilos is a lot of spices: enough to cover the corpse in a mound. There is a suggestion by one scholar that the Greek word *hekaton* should be read *hekaston*, meaning 'myrrh and aloes about a pound *each*'. This would be more realistic.[132] Myrrh we have already encountered; aloes could be either the highly aromatic powdered wood of the eaglewood tree – *Aquilaria agallocha* – native to South East Asia and similar to sandalwood. Or it could be a liquid extract from a member of the lily family, the now-familiar (from shampoos anyway) *Aloe vera*, which had a bitter smell and powerful medicinal properties and was much used in embalming. The implication here is that these were dry spices, so probably some form of fragranced wood is the likeliest option.[133]

He may be the same Nicodemus as is mentioned in rabbinic sources: one Nicodemus son of Gorion. Nicodemus ben Gorion was a member of the council in Jerusalem and one of the richest people in the city. During the Jewish rebellion of AD 67–70, one of his granaries was burnt down. And this Nicodemus had family estates in Galilee. We know from John's account that Nicodemus was rich, for the amount of expensive spices he brought was extraordinarily lavish. Nicodemus probably died during the uprising.[134] His daughter was penniless afterwards.[135]

The site of the burial is within the church of the Holy Sepulchre in Jerusalem, just a short distance from the traditional site of the crucifixion. Mark's concern to mention that the two Marys saw where the body was laid indicates a concern to ensure a chain of witnesses to the correct location. These people saw where Jesus was killed; they saw where he was buried. Also, we know that members of Jesus' family were prominent in the early church. They, too, would have remembered the traditions.

Within fifteen years of Jesus' death, the burial place had been incorporated within the walls of the city, as Herod Agrippa expanded Jerusalem. In AD 135, when the Romans expelled all Jews from the city after the second Jewish revolt, the area was covered by a huge temple to Aphrodite. This, in fact, served to mark the site for the next 200 years. According to Jerome, the rock of Golgotha protruded above the platform of the Temple and served as a base for the statue of the god. So, ironically, it seems as though the Romans accidentally preserved the spot for the later Christians. When Melitto of Sardis came to Jerusalem in the second half of the second century he was taken by local Christians to the site, which he described as being in the middle of the broad streets of the city.[136] It was the perseverance of this tradition that led Constantine's builders, in 325, to dig beneath Hadrian's structures and discover the rock and a cave tomb.[137] Is it the exact place? Who knows. Certainly, if one had been inventing the site from scratch, one wouldn't have positioned it there, because by that time the site was inside the city walls. But its tradition stretches way back. Christians never seem to have come and worshipped at the tomb – a significant factor, as we shall see later. But they remembered where it was.

The trip from the cross to the burial place was not far, for both were in the remains of an old quarry. The quarry made an ideal place for a Jewish burial ground, since it would have had plenty of rock face, where a cave could be excavated. Jewish tombs of the period were mainly what are called *loculi* tombs, consisting of a doorway into a central chamber, with *loculi*, or niches, cut into the walls to hold the bodies. The *loculi* were about sixty centimetres wide and tunnelled into the rock to a depth of around two metres.[138] The arrangement is not unlike those drawers in a morgue, built to hold corpses. There might also be a stone ledge or bench on which bodies could be laid. This seems likely, since, later on, people see someone sitting inside the tomb. Other types of tomb had shelves or ledges for the bodies rather than *loculi* niches. Both types have been found in the area around the Holy Sepulchre.[139]

Joseph had only just had this tomb made, we are told. It was a new tomb, which he had purchased for his family. Loculi tombs were family tombs, but family doesn't just mean the nuclear family of mum, dad and the kids. Cousins, step-brothers, sister-in-laws, aunts – any member of the extended family – might be laid in the 'family tomb'. The actual entrance to the tomb chamber was small, so people would have had to bend down to get in. The tomb was closed by means of a large round stone, which sat in a groove that ran along the front. The stone was rolled across the groove, creating a barrier to any wild animals.

The impression given by the Gospel writers is that Joseph of Arimathea simply thought that something must be done. He had a new, empty tomb. It would do for now.

So that was that. Jesus of Nazareth, Joshua ben Joseph, was dead. The adventure was over. Everyone went home.

The sun set. On the Sabbath they rested according to the commandment (Luke 23.56).

'Then they returned and prepared spices and ointments'

What was it like for the followers of Jesus that night in Jerusalem? For those who had been at the cross, the journey back through the city must have been painful, for all around were the sounds of celebration: the sounds and sights and smells of Passover.

Originally, Passover had to be celebrated in the courtyard of the Temple itself.[140] But as the population grew, and as Herod's rebuilding programme made the Temple much more of a pilgrimage destination, this proved no longer practical. So the rules changed and, for the purposes of Passover, the boundaries of the Temple courtyard were extended to cover the entire city. For one night only, the city was the Temple and the Passover could be eaten anywhere within the walls. The Essenes vehemently opposed this democratisation of the festival and the author of *Jubilees* – a Jewish apocryphal work written around 150 BC – called for the death penalty for anyone who ate the lamb outside the Temple boundary.[141]

The lamb was eaten by groups of ten to twenty people. And since there were so many people in the city, it was celebrated wherever room could be found. A later passage from the Tosefta says that the Jews 'eat it [the Passover Lamb] in their courtyards and on their roofs'.[142] There were Passover ovens in the streets for the roasting of the lambs.[143] So Jerusalem that night must have been alight with fires, with the smell of roasting lamb, with groups of pilgrims taking whatever space they could find – rooftops, alleyways, streets – to eat their meal. If the numbers are correct, Passover night must have been like one huge street party.

And it was through this atmosphere that the women had to trudge back. Did they stay in the city? Did they make their way back to Bethany? Perhaps they went back to the upper room, just a little way from there, where, only the night before, the man who was their hero, their hope – their son – had shared his Passover meal with his followers. And now all that was gone.

And we, like those women who had followed him so far, are left with the question: why did Jesus die?

I've argued the reasons why other people wanted him dead. He had offended the wrong people; he had made what amounted to personal attacks on the economic policy of the Temple. He had accused the Temple aristocracy of being bandits, and the scribes of being spongers. He had attacked their status, by prophesying the destruction of the Temple, and their faith, by having the nerve to raise someone from the dead. When your means of controlling people is through granting them access to the sacred spaces, and someone comes along who says that the sacred spaces don't matter, that the sacred spaces are going to be destroyed anyway, you're in trouble. From the point of view of the Temple elite, that was the problem with Jesus: he didn't obey the rules. He was, literally, uncontrollable. He was a rocker of boats, a troublemaker, a rogue element – someone who could easily give the Romans an excuse.

From the Roman point of view he was a bargaining chip, nothing more. An innocent man, probably, caught up in Judaean politics. It didn't help, of course, that he wouldn't play the game; offer him a way out and he turned the other way; suggest he deny the charges and he just affirmed them.

But what about Jesus himself? Why did he let himself be caught? Why, when he got to Gethsemane, didn't he just keep going? One reason is simply that he died because he let people kill him. Jesus' advocacy of non-violence was, to some extent, part of his Jewish background. Although the Jews had engaged in warfare in the past (and would soon do so again), there is a sense in which they were never entirely happy with the idea. (This may be why, in the ancient world at least, they were never very good at it.) Other cultures celebrated their military victories with parades and arches and festivals, but the only Jewish holiday that celebrated a military victory was Hanukkah: the festival of lights. And that wasn't even in the Jewish Scriptures.[144]

The root of Jesus' non-violence, therefore, lay in his interpretation of Judaism. It lay, in particular, in two ideas: that you should love your neighbour as yourself, and that your neighbours included more people than his compatriots could imagine.

Samaritans, tax-collectors, prostitutes, Gentiles – *enemies*, in fact – were neighbours. And they needed to be shown God's love. Jesus claimed that he had not come to abolish Judaism but to fulfil it. He was pushing Judaism to the max. He was turning it up to eleven.

This is the central irony at the dark heart of these events. Jesus wasn't dangerous because he wanted to destroy Jewish law: he was dangerous because he really wanted to live it. To those whose positions meant that compromise was inevitable, a man who refused to compromise was a threat.

The Temple authorities had compromised with military, political and economic power. They had struck a deal with them so that they could, in their eyes, preserve the state and the Temple. We should not turn them into pantomime villains: they may well have done this deal with the highest of motives. They may have felt they had no choice. But when you make an agreement with dictators, even if that agreement is well intentioned, things tend to go wrong. Military dictators never obey the rules.

What Jesus did was take away their weapons. You cannot use the threat of impurity against a man who doesn't care. You cannot ban someone from your Temple worship if they don't want to come in in the first place. And death is no threat to someone who is prepared to die. This is why Pilate, too, was so baffled. If you are prepared to love someone, even though they kill you, there is nothing that tyrants can do.

Why did Jesus die? Because he wanted to. Because he refused to fight back. Because he'd always said you should love your enemies and this is what happens when you do.

And yet there's more to it than that. Because Jesus could have *not* fought his enemies and still escaped. He could, as we have seen, have just kept going and avoided conflict altogether. So maybe there was more going on here... some kind of test, some kind of strategy, some kind of victory and vindication. Maybe, in the words of Paolo Sacchi: 'Jesus wanted to die and he wanted it for a reason.'[145]

Day Seven: The Silence
Saturday 4 April

The guards at the tomb: The Palace of Herod the Great, Saturday morning

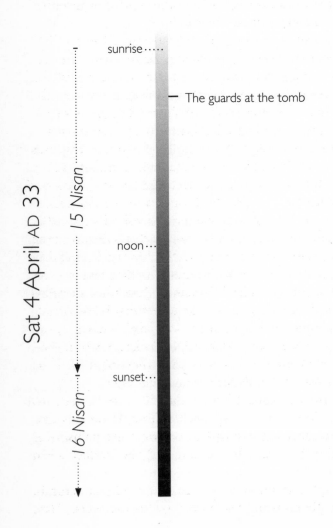

sunrise

The guards at the tomb

noon

sunset

Sat 4 April AD 33

15 Nisan

16 Nisan

The guards at the tomb

Where: The Palace of Herod the Great

When: 8 a.m.

On the Saturday morning, the Sabbath, the festival, all was quiet. Three of the Gospels – John, Mark and Luke – are silent about the Sabbath, picking up the story again on the Sunday morning.

Only Matthew has a small, but important, piece of narrative: a story about the guarding of the tomb.

Pilate must have been a quietly relieved man. Passover had taken place: no major riots, all diplomatic incidents averted. He'd scored some points and cemented some new alliances. Now, however, according to Matthew, a delegation from the Temple has made its way across to Pilate. The news of the burial by Joseph of Arimathea has evidently reached them and some steps need to be taken. They may have assumed that Jesus would have been tipped into an anonymous, unmarked grave; give the man a proper burial and he could become a martyr. Curiously, Matthew includes the Pharisees in the delegation. As we have seen, they were not directly involved with either the trial or the conviction of Jesus. Indeed, this is the only time they appear in Matthew's passion narrative.[1] It may be that they are involved because one of their number – Nicodemus – was involved in the action. Indeed, Joseph of Arimathea may also have been a Pharisee. Mark and Luke tell us that he was 'waiting expectantly for the kingdom of God', which would mean that he was not a Sadducee (Mark 15.43; Luke 23.50). If their followers have angered the Temple elite, they might feel the need to get involved, if only for diplomatic reasons.

There is also the issue of the Sabbath; it seems odd to have a delegation sent across from the Temple on this day. However, presumably there had to be some mechanism for communication between the Temple and the Prefect, even on the Sabbath.

So the Temple authorities want a guard placed on the tomb, to prevent the body being taken away by his followers. Pilate agrees to their request, maybe because, having given an order the day before that could be seen as sympathetic to Jesus, he wants to show a bit of balance. He agrees with their request.

It's not impossible, or even unlikely, that such a tomb would be guarded. The question is: what kind of guard was it? The implication is that it was a Roman guard, but in the second half of the story (Matt. 28.11–15) the guards return not to Pilate, but to the chief priests. Some of the language and terminology used, however, indicates a Roman troop.[2] Perhaps they came from the Antonia, next to the Temple, which would explain why the priests met them first. So it may well be that the Temple authorities set the guard and they went to Pilate to find out where the tomb was – to get official permission.

This event is not recorded in any of the other Gospels; in fact, the soldiers are completely absent from their accounts. It's one of those Matthaean anomalies, a nugget of popular tradition worked into his narrative. However, many scholars claim that the story was invented by Matthew to counter a later allegation against Christians: namely that they stole the body from the tomb and then claimed he'd risen from the dead. Aha! says Matthew, but look, there were soldiers guarding it!

The problem I have with this explanation is that, if it was an invention, it's not actually a very good one. Because the guards are only there from the Saturday morning – or even later. Jesus has already been in an unguarded tomb for well over twelve hours, so the posting of the guard now makes no difference to the charges whatsoever.[3] Even if the story was invented, it presupposes that the tomb was empty. What the theory assumes is that both the early church and their opponents took it for granted that the body was put into a tomb and then disappeared: they are arguing about what happened to the body.

Later, Matthew recounts how the Temple aristocracy bribe the soldiers to say that while they slept, the followers stole the body. The inference is that sleeping on duty would be a serious offence, but the authorities would 'see things right' with the Prefect.

The historicity of this story cannot be confirmed one way or the other, really. But the interesting thing is the final line: 'this story is still told among the Jews to this day' (Matt. 28.15). What that tells us is that the tomb was empty and even the opponents of Christianity never claimed anything different.

One thing more is recorded as happening on Saturday, this time after sunset, with the end of Sabbath. Three of the Galilean women – Mary Magdalene, Mary the mother of James, and Salome, go out and buy some spices to anoint the body (Mark 16.1). That evening they will make preparations. The body will need to be properly washed. Jesus will need to be looked after.

Day Eight: The Return
Sunday 5 April

The empty tomb: The tomb, Sunday daybreak
The Emmaus road: Emmaus Road, Sunday afternoon
The upper room: The upper room, Sunday evening

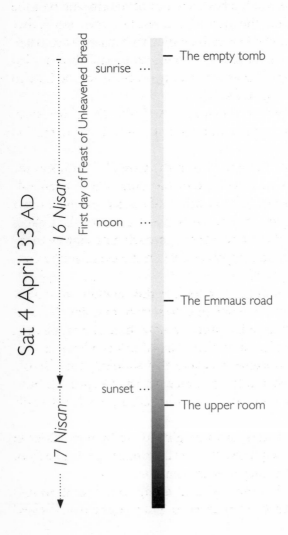

The empty tomb

Where: The tomb

When: 5 a.m.

'Very early' on the Sunday morning, the women make their way through the city to the graveyard just outside the walls. The dawn is hardly breaking; the morning trumpet blast from the Temple has yet to be heard; the city, for once, is quiet. Their route to the tomb takes them out of the city and past the site of the execution, the place where, just two days earlier, they had stood and watched everything die. They have the spices to anoint the body – a last act of honour to the man who has died such a dishonourable death. The only problem will be how to move that enormous stone.

Then they arrive at the tomb. And the stone has been moved; the tomb is open. Someone has already done the job for them.

So far we've been able to look at the Gospel accounts in the light of the history and culture of the time. We've been able to make comparisons, look at other influences, examine other examples and explore the events in the context of the politics and the religion of the time. That approach gets slightly tricky here. You can't make comparisons when the event you're considering is incomparable.

It would be tempting, therefore, at this juncture, to quietly put the idea of history to one side, to start to examine the Gospel accounts as myth or literature or metaphor. The problem is, the Gospels won't let us do that. They don't suddenly change their style, like a documentary film that suddenly turns into a science fiction epic. On the contrary, for the Gospels it's business as usual (or unusual). This, they claim, is what actually happened.

The Gospel accounts, as we might expect by now, differ in their details and emphasis. It's worth exploring what each of them says and what they have in common.

Mark's outline has three women going to the tomb to find the stone rolled back. They enter to find a young man dressed in white, who tells them that Jesus of Nazareth has 'been raised'. He gestures at the place where Jesus had been laid. He tells them to return and tell 'his disciples and Peter' that he has gone out to Galilee. The women flee from the tomb in terror and amazement, saying 'nothing to anyone for they were afraid' (Mark 16.1–8).

Matthew's outline is different. He describes two women – Mary Magdalene and 'the other Mary' – going to the tomb. Then there is a great earthquake (he does love his earthquakes, does Matthew) and an angel descends, rolls back the stone and sits on it. His appearance is like lightning, his clothes 'as white as snow', and when they see him the guards shake and 'become like dead men'. The angel tells the women the same message as in Mark – Jesus has gone to Galilee and they are to go and tell the disciples. The women leave the tomb and return to the disciples, and suddenly Jesus meets them. They hold his feet and worship him, and he repeats the message: 'Go and tell my brothers to go to Galilee; there they will see me' (Matt. 28.1–10).

Luke's women head for the tomb, where they find the stone rolled away. They enter to discover two angels, who remind the women of Jesus' prophecy that he would rise again. The women return to tell all this to 'the eleven and to all the rest'. (It's only then we find out that the women are 'Mary Magdalene, Joanna, Mary the mother of James, and the other women with them'.) The apostles do not believe them, but Peter runs to the tomb, stoops and looks in (he doesn't enter) to see it empty except for the linen cloths (Luke 24.1–12).

John's account has only one woman: Mary Magdalene. She goes to the tomb 'while it was still dark' to find that the stone has been removed. So she runs back and rouses Peter and 'the beloved disciple', who race to the tomb. The beloved disciple arrives first. He pauses at the entrance but sees the linen grave clothes on the floor. When Peter arrives, he enters the tomb. He, too, sees the grave clothes and the piece of linen that would have been placed on Jesus' head 'folded up in a place by itself'. The other disciple goes in for a look, and then they return 'to their homes'. Meanwhile, Mary Magdalene has returned to the graveyard and she stays there, weeping outside the tomb. She looks in to see two angels in white sitting, 'where the body of Jesus had lain, one at the head and one at the feet'. They ask her why she is weeping and she replies that they have taken away the Lord and she does not know 'where they've laid him'. Then she turns round and sees a figure standing there, whom she takes to be the gardener. When she asks the gardener where Jesus has been taken, he says just one word: Mary. She realises who it is and Jesus tells her to go back to the disciples and tell them what she has seen – which she does (John 20.1–18).

So, was it one angel or two angels? Were the angels in the tomb or sitting outside on the stone? Did Peter go in, or didn't he? Did the women tell people or not? Did it happen before dawn or afterwards?

'So they went out and fled from the tomb'

First, I guess we have to start with the ending of Mark. It seems so abrupt. There are two, later, endings, which were added by later editors. The reason for the abrupt ending might be simple. It might be that that's how he finished it. The tomb was empty. And the women went away feeling scared and apparently unwilling to obey the instructions they had been given. But it doesn't add up somehow. I can't see Mark, having taken the trouble to lead us to this point, leaving it there. From a literary point of view, if nothing else, I find it hard to believe that fade-out was how the original ended.

The second explanation is that the original ending is just lost. The presence of the two later endings indicates a widespread belief that Mark's Gospel was never meant to end this way. Indeed, I think in them we might be able to detect the shadow of the original ending. For example, the account of the resurrection appearances in the longer ending is similar in feel to the account given by Paul. Both probably come from early church teaching. The long ending includes the first appearance to Mary Magdalene, the Emmaus road appearance and an appearance to the eleven in the locked room. In other words, it tallies well with the other Gospels accounts of the pattern of events.[1] If we want to look for the ending of Mark, we have to search for it elsewhere. Given that Luke and Matthew based their Gospels on Mark's account, Mark's original ending is most likely in them as well. Perhaps, instead of focusing on the differences, it is simpler to look at what all the Gospels have in common. In all the Gospels:

▷ Women go to the tomb. The women are the first witnesses of what happened and it is they who tell the news to the disciples and the others.
▷ Mary Magdalene visits the tomb.
▷ There is an empty tomb with the stone rolled back and linen cloths on the floor.
▷ Angels appear.

Further, in three of the Gospels, Peter is featured specifically. In Mark the women are told to 'tell Peter'; in Luke and John he goes to the tomb and investigates. This at least allows us to reconstruct a possible outline of events, as follows.

The group of women included Mary Magdalene, Mary the mother of James, Joanna and Salome. They went to the tomb very early, as the sun rose, to find the tomb empty, the stone rolled back and the grave clothes on the floor. They then had an encounter with an angel (or group of angels) who told them that Jesus had risen. The women then returned to the room where the disciples were – probably the upper room, which was only a short walk away. Peter and another disciple went to the tomb to investigate for themselves. They found it as the women said. They were followed by Mary Magdalene, who met Jesus (although at first she thought he was the gardener).

There is, then, a core series of events which makes sense in terms of the narrative. Of course the accounts differ; eye-witness accounts always do differ. But let's face it, people who argue about the differences in the accounts are rather ignoring the big picture. They are, to quote the man who wasn't in the tomb, straining at gnats while swallowing a camel. Because all the accounts agree on one basic fact: Jesus was dead and then, well, then he *wasn't*.

The Emmaus road

Where: Emmaus road

When: Afternoon

Meanwhile, on a road somewhere...

Luke's account contains an intriguing story which happened on that same day. Two disciples – not the eleven, who were still in Jerusalem – are walking to a village called Emmaus. They are joined by an unknown man who starts talking to them about recent events in Jerusalem. These disciples had been in the room that morning, because they had heard the news from the women:

> Moreover, some women of our group astounded us. They were at the tomb early this morning, and when they did not find his body there, they came back and told us that they had indeed seen a vision of angels who said that he was alive. Some of those who were with us went to the tomb and found it just as the women had said; but they did not see him. (Luke 24.22–24)

Now this is interesting, because the phrase 'some of those who were with us went to the tomb' backs up John's account of the event, in which both Peter and the 'beloved disciple' went to have a look. Anyway, the stranger proceeds to explain what has happened and they invite him to share their meal in their home. As he breaks the bread, they realise who it is and he vanishes. Immediately they rush back to Jerusalem to tell the others.

Despite strenuous efforts, Emmaus has never been identified. Different ancient manuscripts of Luke have it as being either sixty stadia or 160 stadia from Jerusalem; probably the smaller number is more accurate, about seven miles. Significantly, we do know who one of the walkers was. Luke identifies him as Cleopas, and a story from the early church tells how the successor to James, as leader of the Jerusalem church, was a man called Symeon, the son of Clopas:

> He [Symeon] was a cousin – at any rate so it is said – of the Saviour;
> for indeed Hegesippus relates that Clopas was Joseph's brother.[2]

It makes sense that, having had one relative of Jesus in charge of the church, his successor would be another relative. Symeon was Jesus' cousin on his father's side. Now if we go back to the account of the women around the cross, we find Mary of Clopas, i.e. Mary, wife of Clopas (John 19.25). The probability that Luke's Cleopas and John's Clopas are the same person is extremely high.[3] That would mean that the person whom Jesus encounters on the Emmaus road is his own uncle. And this fits perfectly with the tradition that Jesus appeared to his brother James, another relative. Indeed, the early church theologian, Origen, took this one step further and identified the unnamed disciple walking along the road as Clopas' son, Symeon.[4] Certainly, this would be a strong qualification for succeeding James: Symeon would be not only a relative of Jesus, but one who had seen him after his resurrection.

All this means that his family – or at least some of them – were in Jerusalem when Jesus died. Two aunts were standing with his mother near the cross when he died. And, according to Luke, he appeared to his uncle after he rose again.

And to others as well.

The upper room

Where: The upper room

When: Sunday evening

By the time Clopas and his companion had got back to Jerusalem, others had seen Jesus as well. Luke records that, when the two excited travellers burst into the room, 'they found the eleven and their companions gathered together. They were saying, "The Lord has risen indeed, and he has appeared to Simon!"' (Luke 24.33–35). When was this? Luke doesn't say. But it actually accords with the earliest accounts of the resurrection as recorded, not in Gospels, but in Paul's first letter to the Corinthians, which predates any of the written Gospels:

> For I handed on to you as of first importance what I in turn had received: that Christ died for our sins in accordance with the scriptures, and that he was buried, and that he was raised on the third day in accordance with the scriptures, and that he appeared to Cephas [Peter], then to the twelve. Then he appeared to more than five hundred brothers and sisters at one time, most of whom are still alive, though some have died. Then he appeared to James, then to all the apostles. Last of all, as to one untimely born, he appeared also to me. (1 Cor. 15.3–8)

Corinthians was written around AD 54, but Paul is recording something that he had been taught much earlier, when he first became a follower of Jesus only a few years after Jesus' death. So this is clearly a piece of very early church doctrine, which was 'passed on' from one follower to the next. It is not, therefore, a detailed account, but an early church formula. It uses generic phrases such as 'the twelve' to mean 'the disciples' (there were only eleven at the time). It doesn't make clear the distinction between Jesus' appearances 'to the twelve' and 'to all the apostles', nor does it include the appearance to Mary. But the account deals with well-known figures, or groups, who would have been known to the wider church. Hence the appearance to the 500, many of whom were still alive. And to 'all the apostles' – a wider group than the twelve and a group that is hard to define, but which would most likely have included some missionaries and teachers known to the early church and to the church in Corinth. Some may be the seven mentioned in Acts 6.1–6.[5]

What it indicates is that there was a tradition of an appearance to Peter, which was separate from the appearance to the group. We don't have a record of that appearance to Peter, but we do have the tradition of the appearance to the group of them.

In Luke it happens immediately after Clopas and his companion have given their account. Jesus appears, 'standing among them', and demonstrates that he has come back as flesh and bone. He even eats a piece of broiled fish (Luke 24.41–43). John's version of the appearance has more detail: the door was locked 'for fear of the Jews' (John 20.19). In both accounts Jesus shows them his hands and feet (Luke 24.40; John 20.20).

In both accounts as well, Jesus goes on to talk about the Holy Spirit (Luke 24.49; John 20.22).

So we have, on that Sunday, four different resurrection appearances: in the garden to Mary Magdalene; on the road to Clopas and friend; in an unnamed place to Peter; and in the upper room to the disciples.

Over the course of the next few weeks, many more people were to see him. The Gospels themselves record subsequent appearances. So, whatever we think of the truth or otherwise of these accounts, what we can't do is simply dismiss them as one person saying 'I saw him again'. Paul is clear, for example, that most of the people who saw Jesus were still alive at the time he was writing. Certainly, when he was writing to the Corinthians, there were people alive who claimed to have seen the risen Jesus. Some of these would have been the 'major' figures – such as Peter and James. But many more would have been ordinary followers of Jesus – some of them undoubtedly known to the Corinthian church. Their names have been forgotten long ago, but their testimony remains.

'He was buried, and that he was raised on the third day in accordance with the scriptures'

All of this is very well, but the key question is: were they telling the truth?

And here's where I have to tread carefully. I hope, in this book, to have demonstrated the credibility of the setting and events of the Gospels, to show that whatever we think of the content of their account, there is nothing in them that is inconsistent with the social and political setting of first-century Judaea. I wanted to write a book that would explore some of the major characters, wander down some of the historical alleyways and generally shed light on the events described in the Gospels.

I don't want to turn this book into a book of apologetics. But I go back to a couple of things I said in the introduction. Whatever we do, let's not patronise these people by pretending that they were just simple folk who didn't know any better.

Whatever else we believe about the ancient world, we should be aware they were far better acquainted with death than we are. They saw it around them on the streets and in the gutters, in the houses and on the execution sites that studded the Roman Empire. So we should credit them with knowing the difference between death and life, between a corpse and a walking, living, fish-eating bloke.

It is popular to see the resurrection accounts as spiritual or metaphorical, but the ancient world didn't think that way and the Gospel writers didn't claim any such thing. The whole point of the hands and the feet and the fish is their physicality. No Gospel writer claims that Jesus went into the tomb as a man and came out as a metaphor. Their claims are that the resurrection was real. It happened. There are no middle, metaphorical exits.

So what, if any, proof can be offered to support the eyewitness testimony?

First, there is the use of women as witnesses. To put it bluntly, no self-respecting religion would rely on the testimony of women. Women were almost completely disqualified as witnesses in Jewish courts of law. During a normal trial in court women's testimony was not sought out and was in fact avoided whenever possible, because 'no man wants his wife to degrade herself in court'. The only way a woman's testimony might be allowed was if there was simply no other choice.[6] So the choice of women as the prime witnesses to the empty tomb would be a terrible piece of strategic planning, unless they genuinely were the first witnesses and the Gospel accounts were trying to get things right. This is also a very strong argument for the fact that the women were a key part of the story from the start. We have seen that in Paul's account of the resurrection appearances – sent to the church in Corinth, a church embedded in the heart of the Græco-Roman culture – there is no specific mention of the women. This is probably because of the cultural considerations listed above, because it wasn't just in the Jewish world that women were discounted as reliable sources of information. The Gospels were written later than Paul's letters; so if we believe that the stories are a later invention, we have to believe that somebody chose deliberately to add the women to the list. It's the equivalent of someone choosing to strengthen reports in *The Times*, the BBC News and *The Washington Post* by adding an account in *Alien Abductees Monthly*. No one would have added the women at a later date. They have to be part of the earliest reminiscences. And the fact that they are there at all has to indicate that these accounts weren't invented.[7]

Second, there is the confusion between the accounts. This might be seen as damaging to their case, but, as James Dunn puts it, 'The conflict of testimony is more a mark of the sincerity of those from whom the testimony was derived than a mark against their veracity'.[8] If the testimonies were invented by later editors, one would expect a lot more uniformity. We would, in fact, expect the inconsistencies to be ironed out and the difficulties to be explained away. But there is none of that, which can be only because the early church believed it important to preserve the original accounts, even where they diverged. When one of the women, say, told her story, she might have remembered things in a slightly different way: but the people listening to her would have remembered her version. That's the point: it was *her* version, so it should not be dismissed. As Wright says, 'stories as earth-shattering as this, stories as community-forming as this, once told, are not easily modified. Too much depends on them'.[9]

Third, there's the honesty of the accounts. We have looked at the ending of Mark, and the possibility that that is, indeed, how it ended, not with a resurrection appearance but with fear and anxiety. I'm not convinced myself, but it may have been so. Nevertheless, the accounts recognise the unreality of the events. Matthew, for example, tells us that 'When they saw him they worshipped him; but some doubted' (Matt. 28.17). I can't imagine why anyone would write that if they were trying to present an air-brushed case. The doubt is there only because some *did* doubt.

Fourth, with regard to the empty tomb, there is a complete absence of any counter-claim. As we saw with Matthew's story of the guards, the idea that the story was made up makes sense only if the tomb was actually empty. The emptiness of the tomb was never, in fact, a subject of controversy. Only the *reason* for its emptiness.[10]

Fifth, there is the fact that the early church did not venerate the tomb. They remembered where it was, of course, but there is no evidence that they went there to worship. No writer of the early church, from Acts onwards, records them meeting at the place even to worship. The reason is that there was nothing there to venerate.

Sixth, there is the evidence from Paul. Within two generations of Jesus' death – while there were still people around who had witnessed the events – there were some 500 people who had seen Jesus. Paul's message is pretty clear: you want witnesses? We've got witnesses and they're still around.

Seventh, resurrection was such a *weird* thing to believe in. We've seen that the Pharisees believed in the resurrection of the dead, but this was a final resurrection, after the day of the Lord. The pagan world dismissed the idea completely. The Christian belief that resurrection had happened ahead of the end, and that it signalled a general resurrection (as reflected in Matthew's dead people walking about), was very strange.

Finally, there is the fact that the early church lived it out. Something changed these people into a force. Something turned a huddle of frightened peasants into a world-changing phenomenon. Acts depicts the rapid growth of the church – 3,000 baptised on the day of Pentecost alone. Even if we dispute the figures, the sheer fact of history is that Christianity flourished and grew. Despite the frequent persecutions to which it was subjected, it spread rapidly. Look, for example, at the transformation in Jesus' own family. At the cross, Jesus' male relatives appear to have been absent, but afterwards his brothers were in Jerusalem:

> When they had entered the city, they went to the room upstairs where they were staying, Peter, and John, and James, and Andrew,

> Philip and Thomas, Bartholomew and Matthew, James son of Al-phaeus, and Simon the Zealot, and Judas son of James. All these were constantly devoting themselves to prayer, together with certain women, including Mary the mother of Jesus, as well as his brothers. (Acts 1.13–14)

Something changed for them. And the answer, according to Paul at least, was that they had seen Jesus. His brother James, who initially thought him deluded, ended up leading the first church in Jerusalem and was eventually martyred by one of Annas' sons. Another of Jesus' brothers, Jude, has a New Testament letter attributed to him. Even if, as some scholars argue, the attribution isn't genuine, it shows that Jude also became a prominent figure in the early church. There would be no point in attributing a letter to someone who had never been a follower.[11] Two, at least, of Jesus' brothers are suddenly turned round from disbelief to belief, from scepticism to adherence.

Personally, I have never been able to come up with an explanation for the growth of the early church and the persistence of belief in this man that didn't involve resurrection. Take the resurrection away from Jesus and all you get is failure. An honourable failure might be the fount of a religious movement in our time, but hardly in the harsher world of the New Testament. Honourable failures do not start religious movements. The martyrs at Masada are remembered, but no one started a religion in their honour.

This, then, is the pattern of the Longest Week. On the Sunday before, Jesus had entered the city in triumph from Bethany. Luke brings us full circle: Jesus leads his disciples out of Jerusalem, up along the Mount of Olives as far as Bethany, where he 'withdrew from them' (Luke 24.51). He entered in triumph and he exits in triumph. It has been a long, hard, strange journey.

And it's not finished yet.

Aftershock: AD 33 and after

It didn't end there, of course. From Jerusalem, Christianity spread like a virus, like a storm, the good news passing from person to person. The first followers of Jesus burst out of the upper room and started to preach and teach and feed the poor, and share their possessions and generally behave in a way that seems to indicate that they've won.

Peter, the disgraced disciple, became the heart and soul of the new movement. Refreshed, revived and apparently reinstated, he stormed around doing everything his master did, including getting arrested by the authorities. After an eventful life he was probably executed in Rome in AD 68. Of the other disciples and followers, little is known of their fates. James the apostle was executed by Herod Agrippa in AD 46. James, brother of Jesus, was, as we have seen, killed by Ananus ben Ananus in AD 63, the final act of revenge of the House of Hanan on the family of Jesus of Nazareth. Of the other followers little is known. They have faded into history.

'Herod and Pilate became friends with each other'

Of Jesus' enemies, we know a little more.

Antipas was to rule Galilee for only another four years or so. When his brother, Philip the tetrarch, died in AD 34, Emperor Tiberius annexed the territory to Roman rule, much to Antipas' disappointment. Then, some time around autumn AD 36, his forces were disastrously defeated in a battle with Aretas, his former father-in-law, who had obviously neither forgotten nor forgiven Antipas' treatment of his daughter. Antipas persuaded the Romans to send forces to avenge his defeat, but before they arrived news came that Tiberius was dead. Caligula was close friends with Antipas' nephew, Agrippa – another in a long and unworthy line of Herodian schemers. He gave Agrippa the territory of his late uncle Philip, and also the title of king. Outraged, Herodias persuaded Antipas to go to Rome to petition the emperor to be made king as well. Against his will, Antipas agreed.

It was a disaster. Agrippa, hearing of their mission, sent a letter to Caligula accusing Antipas of treachery against Rome in making a secret agreement with the Parthians. The emperor, far from rewarding Antipas, accused him of conspiracy and exiled both Antipas and Herodias to Lugdunum Convenarum – now Saint-Bernard-de-Comminges in France. His property and territories were handed over to Agrippa. And that's the last we hear of him. Victim, once again, of his wife's scheming, Herod Antipas and his wife, Herodias, lived out their days in poverty and obscurity on the other side of the empire, thousands of miles away from home.

He never did get to be called 'king'.

Pilate's career ended in late AD 36 or early AD 37. The careers of Pilate and Caiaphas seem to have gone hand in hand, and they ended together. It may have been an attempt to placate Caiaphas that brought about the end of Pilate's career.

It was, as one might expect, a religious dispute that eventually ended Pilate's term of office. An ancient Samaritan belief held that sacred vessels from the Temple were hidden on Mount Gerazim in Samaria. In AD 35, a Samaritan 'prophet' claimed that he would produce these vessels if people assembled on the mountain. And so a huge group of Samaritans began to gather at the foot of Mount Gerazim. The Roman soldiers, fearing a riot, attacked this force, killing many, capturing some and putting others to flight. In the end Pilate executed those he considered the ringleaders, including some of the most respected and distinguished Samaritan leaders. It is difficult to see why Pilate tried to stop them. A group of Samaritans up a mountain was hardly going to be a threat. But it may well be that, once again, he was taking the advice of Caiaphas, who feared that the Samaritans would rebuild a Temple on Mount Gerazim. And a rival Temple and rival priesthood was the last thing he needed.[1] The Samaritans, knowing that the assembly was never going to be dangerous, complained to Vitellus, the legate in Syria. Vitellus ordered Pilate to Rome to account for his actions.[2] After writing to Tiberius for permission, Vitellus also restored the high priest's vestments to Jewish control for the first time in thirty years.[3]

Although Josephus records that Pilate hurried to Rome, he arrived there too late to plead his case before Tiberius, who died in March AD 37. Pilate had done his best to curry favour with the emperor; he had risked taking shields into Jerusalem, he had even built a temple in his honour. Alas, it was a waste of money. The new emperor was Gaius Caligula, and he was not sentimental about his adopted grandfather's memory.[4] Pilate found himself, as he had been warned, no friend of the emperor. According to Eusebius, Pilate committed suicide.[5]

If Caiaphas did accidentally cause the departure of Pilate, he paid for it by losing his own job. In around AD 36, Vitellus removed Caiaphas from his position as High Priest. No more is heard of him until the discovery of his tomb in the twentieth century. However, his replacement was his brother-in-law, Jonathan, one of the sons of Ananus. That canny operator Ananus had once again kept the post in the family.

It may well be that we know where Ananus is buried. Josephus wrote about a wall that was built to encircle the city of Jerusalem during the siege of AD 70. According to Josephus the wall looped round the east of the city, before heading south and descending 'into the Valley of the Fountain, beyond which it ascended over against the tomb of Ananus the High Priest'.

This area is the site of the 'Akeldama' tombs, the most elaborate of which is in the centre of a group of six. It has a triple entrance and may well have been the final resting place of the grand old man, Ananus.[6]

His sons, as we have seen, went on to be high priests. But not everything ended happily for them. Jonathan was assassinated by the dagger-wielding Sicarii around AD 60.[7] His youngest son, another Ananus, became High Priest and, as we have seen, took the opportunity to kill James – a final act of revenge against the family of Jesus. For this, he was deposed by the Romans. He went on to play a major role in the opening years of the revolt against Rome, in which he was a leading figure in arguing for a peaceful solution. His family had, after all, worked alongside the Romans for years: they had property and wealth at stake. Sadly, others no longer shared his family's desire for compromise with Rome. Ananus Jr was hunted down and assassinated, and his bones were denied burial.[8]

'I am with you always, to the end of the age'

And what about Jesus? What happened to him?

Well, we took him and we forgot the history. We stripped away the nasty stuff: the politics and the poverty and all that. Then we washed the blood off, sat him on a throne, dressed him in a robe of purple and turned him into an emperor. We kept him well away from the tables of the moneychangers and we turned the means of his execution into a piece of jewellery.

And, as the final betrayal, we turned him into the leader of a worldwide movement which espoused the very principles he hated. We made him the head of a worldwide official church, which developed a fine line in outdoing the Sadducees, the Romans and the Pharisees wrapped together. While he lived he was all about non-violence and love and poverty and justice; once he'd died he was all about authority and power and wealth and pomp and status and simply butchering anyone who didn't agree with you.

I know, I know... it wasn't always like that. It started well. The early church was a place where Jesus' teaching was empowered by the Spirit of God, where the good news was proclaimed to whomever would listen, where there really was no distinction between slaves and free, between Jew and Gentile, where people really tried to put this stuff into practice. Of course there were arguments and difficulties along the way. There were people who warped the teaching and changed the truth and used the church for their own ends. But the church *grew*. It did what Jesus did – it stood against the power structures of the day. It took the worst the empire could throw at it and it followed the path of its leader.

The early church took Jesus' ideas and changed the world. Then the Roman Empire got its revenge: it took the world's ideas and changed the church. In AD 325 the Emperor Constantine made Christianity the official religion of the Roman emperor. For the first time in its life the church had real power, and suddenly all that other stuff, all the stuff about non-violence and powerlessness and the poor, well, that got sort of embarrassing. Since the time of Constantine the Great, since that moment when Christianity became the 'official' church of the West, the Church as an institution has struggled to conform to the principles of the great outsider who founded it. It became too often a money-making machine, with a seat on the board, a place at the high table, badges and honour and institutions. And it looked at the Jews and, instead of seeing the culture and nation that nourished and fostered its founder, it saw only the chance for revenge.

It has been left, by and large, to the outsiders to keep the vision alive. Outsiders, like the monks who fled into the desert, the teachers who dared to say what they thought, the scholars who wondered why the story of Jesus shouldn't be read by people in their own language. Outsiders, like the Christians who hid the Jews instead of colluding in their death; like the pastors who helped slaves escape their chains and the preachers who marched to show that there is no difference between black and white. Outsiders, who hugged lepers and who tended the sick and helped the prisoners and – oh, the glory of it, the *real* glory of it! There are millions of these people! They don't figure much in the official history, in the long and tedious litany of synods and councils and crusades and heresies, but they are there, looking at the life of their founder and living it out.

This, then, is the message of the Longest Week. It's not really about facts and dates and theories. It's about one man and our response to his life. The real truth is that no one has ever been able to control Christ. He storms down the hills of our theories, wild and triumphant; he marches into the heart of our lives and starts overturning the received ideas that we have carefully organised into neat little piles. The historical Jesus who challenged the oppressive religious and political systems, who was passionately concerned with the plight of the poorest of society, who became, literally, one of the outcasts, who ridiculed authority and made their wisdom look foolish, who walked the road of love to its triumphant conclusion – he's still there. He has slipped off the purple robe and climbed down from the throne and is giving out bread and wine to all those who need it. He's alive and he's kicking: the great rebel, the leader of the upside-down kingdom – Jesus Christ, Joshua ben Joseph – the Son of God.

That's the thing about the Longest Week.

It never really did come to an end.

Notes

Introduction

1. I have suggested at the end a devotional framework for Christians wanting to read and consider the events through holy week. You will find it at my website: http://www.nickpage.co.uk.

2. The early church historian Eusebius mentions the *Acta Pilatii*, but the idea that it was presented by Tiberius before the Senate is clearly legendary. Various other 'Acts' and 'Letters' of Pilate are recorded, but they are all pious forgeries from the fourth century. See, Eusebius, *The Ecclesiastical History and the Martyrs of Palestine*, trans. Hugh Jackson Lawlor and John Ernest Leonard Oulton (2 vols; London: SPCK, 1927), I, 38. See also Ernst Bammel, and C. F. D. Moule (ed.), *Jesus and the Politics of His Day* (Cambridge: Cambridge University Press, 1984), 173

3. Légasse, Simon, *The Trial of Jesus*, (London: SCM Press, 1997), 2–3

4. Goodman, Martin, *The Ruling Class of Judaea: The Origins of the Jewish Revolt Against Rome, A.D. 66–70* (Cambridge: Cambridge University Press, 1987), 5

5. Goodman, *The Ruling Class of Judaea*, 23.

Tremors: Winter AD 32 – Spring AD 33

1. There are also two accounts of trips made as a baby and a child: Luke 2.22–38 and Luke 2.41–51.

2. This account also includes the episode of the woman caught in adultery, which takes place in the Temple (John 7.53–8.11). This is not in the earliest ms. of John and was probably not part of the original Gospel. But it may very well be part of a different recorded tradition about Jesus. At any rate the teaching is radical and eye-opening and turns conventional religious and social custom on its head. In other words, entirely in keeping with Jesus' teaching.

3. Mark 15.42, Matt. 27.62, Luke 23.54, Jn 19.31

4. De specialibus legibus, ii, 144–175, cited in Segal, J. B., *The Hebrew Passover : From the Earliest Times to A.D. 70* (London: Oxford University Press, 1963), 27

5. Ogg, George, *The Chronology of the Public Ministry of Jesus* (Cambridge [Eng.]: The University Press, 1940), 276. Finegan, Jack, *Handbook of Biblical Chronology: Principles of Time Reckoning in the Ancient World and Problems of Chronology in the Bible* (Peabody, Mass: Hendrickson Publishers, 1998), 361–62.

6. Finegan, *Handbook of Biblical Chronology*, 364. Fotheringham, J. 'Astronomical Evidence for the Date of the Crucifixion', *Journal of Theological Studies* XII. 1910. On the moon, see Riesner, Rainer, *Paul's Early Period: Chronology, Mission Strategy, Theology* (Grand Rapids, Mich.; Cambridge: Eerdmans, 1998), 56–57.

7. Beasley-Murray, George Raymond, *John* (Waco, Texas: Word Books, 1987), 172–73.

8. Goodman, *The Ruling Class of Judaea*, 12.

9. Seneca, *On Mercy* 1:2–3

10. Carlton, Eric, *Occupation: The Policies and Practices of Military Conquerors* (London: Routledge, 1992), 18.

11. Xavier Lecureuil, French Consul in Patras, quoted in Mazower, Mark, *Inside Hitler's Greece: The Experience of Occupation, 1941–44* (Yale Nota Bene, New Haven, Conn.; London: Yale University Press, 2001), 3.

12. Wengst, Klaus, and John Stephen Bowden, *Pax Romana and the Peace of Jesus Christ* (London: SCM, 1987), 13.

13. Erhardt, quoted in Wengst and Bowden, *Pax Romana and the Peace of Jesus Christ*, 28.

14. Juvenal, and Peter Green, *The Sixteen Satires* (Penguin Classics, London: Penguin Books, 1974), 293.

15. Plutarch, *Precepts of Statecraft* X, quoted in Lewis, Naphtali, and Meyer Reinhold, *Roman Civilization: Selected Readings* (3rd edn, New York: Columbia University Press, 1990), 231.

16. Reader, John, *Cities* (London: Heinemann, 2004), 83.

17. Wengst and Bowden, *Pax Romana and the Peace of Jesus Christ*, 27.

18. Babylonian Talmud Sabbath 33b. Translation by M. Hadas, *Philological Quarterly* (1929), 8:373. Simeon, reputedly, escaped death, but only by fleeing into hiding and spending the next fourteen years in a cave.

19. Rabbi Gamaliel, quoted in McMullen, Ramsay, *Enemies of the Roman Order: Treason, Unrest, and Alienation in the Empire* (Cambridge, Mass; London: Harvard University Press; Oxford University Press, 1966), 148.

20. Sidebotham, Steven E., *Roman Economic Policy in the Erythra Thalassa 30 B.C.–A.D. 217* (Mnemosyne, Bibliotheca Classica Batava, Supplementum ; 91; Leiden: Brill, 1986), 133, 135.

21. Ant 17.11.4, see Millar, Fergus, *The Roman Near East, 31 BC–AD 337* (Cambridge, Mass.; London: Harvard University Press, 1993), 51.

22. Goodman, *The Ruling Class of Judaea*, 33–35.

23. Goodman, *The Ruling Class of Judaea*, 40–41.

24. Goodman, *The Ruling Class of Judaea*, 44–45.

25. Notley, R. Steven, and Anson F. Rainey, *Carta's New Century Handbook and Atlas of the Bible* (Jerusalem: Carta, Jerusalem, 2007), 235.

26. Goodman, *The Ruling Class of Judaea*, 56.

27. Notley, and Rainey, *Carta's New Century Handbook and Atlas of the Bible*, 235.

28. Horsley, Richard A., and John S. Hanson, *Bandits, Prophets, and Messiahs: Popular Movements in the Time of Jesus* (San Francisco: Harper & Row, 1988), 61.

29. Goodman, *The Ruling Class of Judaea*, 111.

30. Carter, Warren, *Pontius Pilate* (Liturgical Press, US, 2003), 35.

31. Horsley and Hanson, *Bandits, Prophets, and Messiahs: Popular Movements in the Time of Jesus*, 53.

32. m.Shebiith 10.3–4 in Danby, Herbert, *The Mishnah, Translated From the Hebrew* (London: Oxford University Press, 1933), 51.

33. Horsley and Hanson, *Bandits, Prophets, and Messiahs: Popular Movements in the Time of Jesus*, 60.

34. Horsley and Hanson, *Bandits, Prophets, and Messiahs: Popular Movements in the Time of Jesus*, 61.

35. Notley, Turnage and Becker, *Jesus' Last Week*, 204.

36. Paxton, Robert O., *Vichy France: Old Guard and New Order, 1940–1944* (New York: Columbia University Press, 2001), 285–86.

37. Crossan, *The Historical Jesus*, 118.

38. Goodman, *The Ruling Class of Judaea*, 74.

39. Wright, *Jesus and the Victory of God*, 161.

40. Bammel and Moule, *Jesus and the Politics of His Day*, 135–36.

41. Hengel, quoted in Bammel and Moule, *Jesus and the Politics of His Day*, 142.

42. Bammel and Moule, *The Trial of Jesus: Cambridge Studies in Honour of C. F. D. Moule*, 48–50.

43. Moule, C. F. D., *The Birth of the New Testament* (London: A. & C. Black, 1981), 55.

44. Goodman, *The Ruling Class of Judaea*, 123.

45. See also Josephus, *War* 2.162.

46. Bammel and Moule, *Jesus and the Politics of His Day*, 144.

47. Rhoads, David M., *Israel in Revolution: 6–74 C.E. A Political History Based on the Writings of Josephus* (Philadelphia: Fortress Press, 1976), 32.

48. Vanderkam, James C., *From Joshua to Caiaphas: High Priests after the Exile* (Minneapolis, Minn Assen: Augsburg Fortress Van Gorcum, 2004), 435–36.

49. Caiaphas was to be High Priest for another four years after this – he held the position for some nineteen years. Jeremias, Joachim, *Jerusalem in the Time of Jesus: An Investigation into Economic and Social Conditions during the New Testament Period* (London: SCM Press, 1974), 195 n.153.

50. Goodman, *The Ruling Class of Judaea*, 121.

51. Ilan, Tal, *Jewish Women in Greco-Roman Palestine: An Inquiry Into Image and Status* (Tübingen: J. C. B. Mohr (Paul Siebeck), 1995) 71.

52. Millar, *The Roman Near East, 31 BC–AD 337*, 362.

53. Bammel and Moule, *The Trial of Jesus: Cambridge Studies in Honour of C. F. D. Moule*, 63.

54. Carter, *Pontius Pilate*, 39.

55. Jeremias, *Jerusalem in the Time of Jesus*, 97–99.

56. Josephus, *War* 2.397, 400.

57. He may have been alluding to an Old Testament story: the tale of Sheba, son of Bichri, who was beheaded by the residents of the city in which he was seeking refuge. Rather than losing their city and their lives, they threw his head over the wall. See 2 Sam. 20.14–22.

58. See Avi-Yonah, Michael, *The Jews Under Roman and Byzantine Rule: A Political History of Palestine From the Bar Kokhba War to the Arab Conquest* (Jerusalem New York: Magnes, the Hebrew University Schocken Books, 1984), 9.

59. Goodman, Martin, *Judaism in the Roman World: Collected Essays* (Leiden: Brill, 2007), 124.

60. Josephus, *Antiquities* 18.16–17.

61. Josephus, *Antiquities* 13.297–298.

62. Josephus, *Antiquities* 13.173.

63. Goodman, *Judaism in the Roman World: Collected Essays*, 128.

64. Josephus, *Antiquities* 20.198–200.

65. Josephus, *War*, 2.166.

66. Josephus, *Antiquities* 18.16.

67. Josephus, *Antiquities* 18.17.

68. Goodman, *Rome and Jerusalem: The Clash of Ancient Civilizations*, 422–23. Crossan describes the Temple Captain as 'Deputy High Priest' (Crossan, *The Historical Jesus*, 212).

69. *War* 2.409–410

70. Bammel and Moule, *The Trial of Jesus: Cambridge Studies in Honour of C. F. D. Moule*, 35.

The Night Before

1. If John's timetable is correct, it implies that Jesus was travelling on the Sabbath. According to the Torah, a Sabbath day's journey was limited to '2,000 cubits' – about two-thirds of a mile (Num. 35.5; Acts 1.12).

2. Goodman, *The Ruling Class of Judaea*, 132.

3. Tohoroth 7.6, in Danby, H., *The Mishnah, Translated From the Hebrew*, 726.

4. Hagner, Donald Alfred, *Matthew 1–13* (Dallas, Texas: Word Books, 1993), 8.

5. Only once in the New Testament does the word 'disciple' appear in its feminine form – Tabitha is called *mathetria* (disciple). That is not in the

Gospels but in Acts (Acts 9.36), and dates from Peter's visit to Joppa which took place c. AD 37.)

6. Bailey, Kenneth E., *Jesus Through Middle Eastern Eyes* (London: SPCK, 2008), 193.

7. See, for example, Brandon, S. G. F., *Jesus and the Zealots: A Study of the Political Factor in Primitive Christianity* (Manchester: Manchester University Press, 1967)

8. For a refutation of Brandon's theory, see Bammel and Moule, *Jesus and the Politics of His Day*, 1–9..

9. Ilan, *Jewish Women in Greco-Roman Palestine*, 55.

10. Ilan, *Jewish Women in Greco-Roman Palestine*, 67. For example, Berenice, daughter of Agrippa I, married her first husband when she was thirteen.

11. Another possibility is that Martha was the eldest and that she had been married, but was now a widow. When we meet her first in Luke she welcomes Jesus into 'her home' (Luke 10.38). However, in John the household is 'owned'. It has been suggested that Simon the Leper was the husband of Martha, or the father of the family (Nesbitt, *Bethany Traditions* p.120). Nesbitt suggests that the household of Simon was the place where Jesus habitually stayed during his visits to Jerusalem.

12. mSot 3.4 in Danby, *The Mishnah*, 296.

13. (tSot 7.9) Ilan, *Jewish Women in Greco-Roman Palestine*, 191.

Day One: The Entry

1. Wilkinson, John, *Jerusalem as Jesus Knew it: Archaeology as Evidence* (London: Thames and Hudson, 1978), 114–15.

2. Josh 15.63, 2 Sam 5.6–10

3. Ball, *Rome in the East: The Transformation of an Empire*, 261.

4. Bell cites the example of Australia or America, where the streets, with their porches and boardwalks became, effectively, colonnaded. Ball, *Rome in the East: The Transformation of an Empire*, 270–71.

5. Goodman, *The Ruling Class of Judaea*, 127.

6. Josephus, *War* 5.201–206

7. Roller, Duane W., The Building Program of Herod the Great (Berkeley ; London: University of California Press, 1998), 180.

8. Goodman, *Judaism in the Roman World: Collected Essays*, 64–66.

9. Fuks, Gideon, Uriel Rappaport and Aryeh Kasher, *Greece and Rome in Eretz Israel: Collected Essays* (Jerusalem: Yad Izhak Ben-Zvi, Israel Exploration Society, 1990), 143.

10. Goodman, Martin, *Rome and Jerusalem: The Clash of Ancient Civilizations* (London: Penguin, 2008), 316.

11. Feldman, Louis H., *Jew and Gentile in the Ancient World* (Princeton: Princeton University Press, 1993), 293.

12. Ball, Warwick, *Rome in the East: The Transformation of an Empire* (London: Routledge, 2000), 59.

13. Goodman, *The Ruling Class of Judaea*, 97.

14. Lewis, Naphtali, *Life in Egypt Under Roman Rule* (Oxford: Clarendon Press, 1983), 29, 169.

15. Goodman, *The Ruling Class of Judaea*, 48–49.

16. Safrai, Ze'ev, *The Economy of Roman Palestine* (London: Routledge, 1994), 379.

17. Richardson, Peter, *City and Sanctuary: Religion and Architecture in the Roman Near East* (SCM Press, 2002-10-01), 137.

18. Quoted in Reader, *Cities*, 83.

19. Safrai, *The Economy of Roman Palestine*, 34.

20. Scobie, Alex, 'Slums, Sanitation and Mortality in the Roman World', *Klio* 68, 1986, 404.

21. One papyrus from Arsinoë offers to rent a corner house which has three shops in front and two on the side street. Lewis, *Life in Egypt Under Roman Rule*, 51.

22. Scobie, 'Slums, Sanitation and Mortality in the Roman World', *Klio* 68, 1986, 399–433 (402).

23. Neuwirth, Robert, *Shadow Cities: A Billion Squatters, a New Urban World* (New York; London: Routledge, 2005), 181.

24. Neuwirth, *Shadow Cities*, 179.

25. Scobie, 'Slums, Sanitation and Mortality in the Roman World', 402.

26. Scobie, 'Slums, Sanitation and Mortality in the Roman World', 403.

27. Davis, Mike, *Planet of Slums* (London; New York: Verso, 2006), 33.

28. Kearns, Kevin Corrigan, *Dublin Tenement Life: An Oral History* (Dublin: Gill & Macmillan, 1994), 27.

29. Kleijn, Gerda de, *The Water Supply of Ancient Rome: City Area, Water, and Population* (Dutch Monographs on Ancient History and Archaeology, v. 22; Amsterdam: Gieben, 2001), 74.

30. For rainfall in cities, see A. Trevor Hodge, *Roman Aqueducts & Water Supply* (London: Duckworth, 1993), 335

31. As suggested in Wilkinson, *Jerusalem as Jesus Knew it*, 66–67.

32. Aristeas 89 in Hayward, Robert, *The Jewish Temple: A Non-Biblical Sourcebook*, (London: Routledge, 1996), 28

33. Notices were posted on the houses of Pompeii: 'Don't do it here – or else!' Hodge, A. Trevor, *Roman Aqueducts & Water Supply*, 337

34. Suetonius, *Vespasian* 5.4.

35. Suetonius, *Nero*, 26

36. Hodge, A. Trevor, *Roman Aqueducts & Water Supply*, 339.

37. m.Shekalim 8.1 in Danby, *The Mishnah*, 161.

38. Scobie, 'Slums, Sanitation and Mortality in the Roman World', 408, 414.

39. Scobie, 'Slums, Sanitation and Mortality in the Roman World', 416.

40. Scobie, 'Slums, Sanitation and Mortality in the Roman World', 419.

41. Scobie, 'Slums, Sanitation and Mortality in the Roman World', 417.

42. Kearns, *Dublin Tenement Life: An Oral History*, 27.

43. Kearns, *Dublin Tenement Life: An Oral History*, 29.

44. Neuwirth, *Shadow Cities*, 186.

45. Neuwirth, *Shadow Cities*, 4.

46. Scobie, 'Slums, Sanitation and Mortality in the Roman World', 431.

47. Josephus, *Antiquities* 17.213–217.

48. b.Sukk. 37a–b. Cited in Witherington, Ben, *The Gospel of Mark: Socio-Rhetorical Commentary* (William B. Eerdmans Publishing Company, January, 2001), 307.

49. 2 Kings 9.13 shows Jehu being greeted in a similar way. Indeed, the practice of spreading garments before a beloved or celebrated figure was known in the Graeco-Roman world. Plutarch depicts troops spreading their clothes at the feet of Cato the Younger when he left the army. There is also a sarcophagus of Adelphia which shows a man laying some kind of garment beneath the hooves of the horse on which Adelphia is riding.

50. Bammel and Moule, *Jesus and the Politics of His Day*, 319–21.

51. Josephus, *The Jewish War*, (Harmondsworth: Penguin, 1981), 40.

52. Josephus, Williamson and Smallwood, *The Jewish War*, 144.

53. This idea was first suggested, as far as I know, by John Dominic Crossan and Marcus Borg. See Borg, Marcus J. and John Dominic Crossan, *The Last Week: What the Gospels Really Teach About Jesus' Final Days in Jerusalem*, (San Francisco: HarperSanFrancisco, February, 2007), 2–5.

54. Sanders, E. P., *The Historical Figure of Jesus* (London: Penguin, 1995), 23–26.

55. Peters, F. E, *Jerusalem: The Holy City in the Eyes of Chroniclers, Visitors, Pilgrims, and Prophets From the Days of Abraham to the Beginnings of Modern Times* (Princeton: Princeton University Press, 1985), 89.

56. Goodman, *The Ruling Class of Judaea*, 102.

57. The fear of being contaminated by the dead was not unique to Jews. Several Roman sources talk of *contagio funesta*. Kazen, Thomas, *Jesus and Purity Halakhah: Was Jesus Indifferent to Impurity?* (Coniectanea Biblica, New Testament series, 38; Stockholm: Almqvist and Wiksell, 2002), 177.

58. Numbers 19.2–13. The text indicates that the priests kept a store of these ashes for use in these occasions. Kazen, *Jesus and Purity Halakhah: Was Jesus Indifferent to Impurity?*, 185–86.

59. M. Yoma 3.3 in Danby, *The Mishnah*, 164.

60. Bovon, François. 'Fragment Oxyrhynchus 840, Fragment of a Lost Gospel, Witness of an Early Christian Controversy over Purity', *Journal of Biblical Literature* 119 (4), 2000, 705.

61. Bonaccorsi, *Vangeli apocrifi*, 36 and 38, quoted in Bovon, 'Fragment Oxyrhynchus 840, Fragment of a Lost Gospel, Witness of an Early Christian Controversy over Purity', 714–15. Bovon argues that this fragment is a later piece of writing reflecting not Jewish customs, but a controversy over baptism within the Christian church.. His view echoes that of Tripp, David, 'Meanings of the Foot-Washing: John 13 and Oxyrhynchus Papyrus 840', *Expository Times*, 1992. Jeremias and, in the most extensive study, Kruger, argue for the authenticity of the passage and place it in the context of Jewish Christianity.

62. Jeremias, *Unknown Sayings of Jesus* (London: SPCK, 1964), 52.

63. Kruger, Michael J., *The Gospel of the Savior: An Analysis of P. Oxy. 840 and Its Place in the Gospel Traditions of Early Christianity* (Leiden: Brill, 2005), 110–11.

64. Jeremias, *Unknown Sayings of Jesus*, 51.

65 See 'Was the Aksa Mosque built over the remains of a Byzantine church?' *Jerusalem Post*, Nov.16, 2008. See also, http://www.ritmeyer.com/2008/11/28/temple-mount-mikveh/

66. See m.Seqal 8.2. Kruger, *The Gospel of the Savior*, 119.

67. Kruger, *The Gospel of the Savior*, 121.

68. Jeremias, *Unknown Sayings of Jesus*, 52.

69. Kruger, *The Gospel of the Savior*, 136–39.

70. Tos. Kelim B.Q. 1.6 quoted in Jeremias, *Unknown Sayings of Jesus*, 58.

71. Kazen, *Jesus and Purity Halakhah: Was Jesus Indifferent to Impurity?*, 258–59.

Day Two: The Temple

1. The walled city of Jerusalem covered an area of around 115 hectares. The Temple covered 144,000 square metres – 14.4 hectares. *The Anchor Bible Dictionary*, III, 747.

2. Josephus, *Apion*.2.103.

3. Spec. Laws. 1.74, 156.

4. Goodman, *Judaism in the Roman World: Collected Essays*, 50.

5. Schürer, Millar, Vermès and Goodman, *The History of the Jewish People in the Age of Jesus Christ (175 B.C.–A.D. 135)*, I, 366.

6. Josephus, *Apion* 2.104–105

7. Ball, *Rome in the East: The Transformation of an Empire*, 261.

8. m. Kelim 1.8–9 in Danby, *The Mishnah*, 606.

9. m. Yoma 3.10 Goldhill, Simon, *The Temple of Jerusalem* (Profile Books Ltd, 19 January, 2006)

10. Goodman, *Judaism in the Roman World: Collected Essays*, 51.

11. Middoth 4.7. The appearance of the Temple is much debated, because Josephus' description doesn't match the description in the Mishnah. The present-day political sensitivity of the Temple Mount has made excavation all but impossible. One possible reason for the difference is that the Temple complex itself was continually being worked on. Work began under Herod the Great, and continued almost to the outbreak of revolution in 66 AD (Goodman, *Judaism in the Roman World: Collected Essays*, 48). Another is that the Mishnah was written much later and, in the words of Michael Chyutin, 'exploits all the available sources and attempts to weaves them into a coherent picture of a Temple which in actuality did not exist' (Chyutin, Michael, *Architecture and Utopia in the Temple Era*, (Library of Second Temple Studies, 58; London: T. & T. Clark, 2006), 145). Where the Mishnah is concerned the depiction of the Temple in Tractate Middoth is a literary reconstruction, not a historical description.

12. Middoth 3.8. The Mishnah implies that it took 300 men to move it, such was the weight. This is probably an exaggeration, but no doubt the weight required some substantial columns in the hall. On the entrance, see Chyutin, *Architecture and Utopia in the Temple Era*, 161.

13. Bammel and Moule, *Jesus and the Politics of His Day*, 332.

14. Bammel and Moule, *Jesus and the Politics of His Day*, 333.

15. Watts, John D. W., *Isaiah 34–66*, (Revised edn, Nashville, TN: Thomas Nelson, 2005), 820.

16. See, for example, Sanders, E. P., *Jesus and Judaism* (London: SCM, 1985), 68.

17. Fuks, Rappaport and Kasher, *Greece and Rome in Eretz Israel: Collected Essays*, 167.

18. m.Pesahim 4.8; t Pesahim 2(3):19, cited in Safrai, *The Economy of Roman Palestine*, 154.

19. Safrai, *The Economy of Roman Palestine*, 378.

20. Bammel and Moule, *Jesus and the Politics of His Day*, 278.

21. Mekilta, Yithro, Bahodesh I, quoted in Bammel and Moule, *Jesus and the Politics of His Day*, 280.

22. Bammel and Moule, *Jesus and the Politics of His Day*, 283.

23. m.Shek 1.3, Danby, *The Mishnah*, 152. Argued thus Witherington, *The Gospel of Mark: Socio-Rhetorical Commentary*, 316. Lane, William L., *The Gospel According to Mark; the English Text With Introduction, Exposition, and Notes* (Grand Rapids: Eerdmans, 1974), 405.

24. m.Shekal 6.5.

25. Richardson, Peter, *Building Jewish in the Roman East* (Jsjsup, v. 92; Waco, Tex: Baylor University Press, 2004), 245.

26. m.Shekel 2.4 in Danby, *The Mishnah*, 154.

27. t.Ketub 12.

28. *War* 4.105.

29. Richardson, *Building Jewish in the Roman East*, 246.

30. Richardson, *Building Jewish in the Roman East*, 247.

31. Sperber, Daniel, *Roman Palestine, 200–400: Money and Prices* (Bar-Ilan Studies in Near Eastern Languages and Culture, Ramat-Gan: Bar-Ilan University Press, 1991), 74.

32. See m.Shek 1.7. Danby, *The Mishnah*, 153

33. 'The required payment was only a half-shekel, but since the full shekel or tetradrachma was a more valuable coin, the payment for two men with one full shekel was encouraged by a surcharge of 8% on every individual half-shekel payment.' Murphy, Catherine M., *Wealth in the Dead Sea Scrolls and in the Qumran Community* (Leiden: Brill, 2002), 312. There is evidence that this worked well for the Temple authorities. In one coin hoard dating from the first century, archaeologists found 3,400 Tyrian shekels, 1,000 half-shekels and 160 Roman denarii of Augustus. The surcharge was paid in Roman silver denarii. Since the half-shekel was worth two denarii, 8% of the half-shekel was equal to 0.16 Roman denarius. So the coin hoard represents

the Temple tax payments of 7,800 men, 6,800 of whom took advantage of the full shekel discount, 1,000 of whom paid the half shekel. They were charged a further 0.16 denarii each, which amounts to 160 denarii.

34. Josephus, *Apion* 2.195.)

35. Hayward, Robert, *The Jewish Temple: A Non-Biblical Sourcebook* (London: Routledge, 1996), 119.

36. Wright, *Jesus and the Victory of God*, 408–10.

37. Safrai argues that this is too high, and estimates it at 0.5 denarius or less. Safrai, *The Economy of Roman Palestine*, 433. B. Avoda Zara 62a also lists 1 d. as a daily wage.

38. Costs taken from Sperber, *Roman Palestine, 200–400: Money and Prices*, 101. The scribe's wages come from Eccles Rab. 2.17.

39. Sperber, *Roman Palestine, 200–400: Money and Prices*, 103.

40. This is similar to costs elsewhere in the Græco-Roman world: according to Cicero, 1 denarius would buy just over 13 litres of wheat. Jeremias, *Jerusalem in the Time of Jesus*, 122–23.

41. Jeremias, *Jerusalem in the Time of Jesus*, 120–21.

42. m. Menahot 13.8, m. Bava Kama 3.9, cited in Sperber, *Roman Palestine, 200–400: Money and Prices*, 104–05.

43. Murphy, *Wealth in the Dead Sea Scrolls and in the Qumran Community*, 311–12.

44. Peters, *Jerusalem: The Holy City in the Eyes of Chroniclers, Visitors, Pilgrims, and Prophets From the Days of Abraham to the Beginnings of Modern Times*, 99–100.

45. Long, David E., *The Hajj Today: A Survey of the Contemporary Makkah Pilgrimage*, (Albany: State University of New York Press, 1979), 27.

46. Long, *The Hajj Today*, 34.

47. Long, *The Hajj Today*, 14–15.

48. Long, *The Hajj Today*, 5

49. Goodman, *The Ruling Class of Judaea*, 52.

50. Goodman, *Judaism in the Roman World: Collected Essays*, 60.

51. Long, *The Hajj Today*, 102.

52. m. Ker 1.7 in Danby, *The Mishnah*, 564.

53. m.Shekel 4.9 in Danby, *The Mishnah*, 157, 798. In the Mishnah, the prices are in form of *seahs* per *sela*. Modern weight comparisons are tricky, but a *seah* was around 12 litres. See 'Weights and Measures' in *The Anchor Bible Dictionary*, VI, 897–908. Jeremias says it was 13 litres (Jeremias, *Jerusalem in the Time of Jesus*, 122). A *sela* was 2 shekels, or 4 denarii.

54. b.Yoma 35b, Sperber, *Roman Palestine, 200–400: Money and Prices*, 103.

55. See, for example, Sanders, *Jesus and Judaism*, 64–65.

56. Goodman, *The Ruling Class of Judaea*, 52

57. Jeremias, *Jerusalem in the Time of Jesus*, 20.

58. Jeremias, *Jerusalem in the Time of Jesus*, 49.

59. Sifre; cf. j.Pe'a 1.6 quoted in Notley and Rainey, *Carta's New Century Handbook and Atlas of the Bible*, 235.

Day Three: The End Times

1. Woolf, Bertram Lee, *The Authority of Jesus and Its Foundation: A Study in the Four Gospels & the Acts* (London: Allen & Unwin, 1929), 84–85.

2. (BAGD, 793) *The Anchor Bible Dictionary*, IV, 493.

3. Bammel and Moule, *Jesus and the Politics of His Day*, 251.

4. See Bammel and Moule, *Jesus and the Politics of His Day*, 241–48.

5. Wengst and Bowden, *Pax Romana and the Peace of Jesus Christ*, 58–61.

6. Goodman, *The Ruling Class of Judaea*, 79.

7. Saldarini, Anthony J., *Pharisees, Scribes and Sadducees in Palestinian Society* (Grand Rapids: Eerdmans, 2001), 274.

8. m.Aboth 1.2 in Lane, *The Gospel According to Mark*, 434.

9. Lane, *The Gospel According to Mark*, 435. See, for example, Isa. 9.2–7; 11.1–9; Jer. 23.5ff; 30.9; 33.15,17, 22; Amos 9.11.

10. Gundry, Robert Horton, *Mark: A Commentary on His Apology for the Cross* (Grand Rapids: Eerdmans, 1993), 718.

11. Lane, *The Gospel According to Mark*, 440.

12. Lane, *The Gospel According to Mark*, 440.

13. Saldarini, Anthony J., *Pharisees, Scribes and Sadducees in Palestinian Society*, 274–275.

14. Jeremias, *Jerusalem in the Time of Jesus*, 112–13.

15. Jeremias, *Jerusalem in the Time of Jesus*, 115.

16. Jeremias, *Jerusalem in the Time of Jesus*, 114.

17. Leviticus Rabba III, 107 a quoted in Lane, *The Gospel According to Mark*, 443.

18. Zeldin, Theodore, *An Intimate History of Humanity* (London: Vintage, 1998), 350.

19. For example, the definition from the 'Apocalypse Group of the Society of Biblical Literature'. 'Apocalypse is a genre of revelatory literature with a narrative framework, in which a revelation is mediated by an otherworldly being to a human recipient, disclosing a transcendent reality which is both temporal, insofar as it envisages eschatological salvation, and spatial insofar as it involves another, supernatural world.' Webb, Robert L. '"Apocalyptic": Observations on a Slippery Term', *Journal of Near Eastern Studies* 49 (2), 1990, 123. That's cleared that up, then.

20. Webb, '"Apocalyptic": Observations on a Slippery Term', 115–16.

21. Which is not to say that what was originally an outsider's view cannot or has not been appropriated by other groups. There were apocalypses in the Middle Ages supporting the papacy and the empire. Collins, *The Apocalyptic Imagination: An Introduction to Jewish Apocalyptic Literature*, 10.

22. For a more detailed account, see Wright, *Jesus and the Victory of God*, 339–46.

23. Wright, *Jesus and the Victory of God*, 348–49.

24. Wright, *Jesus and the Victory of God*, 349.

Day Four: The Plot and the Perfume

1. Kazen, *Jesus and Purity Halakhah: Was Jesus Indifferent to Impurity?*, 98.

2. Kazen, *Jesus and Purity Halakhah: Was Jesus Indifferent to Impurity?*, 109.

3. m.Neg 13.8, in Danby, *The Mishnah*, 694.

4. m.Neg 12.1, in Danby, *The Mishnah*, 691.

5. Kazen, *Jesus and Purity Halakhah: Was Jesus Indifferent to Impurity?*, 111–12.

6. Vermès, Géza, *The Complete Dead Sea Scrolls in English* (London: Penguin Books, 2004), 207.

7. Dar, Shimon. 'Food and Archaeology in Romano-Byzantine Palestine', in *Food in Antiquity*, edited by John Wilkins, David Harvey and Mike Dobson (Exeter: Exeter University Press, 1995), 327.

8. This was not all bad news. According to the Talmud, village girls who ground the flour every morning had bigger breasts than the city girls who simply bought bread from the bakers. (Tosefta Nida 6.9, cited in Dar, Shimon, 'Food and Archaeology in Romano-Byzantine Palestine', in *Food in Antiquity*, edited by John Wilkins, David Harvey and Mike Dobson [Exeter: Exeter University Press, 1995], 330.).

9. Dar, Shimon, 'Food and Archaeology in Romano-Byzantine Palestine', in *Food in Antiquity*, 327–28.

10. (Yerushalmi Shevitt 5.7.36. Dar, Shimon, 'Food and Archaeology in Romano-Byzantine Palestine', in *Food in Antiquity*, 331.)

11. (Tosefta Baba Metzia 3.27.)

12. We can say, however, that the tradition that the woman in Luke's Gospel was Mary Magdalene isn't found anywhere in the Gospels.

13. Gundry, *Mark: A Commentary on His Apology for the Cross*, 802.

14. 'Spices, Incense, Drugs, and Condiments' in Anchor Bible Dictionary [II, 810–13]. You can still get nard in the form of Spikenard – an essential oil. I suggest, if you want to encounter the Bible story in a new way, investing in a bottle and some massage oil and a foot massage!

15. From Anonymous, *Navigation of the Erythraean Sea* xlix, lvi and Lewis and Reinhold, *Roman Civilization: Selected Readings*, 121–22.

16. Gundry, *Mark: A Commentary on His Apology for the Cross*, 803.

17. Ben Sira 22.3, quoted in Ilan, *Jewish Women in Greco-Roman Palestine*, 44.

18. Ilan, *Jewish Women in Greco-Roman Palestine*, 129

19. m.Ket 9.4.

20. (bQuidd. 80b) cited in Ilan, *Jewish Women in Greco-Roman Palestine*, 124.

21. Ilan, *Jewish Women in Greco-Roman Palestine*, 179.

22. According to the Rabbinic School of Hillel. The School of Shammai argued a man could divorce a woman only for unchastity. mGitt 9.10.

23. (ySot. 7.1, 21b) cited in Ilan, *Jewish Women in Greco-Roman Palestine*, 127.

24. Ilan, *Jewish Women in Greco-Roman Palestine*, 127.

25. Richer Jews got around this by wearing wigs. However, wigs were a luxury which only relatively well-off women could afford, another example of a purity exemption that only the upper classes could afford.

26. Bailey, *Jesus Through Middle Eastern Eyes*, 248; Danby, *The Mishnah*, 794.

27. Bailey, *Jesus Through Middle Eastern Eyes*, 248.

28. Brown, Raymond Edward, *The Death of the Messiah: From Gethsemane to the Grave: A Commentary on the Passion Narratives in the Four Gospels* (London: Geoffrey Chapman, 1994), 1411.

29. Hagner, *Matthew 1–13*, 266. Brown, *The Death of the Messiah*, 1415.

30. Richardson, Alan, *The Political Christ*, (London: SCM Press, 1973), 38.

Day Five: The Arrest

1. Jeremias, Joachim, *The Eucharistic Words of Jesus* (London: SCM, 1966), 22–23.

2. Ogg, *The Chronology of the Public Ministry of Jesus*, 232.

3. Jeremias, *The Eucharistic Words of Jesus*, 17.

4. Segal, J. B., *The Hebrew Passover: From the Earliest Times to A.D. 70* (London: Oxford University Press, 1963), 245.

5. Segal, *The Hebrew Passover: From the Earliest Times to A.D. 70*, 244–45.

6. Ogg, *The Chronology of the Public Ministry of Jesus*, 232–33; Segal, *The Hebrew Passover: From the Earliest Times to A.D. 70*, 244–45.

7. John 18.28, see Jeremias, *The Eucharistic Words of Jesus*, 19–20.

8. Ogg, *The Chronology of the Public Ministry of Jesus*, 230.

9. See Notley, R. Steven, Marc Turnage and Brian Becker, *Jesus' Last Week* (Leiden: Brill, 2006), 49–50. Some have argued that the fact they were reclining indicates the Passover meal. But there are plenty more meals in the New Testament at which they are also reclining, so we cannot assume that major festivals were the only time that guests reclined rather than sat.

10. Brown, *The Death of the Messiah*, 124.

11. Ogg, *The Chronology of the Public Ministry of Jesus*, 239. Paul associates the 'sacrifice' of Jesus with the sacrifice of the lamb, it is true, but also with the removal of all the yeast from the house. 1 Cor. 5.7ff. See Segal, *The Hebrew Passover: From the Earliest Times to A.D. 70*, 243.

12. See Witherington, *The Gospel of Mark: Socio-Rhetorical Commentary*, 371.

13. Segal, *The Hebrew Passover*, 247. There is a calendar of events found at Qumran which does include the Passover, but this may be a Sadducean calendar, rather than one of the community.

14. Chyutin, *Architecture and Utopia in the Temple Era*, 108.

15. See Pixner, Bargil, 'Church of the Apostles Found on Mount Zion', *Biblical Archaeology Review* 16 (3), May/June 1990.

16. John 14.5, 8, 22; 16.17–18, 29–30.

17. Tos. Kelim B.Q. 1.6

18. Pe'a 1.15c. 14 cited in Beasley-Murray, John, 233.

19. Zeldin, *An Intimate History of Humanity*, 7–8

20. Jeremias, *Jerusalem in the Time of Jesus*, 36.

21. Jeremias, *Jerusalem in the Time of Jesus*, 111.

22. Jeremias, *Jerusalem in the Time of Jesus*, 313–14.

23. Jeremias, *Jerusalem in the Time of Jesus*, 314 n.56.

24. You could ask a wife or child to wash your feet.

25. Beasley-Murray, *John*, 233.

26. Notley, Turnage and Becker, *Jesus' Last Week*, 43.

27. According to legend, the Holy Grail was the cup that Jesus used at the Last Supper, and which subsequently, for a reason I've never been able to fathom, was used to collect his blood when he was on the cross. The Holy Grail, as an object, isn't mentioned anywhere, in any literature, before the twelfth century. It features in a poem by Chrétien de Troyes dated sometime between 1180 and 1191.

28. Nolland, John, *Luke* (Dallas, Texas: Word Books, 1989), 1076–77.

29. Jeremias, *The Eucharistic Words of Jesus*, 46, n.6.

30. Murphy-O'Connor, J., *The Holy Land: An Archaeological Guide From Earliest Times to 1700* (Oxford: Oxford University Press, 1986), 106.

31. Murphy-O'Connor, *The Holy Land: An Archaeological Guide From Earliest Times to 1700*, 106–07.

32. Brown, *The Death of the Messiah*, 149.

33. Matthew 26.55. Jeremias, *Jerusalem in the Time of Jesus*, 210.

34. Jeremias, *Jerusalem in the Time of Jesus*, 209–10.

35. Jeremias, *Jerusalem in the Time of Jesus*, 211.

36. See Gen.Rab.70 [45b], quoted in Page, Nick, *What Happened to the Ark of the Covenant?* (Milton Keynes: Authentic Media, 2007), 113, for examples of three acceptable types of public kissing.

37. Harvey, Karen, *The Kiss in History* (Manchester: Manchester University Press, 2005), 197. Brown, *The Death of the Messiah*, 255.

38. See Rom. 16.16; 1 Cor. 16.20; 2 Cor. 13.12; 1 Thess. 5.26. It's also mentioned by Peter in 1 Pet. 5.14.

39. Phillips, L. Edward, *The Ritual Kiss in Early Christian Worship* (Alcuin/Grow Liturgical Study, 36; Cambridge: Grove, 1996), 7–8.

40. Brown, *The Death of the Messiah*, 255.

41. Kreider, Alan, *Worship and Evangelism in Pre-Christendom* (Cambridge: Grove Books, 1995), 28.

42. Page, *What Happened to the Ark of the Covenant?*, 113–16.

43. Bauckham, *Jesus and the Eyewitnesses: The Gospels as Eyewitness Testimony*, 194–95.

44. See Bauckham, *Jesus and the Eyewitnesses: The Gospels as Eyewitness Testimony*, 199–200.

Day Six: The Execution

1. Vanderkam, *From Joshua to Caiaphas: High Priests after the Exile*, 420.

2. m.Par 3.5. See Goodman, *The Ruling Class of Judaea*, 143ff..

3. For a full account, see Vanderkam, *From Joshua to Caiaphas: High Priests after the Exile*, 420ff..

4. Josephus records several incidents of this. Vanderkam, *From Joshua to Caiaphas*, 420.

5. Vanderkam, *From Joshua to Caiaphas*, 476–77.

6. M. Sanhedr, 7.5 in Danby, *The Mishnah, Translated From the Hebrew*.

7. Ritmeyer and Ritmeyer, *Jerusalem in the Year 30 A.D*, 42–43.

8. Ritmeyer and Ritmeyer, *Jerusalem in the Year 30 A.D*, 44.

9. Page, *What Happened to the Ark of the Covenant?*, 180–81.

10. John 13.23–24; 19.26–27; 20.2–4, 8; 21.7, 20–24. Some argue that he is also the unnamed disciple who is called by Jesus in John 1.35ff. See Keener, Craig S., *The Gospel of John: A Commentary* (Peabody, Mass: Hendrickson Publishers, 2003), 1091.

11. A later account describes how his eyes were 'so swollen that they could not be seen' how his body was 'covered with runnings and worms' and how his burial place was left desolate, and 'no one could pass the place without stopping up his nose with his hands.' See *Church Fathers – The Ante-Nicene Fathers*, edited by Roberts, Rev. Alexander and Donaldson, James, 1885

12. b.Erubin 53b in Vermès, Géza, *The Changing Faces of Jesus* (London: Penguin, 2000)

13. See 'Brummie accent is perceived as "worse than silence"', in *The Times*, April 4, 2008.

14. Brown, *The Death of the Messiah*, 601.

15. '...οἱ ἀρχιερεῖς μετὰ τῶν πρεσβυτέρων καὶ γραμματέων καὶ ὅλον τὸ συνέδριον,' (Mark 15.1).

16. Goodman, *The Ruling Class of Judaea*, 113.

17. Goodman, *Rome and Jerusalem*, 327.

18. Flusser, David, R. Steven Notley and David Flusser, *The Sage From Galilee: Rediscovering Jesus' Genius* Grand Rapids, Mich.; Cambridge: Eerdmans, 2007), 138–39.

19. Schürer, Millar, Vermès and Goodman, *The History of the Jewish People in the Age of Jesus Christ (175 B.C.–A.D. 135)*, I, 370.

20. Goodman, Martin, and Jane Sherwood, *The Roman World, 44 BC–AD 180* (Routledge History of the Ancient World, London: Routledge, 1997), 172–73.

21. Goodman, *The Ruling Class of Judaea*, 8.

22. Strabo 5.4.11.

23. Pliny, for example, organised numerous building projects. Pliny, *Epistles* 10.37–44,

24. Josephus, *War* 2.117–118.

25. Goodman, *The Ruling Class of Judaea*, 7.

26. Matyszak, Philip, *The Sons of Caesar: Imperial Rome's First Dynasty* (London: Thames & Hudson, 2006), 143.

27. Juvenal, and Green, *The Sixteen Satires*, 66.

28. See Tacitus, *Annals* iv, 41, 57; Suetonius, *Tiberius*, xli.

29. Matyszak, *The Sons of Caesar: Imperial Rome's First Dynasty*, 143–44.

30. Goodman, *The Ruling Class of Judaea*, 7.

31. Matyszak, *The Sons of Caesar: Imperial Rome's First Dynasty*, 151.

32. Tacitus, *Annals* V.9; Cassius Dio, *Roman History* LVIII.11

33. Carter, *Pontius Pilate*, 3–4.

34. Philo, *De Legatione ad Gaium* xxiv, 159–161.F. The Loeb Classical Library, X, 81–83.

35. Notley and Rainey, *Carta's New Century Handbook and Atlas of the Bible*, 236.

36. Josephus, *Antiquities* 18.60–62.

37. McLaren, James S., *Power and Politics in Palestine: The Jews and the Governing of Their Land 100 BC–AD 70* (Sheffield: JSOT Press, 1991).

38. Josephus, *Antiquities* 18.55–59.

39. Doyle, D. 'Pilate's Career and the Date of the Crucifixion', *Journal of Theological Studies* 42, 1941.

40. Philo, Embassy to Gaius, 299–305. On the dating of these events, see Hoehner, Harold W., *Herod Antipas* (Cambridge: Cambridge University Press, 1972), 178–83.

41. Doyle, 'Pilate's Career and the Date of the Crucifixion', *Journal of Theological Studies* 42, 1941.

42. Bond, Helen K., *Pontius Pilate in History and Interpretation* (Cambridge: Cambridge University Press, 1998), 195.

43. Hoehner, *Herod Antipas* 227–30.

44. Herodias was also his niece. The Herodian family tree is very complicated. See Connolly, Peter, *Living in the Time of Jesus of Nazareth* (Oxford: Oxford University Press, 1983), 39.

45. This was not the only purity law that Antipas broke. To honour the emperor he built a grand new city called Tiberias. Unfortunately the site he chose was the site of a pagan graveyard, meaning that any Jew settling in the city would be impure for seven days (Num. 19.11–16). Antipas was forced to settle the city with slaves and freed prisoners, whom he provided with houses on condition they never leave the city.

46. Mark 6.14–29. See Page, *What Happened to the Ark of the Covenant?*, 19–26.

47. Wilkinson, *Jerusalem as Jesus Knew it*, 142. This was also Agrippa II's place of residence when Judaea was governed by the Romans. Josephus, *Antiquities*, 20.189–90.

48. Hoehner, *Herod Antipas*, 241–43.

49. Brown, *The Death of the Messiah*, 655.

50. Brown, *The Death of the Messiah*, 645.

51. Brown, *The Death of the Messiah*, 644.

52. m.Yoma 5.6 in Danby, *The Mishnah*, 168. Vermès, *The Complete Dead Sea Scrolls in English*, 201–02.

53. Schürer et al., *The History of the Jewish People in the Age of Jesus Christ (175 B.C.–A.D. 135)*, I, 370.

54. Bond, *Pontius Pilate in History and Interpretation*, 199.

55. Some later manuscripts of Matthew have the name 'Jesus Barabbas'. This may be original, since it is unlikely that later Christian tradition would have chosen to give the name 'Jesus' to a villain.

56. Carter, *Pontius Pilate*, 144; Wright, *Jesus and the Victory of God*, 155–56.

57. Goodman, *The Ruling Class of Judaea*, 63.

58. Carter, *Pontius Pilate*, 69–70.

59. See 'λαοσ' in *New International Dictionary of New Testament Theology*, ed. Colin Brown (Exeter: Paternoster, 1986). Brown, *The Death of the Messiah*, 836; Hagner, Donald Alfred, *Matthew 14–28*, (Dallas, Texas: Word Books, 1995), 828.

60. This support may have continued for some time. Acts 5.26 records an arrest of the apostles which has to be done carefully, because people threaten to stone the police.

61. Josephus, *War* 20.179–81.

62. Josephus, *Antiquities* 20.214, cited in Goodman, *The Ruling Class of Judaea*, 139.

63. Brown, Raymond Edward, *The Gospel According to John* (London: G. Chapman, 1971), 881–82.

64. Ilan, *Jewish Women in Greco-Roman Palestine*, 159.

65. Schürer et al., *The History of the Jewish People in the Age of Jesus Christ (175 B.C.–A.D. 135)*, I, 371.

66. Pollard, *Soldiers, Cities, and Civilians in Roman Syria*, 120.

67. See Freeman and Kennedy, *The Defence of the Roman and Byzantine East : Proceedings of a Colloquium Held At the University of Sheffield in April 1986* (Oxford, England: B.A.R. 1986) II 311; Millar, *The Roman Near East, 31 BC–AD 337*, 45.

68. Crown, Alan David, *The Samaritans* (Tübingen: J. C. B. Mohr (Paul Siebeck), 1989), 61.

69. Brown, *The Death of the Messiah*, 701 n.64. Jones, A. H. M., and Michael Avi-Yonah, The Cities of the Eastern Roman Provinces (2nd edn, Oxford: Clarendon Press, 1971), 272.

70. Tractate Kutim 28.

71. Crown, *The Samaritans*, 35.

72. Crown, *The Samaritans*, 35–36.

73. Josephus, *Antiquities* 18.29–30.

74. Gundry, *Mark: A Commentary on His Apology for the Cross*, 942.

75. See Hart, H. St. J., 'The Crown of Thorns in John 19.2–5', *Journal of Theological Studies* 3, 1952.

76. Carroll, John T., and Joel B. Green, *The Death of Jesus in Early Christianity* (Peabody, Mass: Hendrickson Publishers, 1995), 167–70.

77. Zias, J. and Sekeles, E., 'The Crucified Man from Giv'at ha-Mivtar: A Reappraisal', *Israel Exploration Journal* 35, 1985, 22.

78. van der Horst, Pieter, 'Jewish Funerary Inscriptions – Most are in Greek', *Biblical Archaeology Review* 18 (5), 1992.

79. Marshall, I. Howard, *The Gospel of Luke: A Commentary on the Greek Text* (Exeter: Paternoster, 1978), 864.

80. Marshall, *The Gospel of Luke: A Commentary on the Greek Text*, 865.

81. Safrai, *The Economy of Roman Palestine*, 147.

82. Pliny, *Nat.* 14.15 §92 in Evans, Craig A., *Mark 8:27–16:20* (Nashville: Thomas Nelson, 2001), 501.

83. Hengel, Martin, *Crucifixion in the Ancient World and the Folly of the Message of the Cross* (London: SCM, 1977), 25.

84. Josephus, *War* 5.449–451. Josephus, *The Jewish War*, 326.

85. Seneca LA, in Michaelis, H. C., ed. 'De Consolatione ad Marciam', quoted in Maslen, Matthew W. and Mitchell, Piers, D. 'Medical theories on the cause of death in crucifixion', *Journal of the Royal Society of Medicine* 99, 2006, 185.

86. See Haas, N., 'Anthropological Observations on the Skeletal Remains from Gi'vat ha-Mivtar', *Israel Exploration Journal* 20, 1970, 49ff. and Zias, J. and Sekeles, 'The Crucified Man from Giv'at ha-Mivtar: A Reappraisal', 22–27.

87. Hengel, *Crucifixion in the Ancient World and the Folly of the Message of the Cross*, 59.

88. Borg and Crossan, *The Last Week: What the Gospels Really Teach About Jesus' Final Days in Jerusalem*, 146.

89. This event may be the one that is referred to in the Dead Sea Scrolls. 4QpNah 1.7–8.

90. Josephus, *War* 2.293–314.

91. Josephus, *War* 2.74–76.

92. Notley, Turnage and Becker, *Jesus' Last Week*, 201.

93. *Mekilta DeRabbi Ishmael*, cited in Notley, Turnage and Becker, *Jesus' Last Week*, 199.

94. Sidebotham, *Roman Economic Policy in the Erythra Thalassa 30 B.C.– A.D. 217*, 132.

95. Grünewald, Thomas, *Bandits in the Roman Empire: Myth and Reality* (London: Routledge, 2004), 99.

96. Bammel and Moule, *The Trial of Jesus: Cambridge Studies in Honour of C. F. D. Moule*, 163–64.

97. Nolland, *Luke*, 1152–53.

98. Speidel, Michael, 'Roman Army Pay Scales', *Journal of Roman Studies* 82, 1992, 105.

99. Speidel, 'Roman Army Pay Scales', 106. Cavalrymen received more because they had to pay for their horse's hay.

100. Phang, Sara Elise, *Roman Military Service: Ideologies of Discipline in the Late Republic and Early Principate* (Cambridge: Cambridge University Press, 2008), 172. Lewis, *Life in Egypt Under Roman Rule*, 470.

101. Speidel, Michael, 'The Pay of the Auxilia', *Journal of Roman Studies* 63, 1973, 146–47.

102. On Joseph, see Page, *What Happened to the Ark of the Covenant?*, 159–63.

103. Bauckham has suggested that Salome is Jesus' sister, rather than his aunt. See Bauckham, Richard, *Gospel Women: Studies of the Named Women in the Gospels* (Edinburgh: T. & T. Clark, 2002), 225ff..

104. See Page, *What Happened to the Ark of the Covenant?*, 94–95. Mary of Clopas may also be a relative, as we shall see later.

105. Shanks, Hershel, and Ben Witherington, *The Brother of Jesus: The Dramatic Story & Meaning of the First Archaeological Link to Jesus & His Family* (London: Continuum, 2003), 105.

106. Nolland, Luke, 1156–57.

107. Pliny links an eclipse of the sun with the death of Caesar. Natural History 2.30 in Brown, *The Death of the Messiah*, 1043.

108. Josephus, *War* 6.423–425.

109. Jeremias, *The Eucharistic Words of Jesus*, 42.

110. According to the farm welfare council, see http://news.bbc.co.uk/1/hi/uk/3604675.stm. A friend of mine, a vicar who is an ex-butcher, told me that he reckoned a skilled abattoir worker could kill and flay a lamb in around four minutes.

111. Long, *The Hajj Today*, 85.

112. Long, *The Hajj Today*, 86.

113. Brown, *The Death of the Messiah*, 1046.

114. Evans, *Mark 8:27–16:20*, 507.

115. For a list, see Maslen, 'Medical theories on the cause of death in crucifixion', 186.

116. Hengel, *Crucifixion in the Ancient World and the Folly of the Message of the Cross*, 29 n.21.

117. See Page, *What Happened to the Ark of the Covenant?*, 145–151.

118. Beasley-Murray, *John*, 356.

119. Gilliam, J. F. 'The Appointment of Auxiliary Centurions (PMich.164)' *Transactions and Proceedings of the American Philological Association* 88, 1957, 155–156, 167.

120. Gilliam, 'The Appointment of Auxiliary Centurions (PMich.164)', 158.

121. Josephus, Williamson and Smallwood, *The Jewish War*, 303.

122. Some have seen the iconography of this event reflected in Hebrews chapter 9, which is all about access to the sanctuary. But Hebrews makes no specific reference to it.

123. Witherington, *The Gospel of Mark: Socio-Rhetorical Commentary*, 400.

124. Hayward, *The Jewish Temple: A Non-Biblical Sourcebook*, 150.

125. Hayward, *The Jewish Temple: A Non-Biblical Sourcebook*, 150.

126. Hagner, *Matthew 14–28*, 850–52.

127. Brown, *The Death of the Messiah*, 1213 n.17.

128. Witherington, *The Gospel of Mark: Socio-Rhetorical Commentary*, 402.

129. Josephus tells the following anecdote, set in the savage aftermath of the failed Jewish rebellion: 'When I was sent by Titus Caesar with Cerealius, and a thousand horsemen, to a certain village called Thecoa, in order to know whether it were a place fit for a camp, as I came back, I

saw many captives crucified; and remembered three of them as my former acquaintance. I was very sorry at this in my mind, and went with tears in my eyes to Titus, and told him of them; so he immediately commanded them to be taken down, and to have the greatest care taken of them, in order to their recovery; yet two of them died under the physician's hands, while the third recovered.' (Josephus, *Life* 1.420–422)

130. Brown, *The Death of the Messiah*, 1243.

131. m.Oholot 2.2 in Danby, *The Mishnah*, 651.

132. A. N. Jannaris, *Expository Times* 14, 1902–3, 460, cited in Brown, *The Death of the Messiah*, 1260.

133. Brown, *The Death of the Messiah*, 1263.

134. *Encyclopaedia Judaica* (Jerusalem: *Encyclopaedia Judaica*, 1971), 12: 801–802.

135. Flusser, Notley and Flusser, *The Sage From Galilee: Rediscovering Jesus' Genius*, 140–41.

136. Biddle, Martin, *The Tomb of Christ* (Stroud: Sutton, 1999), 60.

137. Brown, *The Death of the Messiah*, 1281–82.

138. Hachlili, Rachel, *Jewish Funerary Customs, Practices and Rites in the Second Temple Period* (Jsjsup, v. 94; Leiden: Brill, 2005), 56–57.

139. Brown, *The Death of the Messiah*, 1249.

140. See 1 Chr. 35.

141. IIQ19 17.8–9 in Vermès, *The Complete Dead Sea Scrolls in English*, 196; Jubilees 49,16–20.

142. Tos Pes 6.11 cited in Jeremias, *The Eucharistic Words of Jesus*, 43 n.3.

143. m.Taan 3.8. in Danby, *The Mishnah*, 198.

144. Kurlansky, Mark, *Nonviolence: The History of a Dangerous Idea* (London: Jonathan Cape, 2006), 13.

145. Sacchi, Paolo, *The History of the Second Temple Period* (London: T. & T. Clark International, 2004), 494.

Day Seven: The Silence

1. Brown, *The Death of the Messiah*, 1289.

2. Nolland, John, *The Gospel of Matthew: A Commentary on the Greek Text* (Grand Rapids, Mich.; Cambridge/Bletchley: W. B. Eerdmans/Paternoster Press, 2005), 1238–39.

3. See Craig, W. L., 'The Guard at the Tomb', *New Testament Studies* 30, 1984, 273–281.

Day Eight: The Return

1. It does include one peculiarity – the idea that followers of Jesus will 'pick up snakes in their hands'. Some cults have taken this literally and go in for snake-handling as a sign of holiness. Probably this comes from a tradition based on Paul's experiences: according to Luke, Paul was bitten by a poisonous snake but suffered no harm.

2. Eusebius, *The Ecclesiastical History and the Martyrs of Palestine*, 78.

3. See Bauckham, *Gospel Women: Studies of the Named Women in the Gospels*, 203–23.

4. Origen Contra Celsus 2.62. See Bauckham, *Jesus and the Eyewitnesses: The Gospels as Eyewitness Testimony*, 43..

5. Orr, William F., and James Arthur Walther, *I Corinthians: A New Translation* (Garden City, N.Y: Doubleday, 1976), 321–22.

6. See Ant 4.219; bKet 74b, quoted in Ilan, *Jewish Women in Greco-Roman Palestine*, 163–65.

7. See Wright, *The Resurrection of the Son of God*, 607–08.

8. Dunn, James D. G., *The Evidence for Jesus: The Impact of Scholarship on Our Understanding of How Christianity Began* (London: SCM, 1985), 65.

9. Wright, *The Resurrection of the Son of God*, 611.

10. Dunn, *The Evidence for Jesus: The Impact of Scholarship on Our Understanding of How Christianity Began*, 67.

11. It would still prove that Jude was believed to be a follower of Jesus; or else why attribute authorship to him?

Aftershock: AD 33 and After

1. Charlesworth, James H., *Jesus and Archaeology* (Grand Rapids, Mich.; Cambridge: William B. Eerdmans, 2006), 334.

2. Schürer, Millar, Vermès and Goodman, *The History of the Jewish People in the Age of Jesus Christ (175 B.C.–A.D. 135)*, I, 386–87.

3. Millar, *The Roman Near East, 31 BC–AD 337*, 55.

4. Tiberius had adopted Caligula's father, the general Germanicus.

5. Eusebius, *The Ecclesiastical History and the Martyrs of Palestine*, 42. Some have doubted this account, but Eusebius does claim ancient sources for the story.

6. Vanderkam, *From Joshua to Caiaphas: High Priests after the Exile*, 423–24. Ritmeyer, Leen and Kathleen Ritmeyer, *Jerusalem in the Year 30 A.D.* (Jerusalem: Carta, 2004), 44.

7. Goodman, *The Ruling Class of Judaea*, 213.

8. Vanderkam, *From Joshua to Caiaphas: High Priests after the Exile*, 481.

Bibliography

Avi-Yonah, Michael, *The Jews under Roman and Byzantine Rule: A Political History of Palestine from the Bar Kokhba War to the Arab Conquest* (Jerusalem/New York: Magnes, Hebrew University/Schocken Books, 1984)

Bailey, Kenneth E., *Jesus Through Middle Eastern Eyes: Cultural Studies in the Gospels* (London: SPCK, 2008)

Ball, Warwick, *Rome in the East: The Transformation of an Empire* (London: Routledge, 2000)

Bammel, Ernst, and C. F. D Moule, *Jesus and the Politics of His Day* (Cambridge: Cambridge University Press, 1984)

—, *The Trial of Jesus: Cambridge Studies in Honour of C. F. D. Moule* (London: SCM, 1970)

Bauckham, Richard, *Gospel Women: Studies of the Named Women in the Gospels* (Edinburgh: T. & T. Clark, 2002)

—, *Jesus and the Eyewitnesses: The Gospels as Eyewitness Testimony* (Grand Rapids, Michigan: William B. Eerdmans Publishing Company, 2006)

Beasley-Murray, George Raymond, *John* (Waco, Texas: Word Books, 1987)

Biddle, Martin, *The Tomb of Christ* (Stroud: Sutton, 1999)

Bond, Helen K, *Pontius Pilate in History and Interpretation* (Cambridge: Cambridge University Press, 1998)

Borg, Marcus J., and John Dominic Crossan, *The Last Week: What the Gospels Really Teach about Jesus' Final Days in Jerusalem* (San Francisco: HarperSanFrancisco, February, 2007)

Bovon, François, 'Fragment Oxyrhynchus 840, Fragment of a Lost Gospel, Witness of an Early Christian Controversy over Purity', *Journal of Biblical Literature* 119 (4), 2000

Brandon, S. G. F, *Jesus and the Zealots: A Study of the Political Factor in Primitive Christianity* (Manchester: Manchester University Press, 1967)

Brown, Colin, ed. *New International Dictionary of New Testament Theology* (Exeter: Paternoster, 1986)

Brown, Raymond Edward, *The Death of the Messiah: From Gethsemane to the Grave: A Commentary on the Passion Narratives in the Four Gospels* (Anchor Bible Reference Library, London: Geoffrey Chapman, 1994)

—, *The Gospel According to John* (London: G. Chapman, 1971)

Carlton, Eric, *Occupation: The Policies and Practices of Military Conquerors* (London: Routledge, 1992)

Carroll, John T., and Joel B. Green, *The Death of Jesus in Early Christianity* (Peabody, Mass: Hendrickson Publishers, 1995)

Carter, Warren, *Pontius Pilate* (Liturgical Press, US, 2003)

Charlesworth, James H., *Jesus and Archaeology* (Grand Rapids, Mich.; Cambridge: William B. Eerdmans, 2006)

Chyutin, Michael, *Architecture and Utopia in the Temple Era* (London: T. & T. Clark, 2006)

Collins, John Joseph, *The Apocalyptic Imagination: An Introduction to Jewish Apocalyptic Literature* (Grand Rapids, Mich.: William B. Eerdmans, 1998)

Connolly, Peter, *Living in the Time of Jesus of Nazareth* (Oxford: Oxford University Press, 1983)

Craig, W. L. 'The Guard at the Tomb', *New Testament Studies* 30, 1984

Crossan, John Dominic, *The Historical Jesus: The Life of a Mediterranean Jewish Peasant* (Edinburgh: Clark, 1993)

Crown, Alan David, *The Samaritans* (Tübingen: J. C. B. Mohr 1989)

Danby, Herbert, *The Mishnah, Translated From the Hebrew* (London: Oxford University Press, 1933)

Dar, Shimon, 'Food and Archaeology in Romano-Byzantine Palestine', in *Food in Antiquity* edited by John Wilkins, David Harvey and Mike Dobson, (Exeter: Exeter University Press, 1995), 326–35

Davis, Mike, *Planet of Slums* (London; New York: Verso, 2006)

Doyle, D. 'Pilate's Career and the Date of the Crucifixion' *Journal of Theological Studies* 42, 1941

Dunn, James D. G, *The Evidence for Jesus: The Impact of Scholarship on Our Understanding of How Christianity Began* (London: SCM, 1985)

Encyclopaedia Judaica (Jerusalem: Encyclopaedia Judaica, 1971)

Esler, Philip Francis, *The Early Christian World* (London: Routledge, 2000)

Eusebius, *The Ecclesiastical History and the Martyrs of Palestine* trans. Hugh Jackson Lawlor and John Ernest Leonard Oulton (London: SPCK, 1927)

Evans, Craig A., *Mark 8:27–16:20* (Nashville: Thomas Nelson, 2001)

Feldman, Louis H., *Jew and Gentile in the Ancient World* (Princeton: Princeton University Press, 1993)

Finegan, Jack, *Handbook of Biblical Chronology: Principles of Time Reckoning in the Ancient World and Problems of Chronology in the Bible* (Peabody, Mass: Hendrickson Publishers, 1998)

Flusser, David, R., *The Sage From Galilee: Rediscovering Jesus' Genius* (4th expanded edn, Grand Rapids, Mich.; Cambridge: Eerdmans, 2007)

Fotheringham, J. 'Astronomical Evidence for the Date of the Crucifixion', *Journal of Theological Studies* XII, 1910

The Anchor Bible Dictionary ed. David Noel Freedman (New York: Doubleday, 1999)

Fuks, Gideon, Uriel Rappaport and Aryeh Kasher, *Greece and Rome in Eretz Israel: Collected Essays* (Jerusalem: Yad Izhak Ben-Zvi, Israel Exploration Society, 1990)

Gilliam, J. F. 'The Appointment of Auxiliary Centurions (PMich.164)' *Transactions and Proceedings of the American Philological Association* 88, 1957

Goldhill, Simon, *The Temple of Jerusalem* (London: Profile Books, 2006)

Goodman, Martin, *Judaism in the Roman World: Collected Essays* (Leiden: Brill, 2007)

—, *Rome and Jerusalem: The Clash of Ancient Civilizations* (London: Penguin, 2008)

—, *The Ruling Class of Judaea: The Origins of the Jewish Revolt against Rome, A.D. 66–70* (Cambridge: Cambridge University Press, 1987)

Goodman, Martin, and Jane Sherwood, *The Roman World, 44 BC–AD 180* (London: Routledge, 1997)

Grünewald, Thomas, *Bandits in the Roman Empire: Myth and Reality* (London: Routledge, 2004)

Gundry, Robert Horton, *Mark: A Commentary on His Apology for the Cross* (Grand Rapids: Eerdmans, 1993)

Haas, N. 'Anthropological Observations on the Skeletal Remains from Gi'vat ha-Mivtar', *Israel Exploration Journal* 20, 1970

Hachlili, Rachel, *Jewish Funerary Customs, Practices and Rites in the Second Temple Period* (Leiden: Brill, 2005)

Hagner, Donald Alfred, *Matthew 1–13* (Dallas, Texas: Word Books, 1993)

—, *Matthew 14–28* (Dallas, Texas: Word Books, 1995)

Hart, H. St. J. 'The Crown of Thorns in John 19:2–5', *Journal of Theological Studies* 3, 1952

Harvey, Karen, *The Kiss in History* (Manchester: Manchester University Press, 2005)

Hayward, Robert, *The Jewish Temple: A Non-Biblical Sourcebook* (London: Routledge, 1996)

Hengel, Martin, *Crucifixion in the Ancient World and the Folly of the Message of the Cross* (London: SCM, 1977)

Hodge, A. Trevor, *Roman Aqueducts and Water Supply* (London: Duckworth, 1993)

Hoehner, Harold W., *Herod Antipas* (Cambridge: Cambridge University Press, 1972)

Horsley, Richard A., and John S. Hanson, *Bandits, Prophets, and Messiahs: Popular Movements in the Time of Jesus* (San Francisco: Harper & Row, 1988)

Ilan, Tal, *Jewish Women in Greco-Roman Palestine: An Inquiry into Image and Status* (Tübingen: J. C. B. Mohr (Paul Siebeck), 1995)

Jeremias, Joachim, *The Eucharistic Words of Jesus* (London: SCM, 1966)

—, *Jerusalem in the Time of Jesus: An Investigation into Economic and Social Conditions during the New Testament Period* (London: SCM, 1974)

—, *Unknown Sayings of Jesus* (London: SPCK, 1964)

Jones, A. H. M. and Michael Avi-Yonah, *The Cities of the Eastern Roman Provinces* (Oxford: Clarendon Press, 1971)

Josephus, Flavius, *The Jewish War* (Harmondsworth: Penguin, 1981)

Justin and Leslie W. Barnard, *The First and Second Apologies* (New York: Paulist Press, 1997)

Juvenal, and Peter Green, *The Sixteen Satires* (London: Penguin Books, 1974)

Kazen, Thomas, *Jesus and Purity Halakhah: Was Jesus Indifferent to Impurity?* (Stockholm: Almqvist and Wiksell, 2002)

Kearns, Kevin Corrigan, *Dublin Tenement Life: An Oral History* (Dublin: Gill & Macmillan, 1994)

Keener, Craig S., *The Gospel of John: A Commentary* (Peabody, Mass: Hendrickson Publishers, 2003)

Kleijn, Gerda de, *The Water Supply of Ancient Rome: City Area, Water, and Population* (Amsterdam: Gieben, 2001)

Kreider, Alan, *Worship and Evangelism in Pre-Christendom* (Cambridge: Grove Books, 1995)

Kruger, Michael J., *The Gospel of the Savior: An Analysis of P. Oxy. 840 and Its Place in the Gospel Traditions of Early Christianity* (Leiden: Brill, 2005)

Kurlansky, Mark, *Nonviolence: The History of a Dangerous Idea* (London: Jonathan Cape, 2006)

Lane, William L., *The Gospel According to Mark; the English Text with Introduction, Exposition, and Notes* (Grand Rapids: Eerdmans, 1974)

Légasse, Simon, *The Trial of Jesus* (London: SCM Press, 1997)

Lewis, Naphtali, *Life in Egypt under Roman Rule* (Oxford: Clarendon Press, 1983)

Lewis, Naphtali, and Meyer Reinhold, *Roman Civilization: Selected Readings* (New York: Columbia University Press, 1990)

Lieu, Judith, John North and Tessa Rajak, *The Jews Among Pagans and Christians in the Roman Empire* (London: Routledge, 1994)

Long, David E., *The Hajj Today: A Survey of the Contemporary Makkah Pilgrimage* (Albany: State University of New York Press, 1979)

McMullen, Ramsay, *Enemies of the Roman Order: Treason, Unrest, and Alienation in the Empire* (Cambridge, Mass; London: Harvard University Press; Oxford University Press, 1966)

Marshall, I. Howard, *The Gospel of Luke: A Commentary on the Greek Text* (Exeter: Paternoster, 1978)

Maslen, Matthew W. and Mitchell, Piers, D. 'Medical theories on the cause of death in crucifixion', *Journal of the Royal Society of Medicine* 99, 2006

Matyszak, Philip, *The Sons of Caesar: Imperial Rome's First Dynasty* (London: Thames & Hudson, 2006)

Mazower, Mark, *Inside Hitler's Greece: The Experience of Occupation 1941–44* (Yale Nota Bene, New Haven, Conn.; London: Yale University Press, 2001)

McLaren, James S., *Power and Politics in Palestine: The Jews and the Governing of Their Land 100 BC–AD 70* (Sheffield: JSOT Press, 1991)

Millar, Fergus, *The Roman Near East, 31 BC–AD 337* (Cambridge, Mass.; London: Harvard University Press, 1993)

Moule, C. F. D., *The Birth of the New Testament* (London: A. & C. Black, 1981)

Murphy-O'Connor, J., *The Holy Land: An Archaeological Guide from Earliest Times to 1700* (Oxford: Oxford University Press, 1986)

Murphy, Catherine M., *Wealth in the Dead Sea Scrolls and in the Qumran Community* (Leiden: Brill, 2002)

Neuwirth, Robert, *Shadow Cities: A Billion Squatters, a New Urban World* (New York; London: Routledge, 2005)

Nolland, John, *Luke* (Dallas, Texas: Word Books, 1989)

—, *The Gospel of Matthew: A Commentary on the Greek Text* (Grand Rapids, Mich./Bletchley: W.B. Eerdmans/Paternoster Press, 2005)

Notley, R. Steven, and Anson F. Rainey, *Carta's New Century Handbook and Atlas of the Bible* (Carta, 2007–12–17)

Notley, R. Steven, Marc Turnage and Brian Becker, *Jesus' Last Week* (Leiden: Brill, 2006)

Ogg, George, *The Chronology of the Public Ministry of Jesus* (Cambridge: Cambridge University Press, 1940)

Orr, William F., and James Arthur Walther, *1 Corinthians: A New Translation* (Garden City, N.Y: Doubleday, 1976)

Page, Nick, *What Happened to the Ark of the Covenant?* (Milton Keynes: Authentic Media, 2007)

Paxton, Robert O., *Vichy France: Old Guard and New Order 1940–1944* (New York: Columbia University Press, 2001)

Perrin, Nicholas, *Thomas: The Other Gospel* (London: SPCK, 2007)

Peters, F. E., *Jerusalem: The Holy City in the Eyes of Chroniclers, Visitors, Pilgrims, and Prophets from the Days of Abraham to the Beginnings of Modern Times* (Princeton: Princeton University Press, 1985)

Phang, Sara Elise, *Roman Military Service: Ideologies of Discipline in the Late Republic and Early Principate* (Cambridge: Cambridge University Press, 2008)

Phillips, L. Edward, *The Ritual Kiss in Early Christian Worship* (Alcuin/Grow Liturgical Study, 36, Cambridge: Grove, 1996)

Pixner, Bargil, 'Church of the Apostles Found on Mount Zion', *Biblical Archaeology Review* 16 (3), May/June 1990

Pollard, Nigel, *Soldiers, Cities, and Civilians in Roman Syria* (Ann Arbor: University of Michigan Press, 2000)

Reader, John, *Cities* (London: Heinemann, 2004)

Rhoads, David M., *Israel in Revolution: 6–74 C.E.: A Political History Based on the Writings of Josephus* (Philadelphia: Fortress Press, 1976)

Richardson, Alan, *The Political Christ* (London: SCM Press, 1973)

Richardson, Peter, *Building Jewish in the Roman East* (Waco, Texas: Baylor University Press, 2004)

—, *City and Sanctuary: Religion and Architecture in the Roman Near East* (London: SCM Press, 2002)

Riesner, Rainer, *Paul's Early Period: Chronology, Mission Strategy, Theology* (Grand Rapids, Mich.; Cambridge: Eerdmans, 1998)

Ritmeyer, Leen, and Kathleen Ritmeyer, *Jerusalem in the Year 30 A.D.* (Jerusalem: Carta, 2004)

Roberts, Rev. Alexander and James Donaldson, (editors) *Church Fathers – The Ante-Nicene Fathers*, (Accordance, 1885)

Roller, Duane W., *The Building Program of Herod the Great* (Berkeley; London: University of California Press, 1998)

Sacchi, Paolo, *The History of the Second Temple Period* (London: T. & T. Clark International, 2004)

Safrai, Ze'ev, *The Economy of Roman Palestine* (London: Routledge, 1994)

Sanders, E. P., *Jesus and Judaism* (London: SCM, 1985)

—, *The Historical Figure of Jesus* (London: Penguin, 1995)

Saldarini, Anthony J., *Pharisees, Scribes and Sadducees in Palestinian Society* (Grand Rapids: Eerdmans, 2001)

Schürer, Emil, Fergus Millar, Géza Vermès and Martin Goodman, *The History of the Jewish People in the Age of Jesus Christ (175 B.C.–A.D. 135)* (Edinburgh: T. & T. Clark, 1973)

Scobie, Alex. 'Slums, Sanitation and Mortality in the Roman World', *Klio* 68, 1986

Segal, J. B., *The Hebrew Passover: From the Earliest Times to A.D. 70* (London: Oxford University Press, 1963)

Shanks, Hershel, and Ben Witherington, *The Brother of Jesus: The Dramatic Story & Meaning of the First Archaeological Link to Jesus & His Family* (London: Continuum, 2003)

Sidebotham, Steven E., *Roman Economic Policy in the Erythra Thalassa 30 B.C.–A.D. 217* (Leiden: Brill, 1986)

Speidel, Michael, 'Roman Army Pay Scales', *Journal of Roman Studies* 82, 1992

—, 'The Pay of the Auxilia', *Journal of Roman Studies* 63, 1973

Sperber, Daniel, *Roman Palestine, 200–400: Money and Prices* (Ramat-Gan: Bar-Ilan University Press, 1991)

Tripp, David, 'Meanings of the Foot-Washing: John 13 and Oxyrhynchus Papyrus 840', *Expository Times*, 1992

van der Horst, Pieter, 'Jewish Funerary Inscriptions – Most are in Greek', *Biblical Archaeology Review* 18 (5), 1992

Vanderkam, James C., *From Joshua to Caiaphas: High Priests After the Exile* (Minneapolis, Minn./Assen: Augsburg Fortress/Van Gorcum, 2004)

Vermès, Géza, *The Changing Faces of Jesus* (London: Penguin, 2000)

—, *The Complete Dead Sea Scrolls in English* (London: Penguin Books, 2004)

Watts, John D.W., *Isaiah 34–66* (Nashville, TN: Thomas Nelson, 2005)

Webb, Robert L. '"Apocalyptic": Observations on a Slippery Term', *Journal of Near Eastern Studies* 49 (2), 1990

Wengst, Klaus, and John Stephen Bowden, *Pax Romana and the Peace of Jesus Christ* (London: SCM, 1987)

Wilkinson, John, *Jerusalem as Jesus Knew it: Archaeology as Evidence* (London: Thames and Hudson, 1978)

Witherington, Ben, *The Gospel of Mark: Socio-Rhetorical Commentary* (William B. Eerdmans Publishing Company, January, 2001)

Woolf, Bertram Lee, *The Authority of Jesus and Its Foundation: A Study in the Four Gospels and the Acts* (London: Allen & Unwin, 1929)

Wright, N. T., *Jesus and the Victory of God* (London: SPCK, 1996)

—, *The Resurrection of the Son of God* (London: SPCK, 2003)

Zeldin, Theodore, *An Intimate History of Humanity* (London: Vintage, 1998)

Zias, J. and Sekeles, E. 'The Crucified Man from Giv'at ha-Mivtar: A Reappraisal', *Israel Exploration Journal* 35, 1985

Index